Project Finance for Business Development

Wiley and SAS Business Series

The Wiley & SAS Business Series presents books that help senior-level managers with their critical management decisions.

Titles in the Wiley & SAS Business Series include:

Analytics: The Agile Way by Phil Simon

Analytics in a Big Data World: The Essential Guide to Data Science and its Applications by Bart Baesens

A Practical Guide to Analytics for Governments: Using Big Data for Good by Marie Lowman

Bank Fraud: Using Technology to Combat Losses by Revathi Subramanian

Big Data Analytics: Turning Big Data into Big Money by Frank Ohlhorst

Big Data, Big Innovation: Enabling Competitive Differentiation through Business Analytics by Evan Stubbs

Business Analytics for Customer Intelligence by Gert Laursen

Business Intelligence Applied: Implementing an Effective Information and Communications Technology Infrastructure by Michael Gendron

Business Intelligence and the Cloud: Strategic Implementation Guide by Michael S. Gendron

Business Transformation: A Roadmap for Maximizing Organizational Insights by Aiman Zeid

Connecting Organizational Silos: Taking Knowledge Flow Management to the Next Level with Social Media by Frank Leistner

Data-Driven Healthcare: How Analytics and BI are Transforming the Industry by Laura Madsen

Delivering Business Analytics: Practical Guidelines for Best Practice by Evan Stubbs

Demand-Driven Forecasting: A Structured Approach to Forecasting, Second Edition by Charles Chase

Demand-Driven Inventory Optimization and Replenishment: Creating a More Efficient Supply Chain by Robert A. Davis

Developing Human Capital: Using Analytics to Plan and Optimize Your Learning and Development Investments by Gene Pease, Barbara Beresford, and Lew Walker

Project Finance for Business Development

John E. Triantis

WILEY

Published by John Wiley & Sons, Inc., Hoboken, New Jersey.

Published simultaneously in Canada.

Library of Congress Cataloging-in-Publication Data:

Names: Triantis, John E., 1944– author.
Title: Project finance for business development / John E. Triantis.
Description: Hoboken : Wiley, 2018. | Series: Wiley and sas business series |
  Includes bibliographical references and index. |
Identifiers: LCCN 2018001354 (print) | LCCN 2018002821 (ebook) | ISBN
  9781119486138 (pdf) | ISBN 9781119486091 (epub) | ISBN 9781119486114 (oBook) |
  ISBN 9781119486084 (hardback) | ISBN 9781119486138 (ePDF)
Subjects: LCSH: Project management—Finance. | Decision making. |
  BISAC: BUSINESS & ECONOMICS / Finance.
Classification: LCC HD69.P75 (ebook) | LCC HD69.P75 T75 2018 (print) |
  DDC 658.4/04—dc23
LC record available at https://lccn.loc.gov/2018001354

Cover Design: Wiley
Cover Image: © Toria/Shutterstock

Printed in the United States of America.

10 9 8 7 6 5 4 3 2 1

To my soul mate, my wife Connie

Contents

Preface

The record of infrastructure project financings provides ample evidence of shortcomings in skills and competencies, adequate project development preparation, and failures in project management. The idiosyncrasies and complexities of large infrastructure projects and the large number of participants account for some of the project failures. However, a number of project failures have their origin in the fragmentation of approach to project finance. That is, sometimes project finance is treated as a financial engineering problem, other times as an interweaving of contracts arrangement and at different times is considered mostly a project management issue. Each of these approaches focuses on subsets of specific issues of the broader discipline of new business development which incorporates elements of strategic planning, portfolio management, and financial and business planning intended to achieve competitive advantage.

Having learned from strategic planning, new business development projects, and project financing experiences, we recognized the need to treat project financing from a broader perspective than prevailing common practices. Why? Because Business Development groups view project financing a responsibility of Project Finance Organizations (PFOs) and PFOs had little knowledge of and interaction with Strategic Planning or Business Development functions. Discussions with project participants and results of a benchmarking study confirmed our assessment. Hence, our focus on integrating the knowledge, processes, and skills and competencies from the two disciplines to deliver significantly improved project financing solutions and make progress towards competitive advantage.

Besides the fragmented approach to infrastructure project finance in the current paradigm and the nonstellar record of project success, other reasons for undertaking the task of writing this book are:

- Treating project finance as an extension of strategic planning and new business development
- Misspelling myths about project financing that it is a matter of legal and financial engineering alone
- Sharing project experiences and findings of benchmarking studies of project financing practices conducted across different types of project participants
- Enhancing understanding of project teams of what is needed to make project finance an instrument to getting competitive advantage

■ Addressing the inadequate development of project financing skills and competencies in different project participant organizations

Some typical misconceptions and wrong impressions the author has encountered are exemplified in the following actual statements by various project financing participants:

■ The main success factors and drivers in project finance are the Sales and Engineering groups

■ We count on relationships with customers to bring in new projects; we don't need project financing

■ Strategic planning has nothing to do with project financing; why complicate things?

■ There is no recourse to the developer in project finance, only to insuring parties

■ Private placements are cheaper than loans to an infrastructure project

■ The World Bank will give us their decision to participate in the project in 2–3 days (*for an estimated $2.3 billion project*)

■ A sponsor does need a project finance organization; Accounting and Finance groups can handle project finance and if not, outsource the financing

■ All infrastructure projects are financeable and if you can't bring financing to the project, we'll bring in investment bankers

■ Project finance is nothing more than good contracts and low cost loans

■ Technical superiority of proposals wins bids most of the time

The problematic segmentation of approach to project finance raised the question: Is there another, possibly better way of treating infrastructure project finance in a more holistic approach? Our research showed that there was nothing to guide a broader treatment of project financing. Yet, we believed that a practical, balanced, broader, and integrative perspective is needed which is more effective. Hence, our treatment of the subject is from a new business development approach which also incorporates the key elements of strategic and business planning with financial engineering, contractual agreement interweaving, and process and project management. However, this book does not claim to be a treatise on infrastructure project financing; it is an eclectic and holistic treatment of its important elements to make it more effective.

In addition to the fragmentation of the approach to project finance, raising funding becomes more complicated and difficult to manage when unharmonized participant interests enter the picture along with under-developed host country and credit impaired customer considerations. To simplify the presentation and make it easier to grasp the essence of project finance, the topic is treated from a sponsor or developer perspective doing projects in countries able to deliver on obligations to the project. On some occasions, when warranted, we deviate from this approach and incorporate other considerations and various participants' viewpoints.

Addressing infrastructure project finance from a new business development, strategic planning, portfolio management, and strategic forecasting elements approach combined with traditional project finance elements is a unique method. The reasons this approach is unique and of benefit to the readers is that it:

- Describes the skills and competencies, processes, analyses, and evaluations required to structure and finance effectively any type of project financing

- Applies knowledge of competitive analysis, forecasting, strategic and business planning, and business development to address project financing issues leading to competitive advantage

- Addresses organizational, project evaluation, process and project management, and funding sources and instrument issues while abstracting from nonessentials that take away attention from major success factors

- Pulls together key factors from each fragmented approach into an eclectic and integrated picture to discuss project finance while leaving the discussion of highly specialized and detailed parts to traditional treatments of the subject

- Helps identify reasons for project failures, key project success factors, and whether a competitive advantage to sponsors is obtainable through highly skilled, high performing PFOs

- Presents a well-considered, balanced, and cost benefit/analysis-based approach to project development, risk assessment and allocation, and project structuring and financing

The expectation is that readers will appreciate how the new business development approach is applied in any project to screen and evaluate opportunities and develop projects more effectively. That is, to bring projects from the prefeasibility study to financing closing quicker, address project stakeholder issues and harmonize interests, deliver winning financing proposals, and create profitable projects for all stakeholders. These are key elements in striving for and maintaining competitive advantage.

Acknowledgments

The idea of formalizing a comprehensive presentation of project finance for new business development has its origins with experiences in projects I did as a business consulting economist. The quest for sound processes, critical analyses, objective evaluations, innovations and continuous productivity improvements have been an integral part of my professional life. I have learned a lot from projects and interactions with financing advisors and colleagues, but it is difficult to ascertain what I have learned from whom or what specific project experiences I benefited from the most.

I took my first steps in project finance under the support and guidance of a most intelligent and capable CFO, Mary Baughman, who placed her trust on my ability to create and manage a professional project finance organization for AT&T Submarine Systems. I owe her gratitude for that which got me into the field of project finance. My skills have been augmented by discussions and work with financing advisors and consultants, financiers, and relationships with official and private funding source managers who shared freely valuable knowledge. I also learned from experiences of other project finance organizations and benefited from interviews of different types of project finance participants and insights from an extensive benchmarking study.

In preparing this book I have had the privilege of benefitting from constructive reviews and seasoned experience inputs and knowledge of Jeffrey Morrison, John Costas, Robert Rieffel, and Julie Hill. I am thankful for their useful comments and suggestions on an earlier draft of the manuscript. The help and guidance of the SAS and Wiley editorial staff are also acknowledged, but all errors and omissions are my own responsibility.

The encouragement and support of my wife during the research and preparation of the manuscript has been invaluable for it enabled me to focus on completing this task. In addition to Mary Baughman, I would like to thank my friend and former advisor Dr. Elizabeth C. Bogan for her guidance and help which shaped my professional life. Once again, I am thankful for and acknowledge the support of the late James Sotirhos; without it none of this would have been possible.

About the Author

John E. Triantis is a retired business consulting economist, business strategist, and former project financing director with a track record of introducing effective processes and practices to develop value creating projects. He is an experienced new business development project leader and a trusted advisor in large investment, international infrastructure financing, and organizational restructuring projects. His passion is to help clients minimize decision uncertainty and project risk by integrating sound processes, analytics, and evaluations with strategic planning and business development principles to maximize project value. He uses unique methods and techniques to create world-class organizations, apply best practices to successful project development and financing, and create sound project value realization measures.

His broad experience encompasses effective analysis for strategic decisions, investment evaluations, project risk management and financing, and productivity enhancements. He has developed practical methods, assessment tools, and early warning systems and uses cost-benefit approaches to minimize time to decision, address risk mitigation effectively, and maximize chances of project success. He delivers knowledge and hands-on coaching to clients on strategic planning and new business development, investment opportunity assessments, project financing, business cases, and business planning. His quest for efficient decision making has produced a proprietary system of quantifying project success at the idea stage before major investment decisions are made.

To address needs and fill gaps in client understanding, he authored numerous position papers and published the books *Creating Successful Acquisition and Joint Venture Projects: A Process and Team Approach* and *Navigating Strategic Decisions: The Power of Sound Analysis and Forecasting* as well as articles in professional domestic and international journals and books. He is the author of this book and currently working on a manuscript for the book *Assessing Project Success at the Idea Stage*. John holds a PhD in macroeconomics and international economics and a master's degree in statistics and econometrics from the University of New Hampshire. His bachelor's degree is in economics and mathematics from Fairleigh Dickinson University. He also served in the U.S. Army during the Vietnam conflict.

Project Finance
for Business
Development

CHAPTER **1**

Introduction

Why Project Finance for Business Development?

The treatment of project finance has primarily been for the infrastructure industry, but the processes and techniques used are also applicable to other off-balance-sheet financings of separate entities, joint ventures, and projects in other industries. Project finance has traditionally been treated from a financial engineering or from a contract finance perspective with applications in infrastructure projects in underdeveloped or developing countries lacking sufficient public and private resources to fund needed projects. Projects of such characteristics are the most challenging and once experience is obtained from such projects, it is easily transferable to projects in other industries and developed countries.

The globalization of business has intensified competition among project sponsors/developers, construction contractors, technology and equipment providers, and some funding sources. The result is coopetition in project development and financing that has increased the need for effective project finance solutions and better-structured partnerships and joint ventures. In this environment, to win large project bids, sponsors need an overall competitive advantage. To create profitable investment projects, they need a disciplined, new business development approach to project finance.

Project finance is not a stand-alone function based on contract finance or legal engineering as it is being treated in the current paradigm. It has been developed to advanced levels for the primary purpose of facilitating new project and business development activities with the nonrecourse aspect as an ancillary factor. It should be treated as part of new business development with its focus on striving to maintain or obtain competitive advantage. Hence, our approach to project finance is different than the one in the current literature and its novelty lies with the value created through addressing it from a broad, new business-development perspective. Why? Because project finance is part of new business development and has to be viewed in that context and not as a stand-alone discipline, and because its key objective is to get competitive advantage through new investments. Other reasons for and benefits of using this approach are explained later in the chapter.

Infrastructure projects are large investments by the public and/or private sectors that require major financial and human resource commitments to build physical assets and facilities needed for economic development and social functioning of a country. Infrastructure projects include power plants, pipelines, railroads, roads and bridges; ports, terminals, and airports; telecommunication networks, and water and sewage treatment plants. They also include social and healthcare facilities such as public housing, elder care facilities, prisons, hospitals, schools, and sports stadiums.

Due to their large and special financing requirements and challenges, infrastructure projects are usually placed in four categories:

1. Greenfield projects, where new facilities are built requiring larger capital investments than investments in existing project companies in operation
2. Brownfield projects, where investment is made to upgrade and refurbish existing facilities and equipment in order to increase productivity or extend their economic life
3. Stock or extraction projects, where natural resources are extracted and sold until depletion, such as coal and mineral mining, and gas and oil extraction
4. Flow-type projects, where the project assets are used to generate income by selling their output or the use of their services. They include pipelines, toll roads and bridges, ports and airports, and so on

There are several definitions of project finance for different types of projects, all valid but each stressing some more than other parts of the discipline. However, we prefer the broader definition shown in the box. To understand what project finance is all about, the definition needs to be expanded to include the structuring of the project company, known as a special purpose company (SPC) or a special vehicle company (SPV); the characteristics of projects, what project finance involves, and the risks associated with a project. That is, it includes:

> Project finance is the art and skill of piecing together new business development elements, financial engineering techniques, and a web of contractual agreements to develop competitive projects and make the right decisions to raise funding for industrial or infrastructure projects on a limited/nonrecourse basis where lenders look to the cash flow for loan repayment and the project assets for collateral.

1. *Structure of the company:* Common SPC structures are corporations, joint ventures, partnerships, limited partnerships, and limited liability companies
2. *Properties of projects:* Infrastructure projects require large capital expenditure, entail massive negotiations and contracts, and require long operating periods
3. *What project finance involves:* It requires the creation of a legally separate, single purpose entity that is a shell company to build the project assets and capture revenues. Financing is of a limited/nonrecourse basis and

it is based on cash flows and the assets owned by the SPC that is responsible for loan repayment

4. *Risks associated with a project:* Financing is provided to the SPC and not to the sponsors and this gives rise to risks usually mitigated through contracts, insurance, and credit enhancements. A common set of risks in project finance includes primarily political, demand, price, supply, currency, interest rate, and inflation risks

5. *Project development complexities:* Addressing them entails the undertakings of project screening and the feasibility study, project development, financial model development, and economic evaluation. It also requires project risk management, due diligence, a financing plan, financial structuring, creation of a project company business plan, and project implementation

A key objective of project finance is to minimize or avoid uncertainty. Unlike asset-based finance, where the asset value determines financing, the adequacy of project cash flow is the foundation of funding. Since infrastructure projects have different types of assets and objectives, capital requirements, and risks; they get different benefits from project financing. However, infrastructure projects have a number of common characteristic due to the common project financing technique. Gatti (2012) names the common elements of project financings as: long economic life assets with low technological risk, provision of essential public services with inelastic demands, regulated monopolies or quasimonopolies with high barriers to entry, and stable and predictable operating cash flow.

The components of project finance are outlined in Section 1.6 and discussed in subsequent chapters, but the basic and common components across projects are the presence of a host government ceding agency, sponsor or developer equity, commercial bank loans, and institutional debt and equity investors. Usually, there is some subordinated debt from sponsors and other project participants, collateral security and revenue assignment, and enhancements provided by sponsors and unilateral and multilateral institutions. Also, there is a common set of project finance prerequisites such as a stable political and regulatory environment, reasonably adequate industry structure, sound project development and planning, thorough risk assessment and mitigation to allocate risks effectively, and contractual agreements to ensure project viability.

The historical origins of project finance and its evolution are traced in Section 1.1 and its advantages and disadvantages are briefly discussed in Section 1.2. The differences between project finance and corporate and structured finance are explained in Section 1.3. To get a sense of the importance of project finance, its size, and the industries it impacts, some of its characteristics are shown in Section 1.4.

Because project finance is part of business development, Section 1.5 provides the rationale for using a new business development approach to evaluate, structure, and fund project finance transactions aiming to create a competitive advantage for the company. The structure of the book and chapter contents is presented in Section 1.6 and how to maximize its benefits to the reader is explained in Section 1.7.

1.1 ORIGINS OF PROJECT FINANCE

The basic idea of project finance is not new, but it has evolved and refined through time and has now become a highly skilled discipline and an art. According to Miller (1991), elements of project finance present in Mesopotamian societies were expanded by ancient Greeks to foster maritime trade and to finance wars. Maritime loans were given to ship owners and merchants to buy goods for sale abroad with the understanding that if the ship returned, the loan would be repaid in full plus a return (often as high as 25% because of risks involved) out of the proceeds of goods sold abroad and out of the proceeds from the sale of cargo brought back. If the ship was lost at sea or did not return with cargo from abroad, in the first instance the loan was not repaid and in the second case was partially paid through proceeds of sales of cargo sold abroad.

The Athenians used project finance concepts to finance war in the following manner: They created an alliance of city-states to fight the Persians using the Persian model that required members to pay an annual tribute. This enabled the Athenians to turn the alliance into an empire and their allies to get a share of the benefits. The Spartans used a different war financing method: They borrowed from a Persian king to fund building a fleet to fight the Athenians "in exchange for the right to levy tribute again on Ionia's Greeks" (Pritchard, 2015). The Romans enhanced the Athenian merchant model with legal agreements and created the *fenus nauticus* (sea loan), in which merchants would get to share the risk with the lender.

A more recent project finance experience is that of the British Crown financing of the Devon Silver mines in 1299, which repaid a Florentine merchant banker with rights to output from the mines in a one-year concession (Kensinger and Martin, 1988). Beginning with the Age of Discovery, the English, French, Dutch, Spanish, and Portuguese lenders financed water irrigation, canal, road, and railroad construction projects in colonies primarily in India, Africa, South America, and the Middle East. The lenders were repaid from revenue proceeds from those projects or from taxation revenues. An example of such projects is the Suez Canal project in late nineteenth century by the French and the railroad network build by the British in India.

In the late nineteenth century, numerous oil and gas exploration and production ventures in the United States were financed with bank loans that were repaid from proceeds of sales of outputs from those projects. Also, in the early twentieth century, the US government financed the construction of the Panama Canal under a project funds transfer syndicated loan arrangement of eight banks led by J.P. Morgan. However, the North Sea project in the late 1970s resembled properties of modern project financing whereby British Petroleum raised a billion British pounds for that project's construction through a forward purchase agreement.

1.2 PROJECT FINANCE ADVANTAGES AND DISADVANTAGES

The reasons for using project finance are the several advantages it yields to different project stakeholders. The benefits of project finance vary by project type and participant and include the following:

1. Raises funding at a reasonable cost for projects not financeable by other methods
2. Minimizes equity contributions and thereby increases borrowing capacity for sponsors or developers through the project company
3. Avoids the risk-contamination issue by diversifying political risk and mitigating other risks through allocation to parties best able to absorb and through insurance contracts
4. Higher leverage than on-balance sheet finance translates into higher sponsor or developer return on investment
5. Well suited to finance large, capital-intensive projects that have long construction periods and no revenue until start of operations
6. Project-financed deals have the benefit and support of high-quality counterparts, such as export credit agencies (ECAs), multilateral institutions, and global insurers
7. Lenders to projects and credit support parties provide incentives for and require careful project evaluation, risk assessment, and due diligence
8. Better managed and improved project company operations because of stringent lender requirements and controls of its cash flow
9. Provides incentives to lenders to cooperate in the project company's restructuring and reorganization and be less likely to foreclose
10. Increases public infrastructure investment than otherwise would be the case and enables governments to get value for their money; that is, greater project value and efficiency
11. Increases tax revenues for the host government and provides tax benefits to sponsors or developers

12. Reduces the cost burden for the host country government authority responsible for the project and affects transfer of technology, training, and know-how to the host country

The other side of project finance is found in its limitations, and its disadvantages are lengthy and costly project development, risk assessment and mitigation, the due diligence process, and finance-structuring challenges. Other disadvantages of project finance include:

1. Protracted contract negotiations and complex, lengthy, and costly project documentation, contractual agreement preparation, and contract negotiations

2. The large number of parties involved in the project, possible divergence of interests and objectives, and difficulties to reach consensus

3. Higher interest rates and fees than other forms of financing and high insurance costs to mitigate project risks and cover hedging contracts

4. Project development complexity and costs, combined with a lack of project financing competencies among project stakeholders, precludes the use of project finance in small projects

5. Lenders require a high degree of supervision over construction, and the SPC's management and operations have stringent reporting requirements

6. Project finance techniques used in one project cannot be easily replicated in other projects. This means that there is no process standardization and the result is higher costs to tailor processes and assessments to each project specifics

1.3 CORPORATE AND STRUCTURED VERSUS PROJECT FINANCE

In corporate finance, also known as direct finance, a company undertaking a new project finances it from loans and not from the project. To do that, the company proves to lenders that its balance sheet assets are of sufficient strength to use as collateral in case of default. Under this arrangement, the lender can foreclose and liquidate the borrower's assets to recover its investment. Unlike corporate finance, project finance is based on debt repayment from project company revenues and not on the sponsor or the developer's balance sheet assets.

Structured finance is a complex set of financial instruments available to large borrowers with needs that a simple loan cannot meet. It was created to help transfer risk though legal contracts, especially when those borrowers are involved in several projects. The crux of structured finance is bringing together mortgages, loans, bonds, and credit default swaps and then issuing tranches against those assets. The prioritization of claims makes the tranches

–safer than the average asset in the pool of assets, and structured finance is used when a number of separate tranches are required to meet project needs. This form of finance has grown in popularity since the mid-eighties and examples of structured finance instruments are collateral bond obligations (CBOs), collateral debt obligations (CDOs), credit default swaps, and hybrid securities.

Development finance, asset based loans, and cash flow and covenant light loans are variants of project finance. Development finance for private or public–private partnership (PPP) projects is used in land acquisition and construction of housing, shopping malls, hotels, schools, hospitals, and sports facilities. It is also used to finance economic development projects such as ports, airports, roads, bridges, etc. On the other hand, asset-based finance consists of revolving lines of credit or loans secured by the borrower's assets and are used for, among other projects, acquisitions, buyouts, and capital expenditures.

Cash flow and light covenant loans are often based on the credit of the acquired company with robust and stable cash flow and entities such as government agencies and regulated utilities. For clarity of presentation, our discussion of project finance is focused primarily on greenfield infrastructure projects although its principles apply to brownfield, extraction, and flow types of projects as well. While our discussion centers around international infrastructure projects, the principal components apply to domestic, private, or commercial new business development projects with a few elements that need adjustment to fit project specifics.

1.4 THE PROJECT FINANCE MARKET

According to McKinsey Global Institute (June 2016), the global infrastructure market is estimated to be $2.5 trillion invested in transportation, power, water, and telecommunications projects. The world needs, however, require average annual investments of $3.3 trillion to support currently expected economic growth with 60% of that to meet emerging market needs. The infrastructure market for 2006–2011 was $1.21 trillion and for the 2016–2030 period the investment need is projected to be $49.1 trillion.

To give a historical perspective, Table 1.4.1 shows the global finance market by amount and percent by region for the 2011 to 2013 period, which shows a decline in those years, but which has since been reversed.

In 2011, the shares of project finance by region show some annual variability, but for the 2006 to 2013 period those shares do not display any trends. The amount of global project finance by sector is shown in Table 1.4.2. Common, average timelines involved in infrastructure projects are shown in Table 1.4.3. It is instructive to observe how debt maturities overlap and appreciate the need for long concession agreements.

Table 1.4.1 Global Project Finance by Region, US$ Billion

	2011		2012		2013	
	Amount	%	Amount	%	Amount	%
North America	23.589	11.0	22.103	11.2	37.711	18.5
Africa and Middle East	16.870	7.9	20.718	10.5	29.335	14.4
Europe	67.443	31.4	46.298	23.4	52.715	25.8
Asia Pacific	91.317	42.6	88.199	44.7	62.762	30.7
Other	15.288	7.1	20.209	10.2	21.618	10.6
Total	214.507	100.0	197.527	100.0	204.141	100.0

Source: OECD Journal, Financial Market Trends, Vol. 2014/1.

Table 1.4.2 Global Project Finance by Sector, US$ Billion

	Amount	%
Power	70.077	34.3
Transportation	40.715	19.9
Oil & Gas	39.862	19.5
Petrochemicals	10.719	5.3
Leisure, real estate, property	7.772	3.9
Industry	16.768	8.2
Water & Sewerage	6.512	3.2
Mining	5.496	2.7
Telecommunications	4.332	2.1
Waste & Recycling	1.887	0.9
Agriculture & Forestry	0.000	0.0
Total Global Project Finance	204.140	100.0

Source: OECD Journal, Financial Market Trends, Vol. 2014/1.

Table 1.4.3 Infrastructure Project Periods Involved

	Number of Years
Mean construction period	2.0
Offtake agreement period	19.5
Concession agreement	28.3
Debt maturity—Bank loans	9.4
Debt maturity—Bonds	13.6

Source: Esty (2004).

Table 1.4.4   Loans During 1994–2003, Percent of Financing

Bank loans	47.0
Bonds	9.0
Multilateral Development Agencies	14.0
Equity	30.0
	100.0

Source: Finnerty (2013).

Table 1.4.5   Bonds Issued During 2002–2012, Percent by Region

EMEA	57.0
America	13.0
Asia-Pacific	30.0
	100.0

Source: Finnerty (2013).

Bank loans are the major source of funding infrastructure projects and the distributions of funding during the 1994 to 2003 period and those of bond issues by region during the 2002 to 2012 period are shown respectively in Tables 1.4.4 and 1.4.5.

1.5   WHY A BUSINESS DEVELOPMENT APPROACH TO PROJECT FINANCE?

There are several ways to approach the discussion of the project finance area, each influenced by the interests and perspective of individual project participants. We mentioned earlier that there are various approaches to the subject, each focusing on line of interest issues and details. Each approach has merits and benefits, all of which are a subset of a necessarily broader treatment of effective project finance. Following are different ways and viewpoints used in the current paradigm to address the subject of project finance:

1. Infrastructure versus industrial project angle
2. Project sponsor or developer perspective
3. Customer viewpoint or host country government ceding authority perspective
4. Lender, multilateral agency, and institutional investor perspective
5. Special purpose company (project company) standpoint

6. Private finance initiative (PFI) versus PPP viewpoints
7. Relationship management, sales, and marketing view
8. Financial engineering perspective
9. Contract finance or legal engineering interpretation
10. Process and project management perspective

Projects cannot receive appropriate evaluations and structuring by project finance organizations (PFOs) and legal teams alone. The main reason for the new business development approach to project finance is that it helps to develop profitable projects and progress toward getting a competitive advantage for the sponsor company. This broader approach is required to address the diverse issues to develop, structure, and finance successfully project finance deals because project finance is an integral part and is used to facilitate new business development. Figure 1.5 shows why project finance has to be treated in that context and is an outline of how and when projects come on the radar of project finance teams, the organizations involved, and how they are processed down to the PFO level.

The great majority of requests for project proposals, investment opportunities, offers, and partnership initiatives never go directly to project finance organizations but first go through business development organizations coming through various venues from:

1. Sponsor company regional sales organizations
2. Different business units of the sponsor company
3. External agents such as government entities, business brokers, and investment bankers
4. Existing or potential new customers making inquiries and submitting request for proposals (RFPs), offers, and partnership initiatives

Figure 1.5 shows that a good part of project analytics and evaluations come from specialized expertise that provides support for the new business development approach. Once projects come to business development organizations, they go through screening and different fit assessments in conjunction with inputs from the corporate strategic planning, portfolio management, and CFO organizations. After projects pass that screening, they are passed on to the project manager, the PFO, and the project team. At that point, a more in-depth screening takes place and project-financing development begins in earnest, which involves several internal organizations and external advisors.

Although it addresses all key elements of every project finance treatment angle, our approach is focused on a new, integrated, business development,

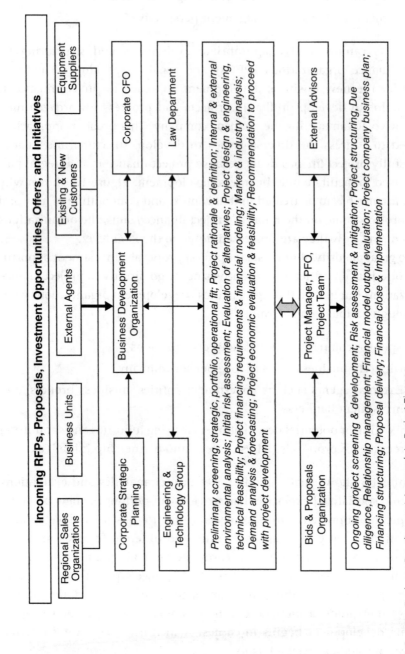

Figure 1.5 New Business Development Approach to Project Finance

business planning, and project-financing method characterized by the following properties:

1. Driven by consistent corporate and project strategies, objectives, and processes, the ability to execute successfully, and taking a comprehensive approach to value creation

2. Extensive and in-depth project evaluation of the driving factors beyond project parameters and financial ratios to determine the likelihood of project success

3. Focus on key project development issues and critical success factors to ensure project viability and successful financing in order to achieve expected value creation for sponsors and customers

4. Emphasis on project management and financing organization skills and capabilities, processes, and critical and objective evaluations

5. Balanced treatment of all project stakeholder interests in cost and benefit assessment, risk allocation, negotiations, and contracts

6. A cost-benefit based, holistic, and wide-ranging approach with the objective of helping sponsors to strive to obtain a competitive advantage through project finance

1.6 STRUCTURE OF THE BOOK

It is generally accepted that infrastructure project finance in developing countries is a complex and difficult undertaking because of credit impairment and a number of other factors involved. Coming from the perspective of project finance for new business development, the intent is to expose the reader to all parts of project finance that are involved in creating successful projects of any kind. To begin with and in order to get a sense of those challenges and difficulties, the essence of project finance is presented in an overview summary of the subject in Chapter 2. The taxonomy of projects is shown along with key activities of project finance processes and SPC ownership and financing considerations. Also, common misconceptions and myths about project finance are presented and dispelled.

To get a better picture of the shortcomings and difficulties associated with project finance and the root causes of project failures, Chapter 3 reviews the record of project financing deals by industry and region and focuses on identifying the main failure factors with the intent to present some valuable lessons learned. One of the project failure reasons is process faults and gaps and Chapter 4 presents project finance process perspectives from different project participants that are indicative of differences in priorities which, if left unresolved, ultimately lead to project failures.

Before discussing project participants and their roles and responsibilities, the PFO is described in Chapter 5. The PFO is a crucial entity and part of the project team and its organizational structure, composition, and business definition are presented along with required PFO associate required skills and competencies. Also, the characteristics of successful PFOs and their contributions are discussed based on the author's experiences, project participant discussions, and findings of benchmarking. Next, the objective of Chapter 6 is to identify the essential parts of the most important elements in project finance. That is, to identify the preparations needed along with the planning and activities that take place in each phase of the project development process. These undertakings lead to obtaining cost estimates and revenue forecasts and driving projects down to sound evaluations and project financing structuring.

Chapter 7 is concerned with project participants and their roles and responsibilities, their objectives and requirements, and how they add value to the development and implementation of projects. We point out the potential for conflict of interest, the importance of an open mind; and unimpeded communication, coordination, cooperation, and collaboration (4Cs). The need for sound competitive analysis, industry and solid market research, persistence, and the balancing of interests is apparent. Due to the crucial importance of accurate project costs and revenue forecasts to project financeability and project viability, factors that determine appropriate forecasting techniques for project financing are discussed in Chapter 8. Sources of analog forecasts, development of assumptions, analyses and evaluations, and forecast sanity checks and sources of forecast failures are also discussed in this chapter.

The purpose, nature, and effects of project contractual agreements are explained in Chapter 9 for the reader to appreciate why project finance has sometimes been called contract finance. The discussion centers around the nature of common project finance contracts, prerequisites, and costs of project contracts as well as the process of contract development and negotiation. Additionally, the main challenges and success factors associated with project financing contracts are cited. On the other hand, how a good part of the work and decisions involved comes down to identifying, evaluating, allocating, and mitigating project risks are the subject matter of Chapter 10. The different types of risk and the use of the risk matrix and other techniques are discussed along with the costs and benefits of effective risk management, which is so important to project financeability. Notice that a crucial component of risk management is the network of contractual agreements that helps to ensure the project's economic viability.

The required project evaluations beyond the feasibility study are given proper attention in Chapter 11 to ensure project viability. Here, we discuss the due diligence process, assessments, techniques, and tools used to test, verify, and validate analyses and results. This is really a continuation of the discussion of the previous chapter and its focus is on the crucial undertaking of due diligence and preparation of its report. Although it is performed by lenders, the early and ongoing involvement of the project team to verify and validate important factors is required. It is because the project team is better informed of issues that outside experts are not in a position to see and it is in a better position to focus the due diligence on those issues. This also helps the sponsor team's objective to drive toward a competitive advantage. The processes and activities discussed in Chapters 11 and 12 are some of the most important areas of project finance organization participation and its contributions to ensure project funding and profitability and build a foundation for competitive advantage.

The different sources of financing for infrastructure projects and the different funding instruments and credit enhancements are covered in Chapter 12. The multilateral, ECA, and US government funding agencies and the support they provide, as well as private funding sources and instruments, are discussed in some detail. This gives an idea of the many options open to funding infrastructure projects. Notice, that many of those funding channels and instruments are available for many other types of projects beyond infrastructure. Next, the crucial element of project and financing structuring is the topic of Chapter 13. Its many elements, determinants, investor requirements, and the decisions and choices that need to be made from ownership structuring to financing structuring and related issues are explored in some detail. Furthermore, the decisive factors of project financing are highlighted and how the integration of various participant deliverables takes place in the financing plan is explained.

Chapter 14 deals with the development of input components, outputs and their use, and evaluations performed through the project financial model. That is because of its central role in determining the project company's funding needs, its ability to raise required funding, repay debt, and estimate the return on investors' equity. Next, Chapter 15 provides a sense of where the state of the project finance industry is headed. For that, we examine project financing trends as a complement to megatrends driving the industry and look at their impact on different project participants. Also, we examine how trends could affect project company operations and look at factors that determine a project team's ability to take advantage of trends and make required adjustments to reinforce progress toward competitive advantage.

Chapter 16 examines the issues of obtaining a competitive advantage through project finance and whether a sustainable competitive advantage can be created. The author's views and the findings of a benchmarking study of different project participants are shown. Participants included sponsors and developers, customers, commercial and investment bankers, ECAs, and multilateral agencies. Law firms, project finance advisors, contractors, and equipment suppliers were also solicited and their views serve as a means of reality and sanity checks on competitive advantage through project finance. The chapter ends with the conclusion that competitive advantage may be obtained through project finance and confirm the initial hypothesis that sustainable competitive advantage may not be long lasting except in a few instances. And, due to the large number of definitions and acronyms used in project finance, appendices A and B contain commonly used acronyms and definitions used in project finance to clarify their meaning.

1.7 USE OF THE BOOK TO MAXIMIZE BENEFIT

Experience from presentations of the book's material suggests that readers will best absorb the material presented, apply lessons learned, and maximize benefit by following the simple outline below:

1. Begin reading chapters with two ideas in the back of the mind:
   a. This is a new approach and a lot of material is presented from a broader perspective that needs to be gradually absorbed
   b. The apparent repetition is intended to clarify issues and orient the reader towards striving for competitive advantage, which is possible with the right mindset, objectives, and focus
2. Read each chapter to understand and make notes on how the material discussed can enhance the current project finance paradigm and help a company's project team move towards obtaining a competitive advantage
3. Continue reading and observe how the different analyses, evaluations, tests, and elements of business development and project finance are interconnected and help assess project viability effectively and affect funding efficiently
4. Record how each chapter's material helps screen, develop, evaluate, and structure a project effectively and how sound risk identification, assessment, mitigation, and comprehensive due diligence enable the project team to create profitable projects
5. Develop increased understanding of how the right project finance organizational structures and charters, skills and competencies, project objectives, processes, assessments and tests, contractual agreements, project financial model outputs, and financing plan decisions come together
6. Recall the roles and responsibilities of all project participants, the importance of managing their interests and expectations effectively,

and the crucial role of project management in integrating different processes and deliverables

7. Assess whether an organization possesses what it takes to obtain a competitive advantage in project financing and if not, make extrapolations on how to go about getting there by following the concepts presented

8. Repetition is the mother of learning and application of lessons learned is certain to enhance project finance team effectiveness, avoid project failures all together, and result in more value creating projects

CHAPTER 2

Overview of Project Finance

The Nature of the Beast

Different models are used for various types of project structures, but a typical project finance model is shown in Figure 2.1, whose central features are equivalent across project finance deals. That is, there are almost the same project participants, similar issues and concerns, comparable processes, and the variants of basic project structuring, financing methods, and instruments. In the basic project finance structure illustrated here, the different participants involved and the agreements necessary to hold the structure together are shown. Details about project participants and their roles and responsibilities are elaborated on in Chapter 7 and the contracts involved are discussed in Chapter 9.

Project finance is well suited for funding infrastructure projects and it is especially useful in the case of projects in developing countries that may not be able to finance such projects in other ways. But to work well, there are some prerequisites that must be satisfied and include the following conditions:

1. A stable political, regulatory, and investment environment in the host country
2. Well-working global markets in a normal functioning environment and accessible financing
3. Adequate industry structure, license protection, regulatory regime, and fair competition
4. Identifiable and quantifiable risks and contracts that allocate risks effectively
5. Viable and sustainable project economics; that is, adequate and predictable cash flows
6. Political support and agreements to ensure long term project viability

The project taxonomy of Section 2.1 introduces the different types of projects and classifications, although projects can be ordered differently depending on the need for further clarification of the project variety. Section 2.2 enumerates the phases common to most project financings, which help define processes and sets the stage for more in-depth discussions, whereas Section 2.3 is a starter discussion of the elements of project finance to be expanded in the chapters that follow. The project ownership and financing structure considerations of Section 2.4 are also a primer of the many project-structuring decisions and funding concerns on the way to financial close. These considerations and decisions are also given attention in chapters that follow.

To complement the discussion of project financing structuring considerations, Section 2.5 deals with the important project finance activities whose recurring themes and key points come up in subsequent chapters.

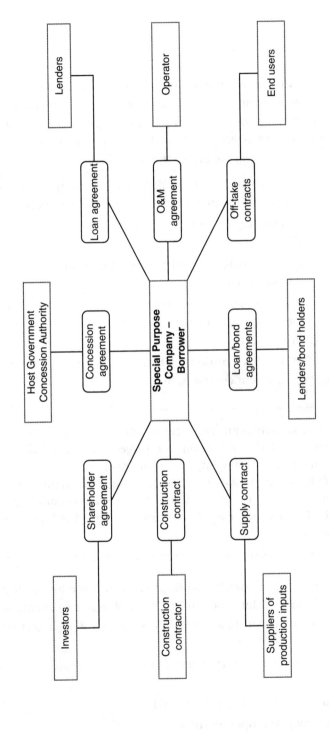

Figure 2.1 Typical Project Finance Structure
Source: Adapted from Merna, Chu, and Al Thani (2010).

And, because there are a lot of wrong impressions about project finance, Section 2.6 addresses some common project finance misconceptions and myths.

2.1 PROJECT TAXONOMY

The first distinction between projects is greenfield versus brownfield; the first referring to investment in new assets and construction, the second to investment in existing assets of companies in operation. Infrastructure projects and finance models are catalogued in various ways and, to clarify the difference in their nature, we group them as follows:

A. *Project types.* The distinction of project types is along the nature the project company and its output which characterize projects such as:

1. Process plants, e.g. power generation, water treatment, waste incineration, etc.

2. Infrastructure, privatized and private sector such as, ports and facilities, airports, etc.

3. Private–public partnerships (PPPs) of different kinds, such as concessions or economic infrastructure, Private Finance Initiative, and availability projects

4. Other PPP kinds of projects, which include privatizations, affermage, management contracts, and leases

Affermage is a contractual arrangement where the operator is responsible for operating and maintaining the project company but is not required to finance it or make large investments in it.

There are instances, however, where it is used in conjunction with another model such as for example the build–rehabilitate–operate–transfer (BROT), in which case the concession period is longer than in other models.

B. *Project classification.* Project classification defines the ownership, type of concession and duration, and transfer of assets to eventual owners. Under this ordering are the following common project types or models:

1. Build, operate, and transfer ownership at project completion (BOT)

2. Build, transfer, and operate (BTO)

3. Build, own, and operate (BOO)

4. Build, own, operate, and transfer (BOOT)

5. Build, operate, maintain, and transfer (BOMT)

6. Design, build, operate, transfer (DBOT)

7. Variants of the above models

Project finance purists maintain that project financings are only commercial property and real estate development projects, single-purpose holding companies of physical assets, and PPP projects. This view excludes real estate investment trusts (REITs) not holding real assets, privatizations, leases, and vendor debt-financed projects. However, the reality is that while the purist view is consistent with a common definition of project finance, actual project financing deals involve all types of different kinds of transactions funded by different financial instruments.

2.2 PROJECT FINANCE PHASES

The typical phases of project finance are shown in Figure 2.2, which is a simplified view of fairly common areas across different types of projects which help define the necessary project finance processes. It is a summary view of discussions that follow and worth noting that the phases shown here are in sequential order, whereas in practice they may be tackled in parallel or in a different order depending on a variety of project needs. The numerous intervening deliverables which are produced by the project team are addressed shortly. Project finance processes are discussed in Chapter 4, but the general project finance process defined by deliverables of Figure 2.2 can be adapted to fit different types of projects and situations and it serves as an introduction to the complex tasks and activities of project financing processes discussed in detail in Chapters 6 and 13.

The deliverables from different project finance phases shown are almost the same across project finance deals. The most important are:

1. The host country's political, economic, legal and regulatory, and social and environmental assessment

2. Strategic, portfolio, and operational fit assessment

3. Technical feasibility and economic viability evaluation

4. Project development processes and planning for project delivery

5. Structuring and formation of the SPC ready to begin financing negotiations

6. Development of the project financial model to determine required funding and adequacy of cash flow

7. Risk identification, assessment, quantification, and mitigation

8. Creation of the project company business plan

9. Project financing structuring decisions and development of an interim project financing plan

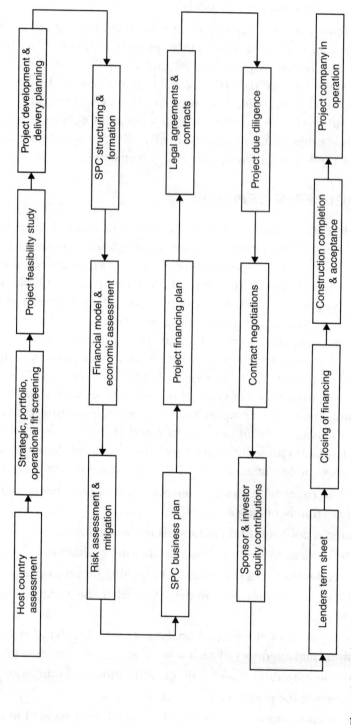

Figure 2.2 Major Project Phases

Once the expected outputs above have been produced, the next series of deliverables and necessary functions performed include the following:

1. Finalized project documentation and negotiation of legal agreements and contracts
2. Project due diligence jointly performed with the lender's advisors and the due diligence report
3. Funding issue negotiations finalized and sponsor and other investor equity contributions secured
4. Lender's term sheet with final terms and conditions delivered
5. Closing of financing takes place with all necessary enhancements and support
6. Construction completion and project acceptance and the project company begins operations

2.3 KEY ELEMENTS OF PROJECT FINANCE

The major elements in project finance investments are certainty of revenues, solid financial ratios, effective risk mitigation and lender protection, and effective contractual agreements and project termination. Underlying these major elements are the project characteristics and definition, the structure of the project company, also known as SPV or SPC, the risk mitigation plan and contracts and agreements, the project company's business plan, the due diligence report, the project financial model and the financing plan and the information memorandum. Details about the underlying factors are discussed in later chapters and here we only touch on them.

The project company structure refers to the ownership and governance structure of the special purpose vehicle taking forms such as a development consortium, corporation, general partnership, limited partnership, unincorporated joint venture company, limited liability company, etc. The project company is a vehicle created to develop agreements and enter into contracts, manage project operations, and receive and disperse money flows. On the other hand, the financing structure refers to the composition of the funding raised for the project and includes the following parts:

1. Equity—Sponsor or developer equity, consortium partner equity, private placement equity, mutual fund investments, and other facilities
2. Debt—Senior debt and subordinated or mezzanine debt from commercial banks, sources like insurance companies and pension funds, and other funding channels
3. Bonds—Rated or unrated, the former carrying higher interest rates

4. Credit enhancements—Sponsor or developer, host country public sector, and unilateral and multilateral agency enhancements

5. Lender protection—Protection from the effects of risks materializing and recourse to the project company's cash flows and assets

Project risk mitigation involves identifying risks around construction, technology, design and engineering, equipment used; the host country's political, social, and economic conditions; and the project company's operating environment. Assessment of risks is performed to determine the likelihood of risks materializing and extent of impacts. The task of balanced risk mitigation is achieved through allocation to the party best equipped to handle on a cost-benefit basis. The project company's business plan reflects all planning data, assumptions, and decisions concerning its operations and costs involved as a stand-alone entity.

The internal organization due diligence is an ongoing effort which is part of project evaluation to determine the organization's ability to execute the project successfully and to establish the merits of decisions made as the project moves along different development phases. On the other hand, the project's due diligence is an independent verification and validation by an agent of the lender(s), in conjunction with the sponsor's project team, of technical and financial data and information. Verification and validation extend to assumptions and tests thereof, forecasting techniques and models used, analyses and evaluations, project financial model and its outputs, and the security package to determine project financeability and viability.

The project financing plan is where all the work of the project team comes together through the development of a detailed project financial model of the company's upfront capital expenditure requirements and operating expenses, the drawdown schedule, taxes and accounting factors, and the repayment schedule, along with attached lender covenants and restrictions. The other side of the equation is the project revenue forecast which consists of demand and pricing forecasts. The key outputs of the project financial model are the project's net present value (NPV), the estimated sponsor internal rate of return (IRR), and return on investment (ROI), and the different ratios used to determine the project's borrowing capacity and its ability to meet repayment obligations. However, in infrastructure projects, negotiated contractual agreements are the glue that holds together the financing plan and makes project finance possible.

A key element of project finance that is often given insufficient attention or assigned to external advisors but is important in new business development undertakings is the project's information memorandum. It is a document used to market the project to potential debt and equity investors. The information memorandum describes in detail the project rationale, strategic and operational fit, the feasibility study results, the project risk profile, the due diligence findings, the project financial model and its findings and evaluations, and the financing structuring. The information, data, analyses, and evaluations appended in the information memorandum are of high quality in nature and in its presentation.

2.4 OWNERSHIP AND FINANCING STRUCTURE CONSIDERATIONS

The first question of sponsors when structuring a project is how the special purpose company should be organized. It is an important question because different structures have different advantages and disadvantages and selection of the best project company organization requires taking into account a number of considerations. A schematic that summarizes the main ownership considerations of the project company is shown in Figure 2.4.1, which include:

1. The number of owners, shareholders, or partners and equity contribution interests
2. The sponsor or developer's objectives and the internal consistency of these objectives
3. The project company management and decision making structure
4. Host country government participation in the project and its requirements
5. Local law and regulatory requirements and tax jurisdictions and laws
6. Project company debt funding needs and sponsor equity requirements

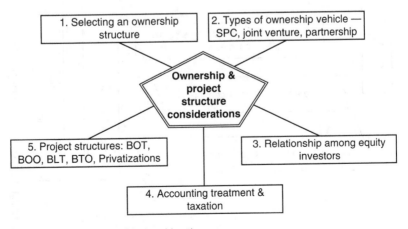

Figure 2.4.1 Key SPC Ownership Considerations.

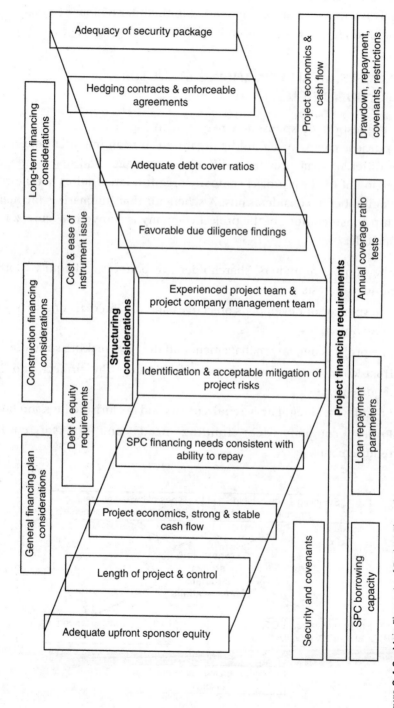

Figure 2.4.2 Main Elements of Project Financings

7. Lender requirements, covenants and restrictions, and security package
8. Accounting treatment of the project company and ease of profit distribution outside the host country
9. Minority shareholder protection and dissolution concerns

The various elements of project financing considerations are condensed in Figure 2.4.2, which shows that besides company ownership, other concerns in developing the project financing structure that are given close attention include the following:

1. Project company funding requirements and the amounts and timing of equity contributions
2. Parties currently involved and those likely to be involved later in the project
3. Estimated construction costs, operating costs, and costs of project company production inputs and supplies
4. Loan tenor and timing of drawings on debt finance versus the repayment schedule
5. Risk analysis and mitigation (along the risk matrix) and the security package for lenders
6. Type of concession agreement and the contractual agreements involved
7. Funding parameters which include the debt to equity ratio, terms of financing and interest rates and fees, project NPV, payback period, IRR, and different debt ratios
8. Contingency financing to cover unexpected costs during construction
9. Allocation of cash available to investors based on equity contributions or risks assumed

Notice the structure of the project company and the financing structure have elements that are considered together in order to maximize the project benefits and optimize financing. These issues are further examined in Chapters 12 and 13.

2.5 PRIMARY PROJECT FINANCE ACTIVITIES

The nature of project finance necessitates several assessment steps that corporate financed projects do not usually involve to pass financeability tests. In project finance though, financeability tests are crucial and after project identification the project teams go through a sequence of processes and activities, analyses, and evaluations in different project stages, which include the following undertakings:

1. Assuming the project management function and obtaining internal and external support
2. Describing project attributes; strategic, portfolio, and operational fit assessments, project rationale, and development of broad timeline targets
3. Project development planning and preparation and allocation of appropriate resources to the project
4. Formation of the project team, assignment of the PFO, and engagement of outside advisors and consultants
5. Creation of project objectives and processes and assigning roles and responsibilities to the project team and other participants
6. Assessing true customer needs and their ability to meet required contributions and harmonizing project participant interests and objectives
7. Conducting host country and external environment assessments, technical, and economic evaluations, and preparing a project feasibility study
8. Developing and validating assumptions and preparing cost projections and revenue forecasts

By this point the project team is prepared to undertake other important activities to drive decisions and usher the project forward. These activities are centered around:

1. Ensuring sufficient internal and customer organization political support
2. Conducting a project risk identification, assessment and mitigation review to ensure a fair and balanced allocation of risks
3. Completing a thorough project due diligence to validate analyses, evaluations, scenarios used, and cost and revenue projections
4. Creation of a detailed project financial model and evaluation and testing of its results for sanity and internal consistency
5. Reassessing the special purpose company ownership and financing structure considerations and finalizing them
6. Preparing project documents and negotiating contractual agreements
7. Ensuring unimpeded communication, cooperation, coordination, and collaboration and paying attention to the customer relationship management function

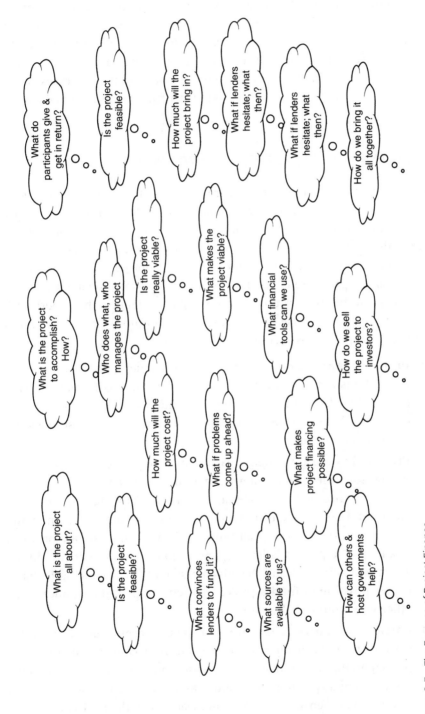

Figure 2.5 The Essence of Project Finance

The project financing process, the activities involved in it, and the deliverables produced provide a basis for decisions that are important because they determine the success of projects and are discussed in more detail in Chapter 4 and subsequent chapters. The crux of project finance was illustrated by the author at a client meeting with Figure 2.5 in answer to the question: What is the essence of project finance? Answers to surrounding questions describe what project finance is all about and the processes, activities, analyses, and evaluations required to structure projects to make them financeable effectively.

2.6 COMMON MISCONCEPTIONS AND MYTHS

Misconceptions about project finance are present not only in groups outside this area but also, among some project participants due to limited exposure to, knowledge of, and experience in project finance. These misconceptions manifest themselves in errors of judgment, incomplete evaluations, miscalculations, wrong assumptions and decisions, poor negotiation positions and posture, and protracted negotiations and re-work of agreements. Project finance misconceptions account for a good part of lengthy back and forth negotiations and are a cause of project failures. Opinions or beliefs behind expressed misconceptions include the following:

1. **Project finance is nonrecourse finance.** True; there is no recourse to the sponsor(s) balance sheet, but in the event of risks materializing that lead to discontinuing operations and dissolution of the project company, there is a loss of their investment. No recourse does not equal no loss in any case.

2. **Project financing is cheap.** True, but it depends. There are cases where subsidies from international development associations or donor organizations, unilateral and multilateral agency enhancements, and government in-kind contributions make the financing costs of a project lower than without them. But, corporate or direct financing of a project is less expensive than project financing in the absence of subsidies and the advantage of project financing is that it makes possible to fund a project of credit impaired customers than otherwise would be the case.

3. **Barriers to entry guarantee project success.** Because infrastructure projects ordinarily involve the host country government's participation, the issuance of licenses and permits, a monopoly project-company status, and substantial upfront investment, these factors usually ensure the economic viability of the project company. Because of the project-security package, this thinking does not take

into account fluidity of developing country political and economic conditions and industry and market changes and often leads to complacency. Complacency in the quality of the project company's products or services and management of the relationship with the host country's government agencies invites competition that usually come in the form of a second operating license or regulatory regime changes.

4. **Build it and they will come.** This belief assumes that because there is a need for the project company's products or services and the characteristics of the project will satisfy customer or user needs. Therefore, the project will attract a sufficient number of customers or users and create adequate demand to make the project a success. However, without market research to establish desire for the product or service and the willingness of customers or users and their ability to pay, such view is baseless. That is, it does not really understand needs and pricing that would make the products or services affordable, it is plagued with overoptimistic revenue forecasts, and is prescription of project underperformance and even failure.

5. **Project approvals for developing country projects are routine.** This misconception has to do with the presence of ECA and multilateral agency enhancements, support, and project reviews flexibility which make approvals easier to get because of the urgent help needed by developing countries with no public budgets to undertake infrastructure projects. This is not true and comes from ignorance of processes, evaluations, and requirements of these institutions that are accountable for investments to all projects they support and, therefore, they ensure that their investments or support are in viable projects. Export credit agencies and multilaterals have expertise in scrutinizing projects using well-developed processes and requirements that take time to complete before final board review and approval. That is to say, sponsors or developers should not expect immediate project support approvals; not even an indication of their interest in participation.

6. **If the project passed due diligence, there is no problem.** Unlike lenders, other project participants are under the impression that raising funds for the project is forthcoming simply because the due diligence found no glaring major errors, omissions, discrepancies, technical issues, and objections and that funding is then only a formality. The due diligence is only one hurdle the project must pass to make it bankable. Other hurdles, such as stress testing the validity of assumptions and financial ratios under less favorable scenarios and

validating creditworthiness of parties behind the security package must also be performed.

7. **The project advisors know; we do not need to know.** This mindset of sponsor or developer project teams is troubling because it assumes that project financing advisors fully understand sponsor and the customer true needs, interests, objectives, and requirements. It also assumes that advisors have the ability to conduct appropriate analyses and evaluations and their capacity to deliver on all expectations. This mentality leads to delays, rework, and inefficiencies throughout the process and increase advisor and project costs. Also, it does not ensure that these participants receive the benefits they expect to receive from the project.

8. **Any project can be project financed.** This view is too naïve to hold true universally. Projects need to meet the basic criteria of project finance. That is, they must have adequate and stable cash flow and reasonable debt ratios, sufficient sponsor equity and debt funding, credit enhancements, and adequate lender protection, all of which necessitate development and negotiation of agreements. There is also a project size requirement because of the high cost of project development and preparation and negotiation of contractual agreements: The minimum project size for project financing purposes is in the neighborhood of US$75 to $100 million. Otherwise, the project costs are overbearing and projects become unprofitable.

CHAPTER 3

The Record of Project Finance

Lessons to Avoid Failures

roject finance deals are commonly viewed as sound investments because of the security packages and the web of negotiated contracts. The prevailing view is that failures are limited and losses are minimized when the security package includes a security agreement, a pledge of assets agreement, a mortgage or a deed of trust, and a direct agreement. Other considerations that limit failures are the following:

1. Sponsor equity investment is usually adequate in the 20% to 40% range of project costs
2. Sufficient risk insurance across all common project risks and strong host government guarantees are pledged
3. Tight engineering, procurement, and construction (EPC), offtake, supply, and operations and management (O&M) contracts are negotiated and signed
4. Interest rate and foreign exchange rate hedging contracts are in place
5. The ECA and/or multilateral agency providing support and help in project approvals is present
6. Lenders always get rights to control project company assets in the event of underperformance
7. Waterfall accounts, covenants, and restrictions are included in the financing documentation
8. Depository account agreements control the flow of cash from the project company

For large capital investment projects, it is difficult to measure success or failure for three reasons: Assessment is done along several dimensions, political considerations cloud project performance ratings, and failure grading is usually subjective. For example, Global Infrastructure Basel (2014) grades sustainable infrastructure along a number of dimensions, most of them being qualitative, such as:

1. Meeting host government financial and social objectives
2. Proactive and effective risk project lifecycle management
3. Equitable and balanced project cost and benefit agreements
4. Transparency of procurement processes and practices
5. Sound and efficient project financing is obtained
6. Sufficient project output to fill consumer or user needs
7. Project economic value creation according to project evaluations and project company business plan

Project finance success is difficult to measure and the alternative is to define project failure by the default rate of project finance loans. A Moody's

Investor Services 10-year study shows that "project finance is a robust class of specialized lending" and that "default rates of project finance loans are consistent with those recovery rates of low-grade corporate issuers and recovery rates of 80.3% as defined by Basel II." Notice, however, that the number of projects that failed to achieve the expected economic value is greater than the number of bank loan defaults because projects may not create the expected economic value and yet, not have loan defaults.

> The definition of Basel II default rates is based on a complex formula, but for practical purposes they are bank losses that include unpaid principal and accumulated interest, discounts, and the costs of collecting on default loans.

In the next section we present findings from different studies of project finance loan defaults by industry and region. For our purposes, loan defaults constitute project failures that are commonly accepted as a reasonable quantitative way to measure objectively if a project has met financial expectations. Section 3.2 is a discussion of common reasons for project finance failures along major categories and prepares the stage to avoid pitfalls in different project stages. Section 3.3 presents a summary of valuable key lessons learned help avoid failures and increase chances of project success.

3.1 THE RECORD OF PROJECT FINANCE DEALS

To get a sense of the size of the project finance market and the extent of project finance failures Table 3.1.1 shows the total number of 7,959 projects in the 1987 to 2014 period by industry. Table 3.1.2 displays the number of project defaults for the same period by industry where we observe an average default rate of 9%. However, the telecom and media industry has the highest default rate (90.9%) and the industry with the least defaults is the transportation industry with 4% default rate.

Table 3.1.3 gives another perspective of default rates for the 1987 to 2014 period by region and one gets an immediate impression that Western Europe and North American projects have the most defaults. This is not true when considering the large project finance deals in Western Europe and North America.

It is very instructive, however, to look at the reasons for project finance defaults across all projects during the same period in Table 3.1.4. Market exposure factors count for 26.5% of bank loan defaults followed by 20.6% failures due to technical design issues, while changes in host country regulatory changes are responsible for only 2.9% of default rates.

Table 3.1.1   Total Projects by Industry, 1987–2014

Power	3022
Infrastructure	2298
Oil and gas	1108
Telecom and media	88
Metals and mining	420
Chemical production	174
Manufacturing	111
Transport	110
Leisure and recreation	88
Total	7959

Source: Annual Project Finance Default and Recovery Study 1980–2014.
S&P Global Market Intelligence (June 2016).

Table 3.1.2   Defaults by Industry 1987–2014

Power	277	41.1%
Infrastructure	149	22.1%
Media and telecom	80	11.9%
Oil and gas	65	9.6%
Metals and mining	49	7.3%
Chemicals production	21	3.1%
Manufacturing	16	2.4%
Leisure and recreation	10	1.5%
Transportation	4	0.6%
Other	3	0.5%
Total	674	100.0

Source: Annual Project Finance Default and Recovery Study 1980–2014. S&P Global Market Intelligence (June 2016).

Table 3.1.3   Total Default Rates by Region, 1987–2014

Western Europe	246
North America	159
Asia Pacific	80
Latin America	71
Oceania	32
Africa and Middle East	20
Eastern Europe	16
Total	624

Source: Annual Project Finance Default and Recovery Study 1980–2014. S&P Global Market Intelligence (June 2016).

Table 3.1.4 Reasons for Project Defaults
Across All Projects

Market exposure	26.5%
Technical design	20.6%
Counterparty problems	18.0%
Structural weaknesses	17.7%
Operational issues	8.8%
Hedging/commodity exposure	5.9%
Regulation related changes	2.9%

Source: Ben MacDonald. "Lessons Learned from 20 Years of
Rating Global Project Finance Debt," *Standard & Poor's Ratings
Services Credit Week* (January 21, 2015).

A source of project finance defaults is Moody's survey of 1983–2013
project finance loans, which shows a cumulative default rate of 6.4% that is
consistent with low investment-grade corporate issuers (Davison, 2015).
A different Moody's survey of 2,639 projects from 1983 to 2008 showed that
213 of the projects had a senior loan default, of which the ultimate recovery
rate was 76.4%.

Table 3.1.5 shows default rates by industry based on Moody's review
of 4,069 project finance loans and it is interesting to note that it shows a
different view of project finance default rates by industry than the picture
obtained from Table 3.1.2, explained mostly by the difference in the study's
longer time period.

It is almost impossible to isolate individual factors causing project failures, but the results of a KPMG study of projects not project financed are
instructive and may be comparable for project finance deals. In 2012, only
33% of projects reviewed by KPMG (2013) were delivered on budget and
65% of them delivered on time, but these statistics are not necessarily causes
of project failures. Thus, one must be careful is assigning failure cause to a
single dimension without taking into account all the project stakeholders'
perspectives.

Table 3.1.5 Project Default Rates by Industry

Manufacturing industry defaults	17%
Metals and mining projects	12%
Telecom and media projects	12%
Infrastructure projects	4%
Oil and gas projects	8%
Power generation projects	8%
PPP project defaults	2.6%

Source: Thomson Reuters Project Finance International.

Table 3.1.6 Examples of Project Finance Deals and Reasons of Failures

Project	Reasons for Failure
Road Concession Program in Mexico	25% cost overruns and 30% revenue shortfall; government took project over.
Chad–Cameroon Oil Pipelines	Government diverted money from repayment to purchase weapons.
St. Helena Airport—UK	Poor engineering and technical feasibility study.
Advanced Passenger Train—UK	Wrong technical design and engineering.
Lesotho Highlands Water Project	Higher than expected electric costs, pervasive corruption.
Lake Turkana Fish Processing Plant—Kenya	Unexpectedly high costs, plant shutdown.
Bolivia Cochabamba Water System	Excessive water bills lead to violence, consortium withdrew from the project.
Portugal PPP projects	Lack of experience, government decision delays, cost overruns.
Tacoma Narrows Bridge—US	Financial and time constraints, poor construction; bridge collapse.
The Millennium Dome—UK	Overoptimistic forecasts, failure to attract enough visitors, and financial problems.
Denver International Airport Automated Baggage System	Underscoped project, unrealistic time schedule, unnecessary risks taken, airlines (customers) excluded from planning.
The Channel Tunnel—UK and France	Conflicting interests and objectives, 20% longer construction period, 80% over budget.

Source: International Project Leadership Academy.

There have been many project finance failures over the years, but a small sample of projects considered failures and the main reasons for failures are shown in Table 3.1.6. It is instructive to examine the many and varied causes of project failures.

3.2 REASONS FOR PROJECT FAILURES

Based on project post mortem experiences and project finance participant discussions, in the sections that follow we identify failures factors using the Fishbone diagram shown in Figure 3.2 and discuss root causes of failures by key areas of project finance. These root cause factors, in turn, provide motivation for developing better alternatives, processes, and approaches that can minimize these failures. The analysis is focused on 12 main categories of problem areas that lead to project failures; namely: strategy and project objectives, screening and preparation, bidding and procurements, skills and competencies, processes and practices, project economics, technical

Purpose of root-cause analysis: To identify, break down, and eliminate the root causes that contribute to strategic decision challenges and problems.

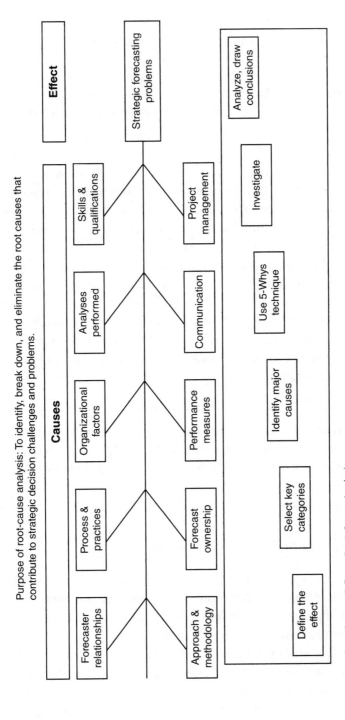

Figure 3.2 Project Finance Failures Root-Cause Analysis.

issues, risk management, project management, contracts and agreements, financing, and organizational and operational factors.

> The fishbone diagram is also known as a cause-and-effect diagram that gets its name from its design, which looks like fish bones. It is a tool to visualize and categorize the potential reasons of a problem and identify its root causes. The purpose of root-cause analysis is to identify, examine closely, and help eliminate the factors causing failures.

The purpose of project failure root-cause analysis is identify, break down, and eliminate the root causes that contribute to project finance challenges and failures. The process used is shown at the bottom of Figure 3.2 and it starts with first defining the effect or problem and selecting key categories to examine. Then major causes are identified using the 5-whys technique and further investigation is conducted to provide enough evidence and evaluation to draw conclusions. In the subsections that follow each problem category is examined and the predominant factors identified. The analysis is by no means exhaustive, but it covers the majority of reasons that contribute to project failures and while individual factors may not be sufficient to derail a project, in most cases there is a confluence of factors that cause project failure.

> 5-Whys technique: It is a method used in Six Sigma used to identify the root cause of a problem by asking repeatedly five times why to get beyond symptoms and to determine relationships between different root causes.

3.2.1 Strategy and Project Objectives

One of the first reasons for large capital expenditure project failures is an apparent disconnect between undertaking projects and corporate strategy and project objectives. That is, projects do not have the benefit of a sound rationale justification and thorough strategic and portfolio-fit assessment. Because of that, and in the absence of a well-thought-out project strategy, project objectives are vague, confusing, and unsupported by facts. In such a context, project objectives are influenced by excessive optimism and the problem is compounded by wishful thinking begetting unrealistic expectations. This is true of some project sponsor or developer and other project stakeholders' objectives, including those of the host government ceding authorities.

In the absence of a clear project strategy that is consistent with the overall project stakeholder strategy, conflicting participant interests and objectives can create cooperation problems and result in longer negotiations of contracts and project delays. This kind of environment is characterized by impeded communication, coordination, cooperation, and collaboration all of which result in mistrust and indecision. What comes out of that context is a set of different and unreconciled individual project stakeholder objectives which drive project forecasts and financials everywhere. This is not a correct, consensus, reality checking, and validating-assumptions environment. Another factor contributing to project failures is that project objectives do not align with project requirements. That is, a gap exists between project specifications and performance requirements and unrealistic sponsor expectations and objectives which results in wrong cost estimates and different perceptions of project financeability.

A different failure factor related to project sponsor strategy and project objectives has to do with project portfolio management, or more precisely, with little consideration and analysis given to the project impacts on the portfolio allocation and risk composition in current project finance practices. So, why is that a problem? It is because it results in unbalanced portfolios in terms of risk exposure, blurred strategic intent and clarity of purpose, and suboptimal allocation of capital investments. It is also because successful project portfolios require correspondingly appropriate allocation of scarce financial and human scarce resources possessing the right skills and competencies. This is true of all types of project stakeholders, but particularly true of project sponsors or developers initiating large projects.

3.2.2 Screening and Preparation

Projects starting with unclear strategy and project objectives are followed by inadequate preparation and project screening, which are then complicated by a series of other project failure factors. Screening is usually limited to technical achievability and financial viability while ignoring other tests, such as the ability to execute successfully, compatibility of technical platforms, and alternative project investment prospects. Poor sponsor-team preparation for a large project begins with reliance on the initiating organization to move the project forward and not creating early on a dedicated project team with experienced personnel supported by external advisors and consultants. But, even in cases of early project team formation, failures occur when teams are inadequately resourced or not fully dedicated to project screening, preparation, and development. Also, when little attention is paid to processes and required financial and human resource systems to ensure proper screening and preparation, disappointing project evaluation and performance follow. Other project failures related to screening and preparation are due to inadequate host government preparation, systems, resources, and project development plans and processes.

Failure factors caused by host governments originate with inadequate ceding-agency preparation, issuance of bids with unclear project requirements, and underestimating the financial support needed for the project. On the sponsor side, inadequate understanding of the host country macroeconomic and operating environment; partial knowledge of industry structure, capacity, and dynamics; and little appreciation of the effects of megatrends and subtrends are factors causing false assessments of project viability and subsequent project failure. Also, poor assessment of host country social and living conditions for skilled project company expatriates result in difficulties recruiting talent needed to manage the project company. The combined effect of these factors leads to poor risk assessment and inadequate risk allocation and mitigation.

The main factors resulting in project failures from the screening and operational fit assessment side are inadequate understanding of project equipment requirements and design specifications, and ambiguity of performance specifications that result in flawed cost estimates and financing requirements. While the absence of standardized project screening and evaluation templates is sometimes blamed for project finance failures, the reality is that projects are unique and require the tailoring of processes and assessments throughout the project stages. However, there is cursory, if any, sponsor-company strengths, weakness, opportunities, threats (SWOT) analysis, which impedes the project team's ability to execute a project successfully. The absence of early and comprehensive political, economic, social, technical, legal, educational, and demographic assessments produces erroneous project-feasibility studies. Time after time, weak industry, market, and competitor assessments and a lack of benchmarking data result in the creation of faulty assumption sets and skewed economic evaluations. These factors complicate the due diligence process and result in incomplete risk assessments and weak due diligence reports that weaken the major cornerstones of project finance.

The failure factors mentioned above are project-preparation causes, but factors related directly to raising financing failures have to do with poor PFO and project team preparation and planning with respect to ensuring clear and complete processes, integrated planning and budgeting, sound financial models development, and correct data and assumption inputs. Just as damaging a factor is the inability of sponsor PFOs to educate, prepare, and help the host government ceding agency understand all project finance requirements and what it takes to complete a project successfully. Also, a failure to cultivate good working relationships with funding sources globally, and to know well their processes and requirements for different types of projects, is another factor leading to project finance complications and delays.

3.2.3 Bidding and Procurement

Many of the bidding and procurement-related reasons for project failures stem from confusion among project stakeholders, misunderstandings of requirements, protracted fact finding, and back and forth clarification seeking discussions. More often than not, a lack of host-government bidding process transparency and clear selection criteria throws projects off track. This is a prime factor for frictions, delays, and project failure. Also, the difficulties of inexperienced sponsor teams working with different cultures and host-government bureaucracies add to mistakes, delays, and inefficiencies, as does the absence of rigorous bidding and procurement processes, which lead to wrong assessments of project development costs.

Ambiguous bid requirements and project specifications even in the presence of good intentions result in project changes, delays, technical difficulties, longer negotiations, and cost overruns. But, the effect of low ball bids by competitors not bound by laws such as the US Foreign Corruption Practices Act, causes sponsors going back to the drawing board, making costly technical changes and price adjustments in order to prepare more competitive bids to win a project and in the process end up with a losing proposition. More factors responsible for failures, however, have to do with rigged bid processes and procurement practices and, sometimes, with host government officials' corruption and fraud. And, one cannot ignore the effect of loss of proprietary information contained in bids which are assessed by independent agents hired by the ceding authority and leaks to competitors on the current and future project chances of structuring profitable deals.

3.2.4 Skills and Competencies

It is widely recognized that an all-around project finance knowledge deficit is a leading cause of project finance failures. Just as important, however, is the point that because the knowledge, skills, and experience required in project finance are so broad that, by necessity, they are rare. To work around that constraint, they are compartmentalized and highly specialized. Engineers know project design and technology; project finance associates know accounting and tax, financial modeling, and instruments; legal teams know law, contract development, and negotiation of agreements; but they do not know each other's area. Therefore, all the responsibility of integrating the vast amount of diverse knowledge, analyses, and evaluations rests with the project manager supported by the PFO. In large capital investment projects, if the set of required project finance and project management skills and competencies is weak and not outsourced, it is a common and major cause of project failures. This is primarily because the inability to direct and integrate effectively results and deliverables of varied and specialized assessments into a unified evaluation that results in erroneous conclusions and project failures.

A sponsor project team's lack of international business experience and its inability to work with different cultures and government bureaucracies to gain political support and negotiate contracts effectively is another failure factor. This manifests itself in long negotiations and contract revisions and an inability to implement the project company's business plan successfully. Similarly, weak and ineffective PFOs are responsible for project failures in three ways: The lack of project finance skills and experience, the inability to screen and select qualified external advisors and consultants, and failure to create processes that are best suited for each project and assign roles and responsibilities appropriately.

A lack of adequate PFO skills and competencies extends to unfamiliarity with specific duties in the different project stages, and failure to lead and manage project finance processes and create sound project company business plans. This is partly due to lack of critical mass of project finance transactions for a sponsor company and excessive reliance on the skill set and guidance of external advisors, who may not have a thorough understanding of the sponsor company's needs, strategy, and objectives, nor the customers' needs and requirements. A more common factor, however, is the limited set of established, good working relationships with associates in funding sources and partial knowledge of financial instruments and their proper application in different projects. Lack of innovation added to each of these factors individually can lead to project failures, but when combined they undoubtedly lead to unsuccessful project structuring and financing.

3.2.5 Project Processes

Processes in project finance are important because (1) they serve as clear maps and blueprints that guide the project team through the maze of activities to be performed and do it consistently well, and (2) of the necessary integration of each process' analyses and evaluations into other processes with minimal frictions and adjustments. Sound processes are complete, efficient, parsimonious, and effective procedures that have been executed successfully a number of times and lead to the least time to completion and lowest costs of doing a project. Such processes are not a common occurrence in many project finance deals in the current paradigm. In fact, the opposite is true; that is, project failures result from flawed or incomplete processes that are developed with an orientation towards expediency and weak organizational cultures, or when dictated by wrong or misguided project objectives.

The creation of effective project finance processes involves skilled associates, good preparation and planning, and the right financial and contract management systems, lack of which leads to wrong evaluations, schedule slippages, and errors. Even when there are sound processes in place, a lack of adherence to tested processes and procedures, and difficulty managing the integration of the various processes, leads to failures to meet project financing requirements as well as compliance with lender, ECA, and multilateral institution guidelines and requirements. Project failures due to process defects are usually related and traced to the following causes:

1. Compartmentalized sponsor-company processes of sales, engineering, finance, legal, and external affairs organizations with individual needs, processes, and objectives

2. Difficulties in dovetailing internal sponsor company processes to create a seamless, consistent, and complete end-to-end project finance process and winning proposals

3. Incomplete, inconsistent, faulty host-government processes that are challenging to reconcile with sponsor and funding source processes and requirements

4. Impeded all-around communication, coordination, cooperation, and collaboration within the sponsor entity and between project participants leading to inability to manage processes effectively and to project delays, errors, and omissions

5. An unwarranted, single focus on engineering, finance, or legal processes at the expense of others, and selecting project managers from the project initiating organization who may not the most qualified managers

6. The exclusion of valuable skills and expertise due to the internal, competing interests and politics of the project sponsor company

7. Unreasonable timelines, misguided objectives, wrong assumptions driving project finance processes, and duplication of work trying to reconcile different process outputs

3.2.6 Project Economics

A major part of project finance failures is due to insufficient and unsatisfactory economic evaluations; that is, inadequate project cost/benefit analyses.

Deficient or faulty project economic evaluations are the direct result of poor environmental assessment, lack of megatrend and subtrend evaluations, and scanty market, industry, and competitor analysis; underestimated creeping project costs, and overestimated revenues. Inadequate economic evaluations can be due to erroneous data and information which, in turn, cause wrong assumptions, the effect of which is to contaminate the results of forecasting and financial models. However, it is not only deficient or unreasonable assumptions that cause the failure of projects; it is also the casual use of assumptions without reality checks and an absence of reasonableness checks of the resulting analyses and assessments.

Deterministic project cost modeling may be appropriate under conditions of certainty of project specifications and requirements and stability of economic and market conditions of the host government and the sponsor countries. In the absence of those conditions, miscalculations and underestimation of cost overruns become common and significant. Also, limited consideration to possible specification, technology, design revisions, and cost changes, and their inclusion in cost analyses along with lack of provisions to handle cost escalations, lead to wrong cost projections. More important, however, are project finance failures related to deterministic project revenue modeling using overly optimistic operating scenarios and optimistic pricing and project-output demand that yields unjustifiably high revenue projections.

Inadequate economic evaluations are frequently traced back to deficient screening in feasibility studies, weak due diligence reports, and erroneous risk assessment assumptions and ineffective risk allocation. These factors lead to project failures in the presence of incomplete, and inaccurate financial models and evaluations that are usually coupled with inadequate or optimistic project company business plans. In many projects, little attention is paid to performing sensitivity analysis of financial results to changes in controllable factors. This is a problem because good project forecast realization plans cannot be developed for simulated scenarios that do not capture the effects of the sensitivity of revenue drivers under less optimistic views. The end result is untested and unreasonably high estimates of project value creation that cannot materialize.

Repeatedly, the point has been made that inadequate reasonableness checks of assumptions and evaluations result in project failures. This is a crucial requirement in the project economic evaluation and financial model development well ahead of the due diligence report, prior to the start of operations, and also in the operating stage. Checking the reasonableness of assumptions in the operating stage presumes development of a sound business plan and an early warning system to alert the project company's management team of risks appearing on the horizon so that measures are taken to course correct and avoid invalidation of the economic evaluation which was the basis of decisions to implement the project. Lastly, an obsession with project risk management and security arrangements and insufficient attention paid to sound project economic evaluation also causes project finance failures.

3.2.7 Technical Issues

Technical factors contributing to project failures begin with unclear, conflicting, wrongly stated, unreasonable, misinterpreted, or misunderstood project requirements and specifications. In this case, sponsors and the host government ceding authority share responsibility equally, but lack of host-government project team technical know-how and an unwillingness to invest in getting technical knowledge accentuates the likelihood of technical issues causing project failures. Faulty project design and engineering are factors that lead to project failures when cost considerations create rigid designs that require subsequent modifications, expensive changes, and protracted negotiations.

Project scope creep and associated changes of requirements are failure factors because of capital cost overruns and schedule delays well beyond planned levels. Overlooked physical project-asset security needs and cyberspace security protection end up increasing costs when projects are retrofitted and cause operational disruptions, which mean revenue losses. Additionally, new and untested technologies intended to increase productivity and project efficiency can lead to project failures because they require changes, schedule slippages, and cost overruns. At other times, the poor reliability of technology components used causes construction delays and cost increases beyond insured levels, as does the problem of technology, equipment, and systems integration in large, complex projects.

Conflict between technology suppliers and noncooperation or sabotage during construction lead to project completion delays and, often, to price increases in the operations stage of the project. Another factor related to technology is the inability to attract qualified talent to manage technology update issues in the operations stage and this leads to higher operating costs and revenue loss. As importantly, underestimating technology transfer costs and long training periods of local personnel cause large adjustments to the project company business plan projections which alter the project's profit profile. Finally, inadequate monitoring and management of technology issues throughout a project's lifetime, the absence of reserves to cover cost increases, and provisions to handle schedule delays throw projects off the planned track and into eventual failure.

3.2.8 Risk Management

Project risks are events, developments, or changes whose occurrence adversely affects a project's ability to achieve expected objectives. Risk management is the process of identifying those factors, assessing their impact, analyzing and prioritizing, mitigating, and monitoring them to control chances of occurrence and manage their impact. One of the risk management factors is the reality that not all project risks are knowable before agreements are negotiated and signed in order to subject them to the risk management process. Also, the inability to identify sources of new risks in the operations stage has the same effect and sometimes projects fail because there is no ongoing, proactive risk management for the duration of the project and only reactive and inadequate risk management. In other projects, risk management processes and activities are poorly carried out and end up in construction delays and the project risk management in the operations stage relying entirely on signed contracts and insurance, which causes friction among project stakeholders and further delays.

Disconnects between corporate risk tolerance and project risk levels lead to internal sponsor organization frictions, project changes, and delays. This happens partly because of incomplete risk identification and assessment or due to a lack of skills and experiences across the management structure, both of which are project failure factors. Frequently, inadequate risk management happens because it is based on shaky assumptions and erroneous feasibility studies and due diligence reports. While these are the main reasons that risk assessments are inadequate, in some instances it is the inability to quantify correctly the likelihood and impact of risks that result in inadequate risk mitigation. Also, incorrect risk identification and assessment are sometimes due to incomplete or flawed external environment and project analyses and evaluations.

Project failures can also be due to inadequate risk allocation; that is, imbalanced, inequitable, disproportional allocation to benefits obtained; or allocation to parties other than those best able to handle them. Often, inadequate risk mitigation factors that cause project failures have to do with weak security packages, insurance, and hedging contracts. Occasionally, some risks considered small are left uninsured, but their occurrences in conjunction with other factors lead to failures. Unbalanced or inequitable risk allocation creates resentments among the stakeholders bearing the risks, noncooperation, and delays in completing project negotiations. This is often a reason for intervention by regional development banks or multilateral institutions to remedy the situation and improve the project risk profile by a more equitable allocation of benefits and risks. Delays associated with multilateral agency intervention may sometimes produce residual resentment and reduced cooperation can then lead to project delays.

A good part of risk-related failure factors has to do with insufficient attention to managing project design, changes to requirements and specifications, scope creep and subsequent cost overruns, and project-site conditions risks. In the operating stage, an inability of the project company to compete in changed regulatory or commercial environments leads to project failures due to the lack of using a business plan realization strategy as a risk minimization tool. More importantly, risk-related project failures occur because far more attention is given to risk management issues than to sound assessment of project economics. In an effort to improve risk management and reduce project failures, sponsors are initiating efforts such as education, increased senior management engagement, communication of the approval risk framework, and alignment of project risk with organizational risk framework (KPMG, 2013).

3.2.9 Project Management

Many project management-related failure factors have to do with knowledge and experience deficits, which is further aggravated by the lack of project management infrastructure systems and tools. Another significant factor is the assignment of the project management responsibility to associates who initiated the project instead of assignment to the best-qualified project managers in the sponsor company. Inadequate project management governance is a failure factor that goes beyond the project management team skill and competency deficits and includes issues related to the processes used and inadequate resources allocated to the project-management function.

Unclear roles and responsibilities and overlaps create confusion and resistance to cooperate during handoffs of responsibilities and deliverables and in inability to project manage effectively large capital investment projects. However, most project management-related failure factors have their origin in the following:

1. Conflicting or inconsistent project stakeholder expectations and objectives
2. Inconsistent or flawed project stakeholder processes across all participants
3. Poor project management of individual project stakeholder processes and their integration with those of the sponsor project team
4. Impeded and ineffective communication, coordination, cooperation, and collaboration among different stakeholder project managers
5. Difficulties in coordinating individual process outputs with input requirements of other project stakeholder processes

At times, poor management of project stakeholder expectations from the start is a root cause of project management inadequacies, especially in the presence of inadequate project monitoring capabilities and strong project controls. Aggressive and unrealistic project schedules and inadequate staffing with qualified project management associates and support cause coordination problems that translate into project failures. Also, creeping project scope causes project management problems that are magnified by personnel turnover over long periods. Additionally, motivational issues over long periods of project management occur due to stressful confrontations in project evaluations, coordination, and negotiations that lead to project management ineffectiveness that take attention away from project financing needs and lead to project failure.

3.2.10 Contracts and Agreements

One of the first reasons usually cited for project failures is related to contracts and agreements; namely, weak host-country legal and regulatory systems and enforcement of contracts. Differences in sponsor country and host country languages and laws complicate effective negotiation, implementation, and arbitration of contractual agreements due to misinterpretations or inability to grasp the impact of differences in legal intervention for conflict resolution. International project contract development and negotiation is a highly specialized discipline that needs input and validation of facts, assumptions, analyses, and assessments by external, independent experts. Yet, at times contracts and agreements are based solely on the project due diligence report findings and risk allocations, and the result is deficient contracts that do not provide protection against project failures.

Contractual misunderstandings are a cause of project construction delays and financial closings, which lead to a failure to negotiate reasonable, balanced, and sustainable contracts with acceptable terms for the parties involved. The lack of a contract that balances project costs, benefits, and its sustainability are linked to eventual project failure. Furthermore, aggressive contract schedule pressures to complete construction and financing can lead to drafting weak or faulty agreements, especially concerning contract enforceability of offtake agreements which are commonly thought of as viable and fairly secure arrangements.

Legal teams involved in drafting and negotiating project contracts are primarily composed of external legal expertise with the sponsor legal group taking a lesser role in the creation and management contracts unless, of course, there is a critical mass of projects in the pipeline and the required in-house expertise is developed. This makes the integration of the various legal processes and analyses, evaluations, and desired terms and conditions with those of other project stakeholders difficult. Lack of harmony and cohesion in legal document development leads to project failures, especially when sound contract management systems and required specialized expertise are absent. Also, complications in managing a multitude of contracts by reams of paper make it impossible to effectively handle changes to the web of the contractual project basis without major delays.

In some projects, there is an excessive focus on contracts and agreements to manage sponsor risks and lesser attention to project economics and funding needs, sources, and implements. In the midst of such excessive focus, inadequate insurance contracts are concluded because of misguided and misinterpreted project objectives. At times, insufficient insurance and interest rate and foreign exchange hedging contracts are signed that expose the project company to adverse costs and the sponsor company to profit variability. It would be a serious omission if the high costs of project contract development, negotiations, changes and revisions, and renegotiations are not included in contract-related factors that lead to project cost underestimation and a failure to meet financial expectations.

3.2.11 Project Financing

Universal project failures across all types of projects, host countries, sizes, and complexities begin with two major factors: Inadequate project finance skills and competencies in the sponsor company and the host-government organizations, with overoptimism permeating all aspects of project development, assessment, financing, and operations. The next factor is insufficient, upfront project sponsor equity investment resulting in an unwillingness among lenders to provide debt financing, which results in delays and higher loan costs, and more stringent loan covenants. But, so does the host-government's inability to make debt or equity contributions in hard currency and deliver on agreed-to terms of contracts and agreements. These situations are further worsened by the inability to deliver on future obligations and credit support to raise permanent financing. The result is project failure on several dimensions.

The lack of strong project-sponsor senior management commitment and host-government political support, along with failure to dedicate sufficient and properly qualified resources to do the project right at the start of the project, are common causes of project failures. Again, inconsistent and conflicting project stakeholder objectives, the misinterpretation of requirements and deliverables, and even unintentional misrepresentations lead to delays in drafting and wrapping up financial documentation negotiations. These factors cause increases in project costs and more expensive debt financing, which are cited as common factors of project failures.

PFOs of sponsors with a critical mass of projects are staffed with competent and experienced associates who develop individual project plans and processes. But, an absence of standardized project financing templates is often given as a reason for the financing failures of small and inexperienced PFOs. A lack of project finance experience is linked with the use of erroneous, untested, and overly optimistic assumptions that generate unreasonable project forecasts that are not realized. Also, inadequate feasibility studies and project economic evaluations are characterized by omissions and errors and incomplete financial modeling, and the evaluation of financial model outputs that give a false sense of cash-flow adequacy. In some instances, shaky project company business plans and operational models are used to support financing and end up not enabling the project company to realize its potential value creation and benefits in all areas, including sponsor tax advantages and increased tax revenues to the host government.

Poorly structured projects fail to make projects bankable because of their opportunistic nature, expedience, and unwarranted optimism. Such projects experience delay eventualities and unfavorable consumer or user acceptance of the project company's product or service, competitor entry to its industry, and disappointing regulatory rulings. Structural, financial, and operational weaknesses lead to poorly structured projects and higher financing costs and such projects fail to negotiate advantageous loan terms and conditions. Additionally, the absence of good sponsor-project team working relationships with associates and decision makers of funding sources precludes getting the benefit of their sound, early advice and guidance. A more important factor, however, is a lack of experience in integrating technical, contractual, and financing facilities and instruments in the marketing of projects to investors effectively. Projects marketed ineffectively take longer to complete financing and at higher costs and have lengthy sponsor, host government, ECA, and multilateral agency approval times.

Earlier, we mentioned that a number of project finance failure factors have to do with inadequate project risk identification, assessment, and mitigation. Some failures occur because not all risks are identifiable or because risks viewed as having a small impact that can be easily absorbed and should not affect financing may turn out to have larger than expected impacts. Large impact risks cause project failures if not all their sources and timing of occurrence are identified correctly and financing proceeds based on shifting conditions. There is a lack of a common standard among stakeholders to judge risk-mitigation effectiveness and a clear measure of successful risk coverage; however, having adequate coverage is a requirement. When the inadequacy of security packages and insufficient risk coverage are present in the interest rate, exchange rate, and local currency convertibility and commodity hedging contracts, project failures often occur. Likewise, weak guarantees, insurance contracts, and host-government support used to raise financing can lead to project finance failures. This is especially true in the absence of early warning systems for risks and corrective steps to be implemented.

3.2.12 Organizational and Operational

There are project finance failures caused by organizational and operational factors, starting with the many decision-making layers in sponsor and host-government organizations that have different views of organizational risk tolerance versus those present in the project. This results in long project duration and additional delays, which leads to decision maker and project-team weariness, which is pronounced when there is impeded all-around communication, coordination, cooperation, and collaboration. Additionally, high project team and senior management turnover in project stakeholder organizations creates discontinuities in handoffs of responsibilities, earlier work, and deliverables. Agreements come into question, it takes more time to understand and accept what was decided earlier, and such discontinuities and delays contribute to project failures.

Weak organizational structures, a lack of project-finance knowledge, and a lack of interdisciplinary training and development in the technical, legal, project finance, and project management areas can cause project failures. Also, shortages of qualified local talent cause expensive international human-resource searches and costly local personnel training and technology transfers that result in cost overruns and less effective management of the project company. Furthermore, an unwillingness to fund project-company management and leadership development amplifies shortages in the effective monitoring of large project performance and the inability of the project company to course correct when faced with adverse commercial developments. Occasionally, poor living and educational conditions for expatriates in the host country necessitate reliance on contracts with the O&M company for required project performance and costly incentives to achieve it.

Shortages and a low quality of production inputs and materials result in poor project-company performance, as do some host government requirements to use local resources and materials. Project-company management complacency and their heavy reliance on regulations that protect them cause an inability to effectively address changes in capacity and output requirements, or to respond to the entry of new competitors and variations in user or consumer needs. These factors are often cited as factors for project failure as well as for the inability of the project companies to implement business plans, especially under host-government regulatory authority interference.

Lastly, project stakeholder misrepresentations of facts and requirements due to their lack of experience working with different cultures also creates conditions for project failure.

3.3 LESSONS LEARNED

The intent of this section is to highlight some lessons learned in past projects and not to itemize project finance success factors since they are the opposites of the causes of project failures. The first lesson learned is confirmation that it is easy to judge the failure of private project finance deals from the sponsor perspective if the expected project NPV or IRR are not realized or if loan default are the criteria used. However, when it comes to large capital projects involving host governments, ECAs, and multilateral institutions one should not rush to judgment. Project failures in those instances need to be seen from the individual project stakeholders' perspective and a project has failed if it has not met that stakeholder's expectations. Hence, the need to manage all-around stakeholder expectations to balanced and realistic levels using widely accepted performance measures and benchmarks that are appropriate for each project.

In PPP projects success is judged in three dimensions: government policy implementation success, project value-creation success above value for money, and social and economic benefit success. Others believe that success should be declared only if political, economic, and execution objectives are met to a large degree since PPPs are primarily political decisions for the efficient use of limited public sector resources and are not really based on financing goals. Here, political buy-in and sensitivity to host-government needs as well as the involvement of project stakeholders early in the process are essential to avoid failures. The sustainability aspect of infrastructure project success is even more difficult to grade with the introduction of additional dimensions and considerations to rate a project. As expected, the more infrastructure projects a host government undertakes, the quicker and more efficient financing becomes and the better its credit ratings.

Project post-mortem analysis is a useful tool to improve future project chances of achieving expected performance by applying lessons learned from past failures and mistakes of competitors. It helps avoid problems or repeat failures and this is the most prudent approach to engaging in international project finance: Learn from earlier project post-mortem analyses. Creating project teams early with the right skills and competencies in the different areas of desired expertise needed and early planning and preparation sets the stage for sound assessments and for better shaping and managing the project risk profile. Assigning professional project managers with considerable experience managing large projects to lead the project team, and not picking managers involved in the initiation of the project, reduces failures. It is also important to clarify project participant roles and delineate responsibilities early, prepare a complete and sound project process, and create an implementation plan to be executed by skilled managers.

From a new business development perspective, it is necessary for all projects to have several layers of reality and reasonableness checks, tests, and validations and to insist on independent, critical, and objective analyses and evaluations. The sponsor's PFO or the project finance advisors should be prepared to educate the personnel of the host-government agency responsible for the project in key aspects of project finance. It is equally important that sponsor organization skills and expertise be developed in marketing large projects to funding sources and potential investors. Localized expertise must be integrated early in PFO processes because each participant has only a limited understanding of the others' functions, processes, and focus. This is important because:

a. Sponsors and external advisors know their industry

b. Funding sources know financial instruments

c. Engineering experts know technology and project design

d. PFOs know project and financing structuring, financial models, and funding channels and instruments

e. Project company and O&M personnel are focused on managing daily operations

f. Legal teams know law and contracts and negotiation of contracts

g. Specific area experts do not know the other project team members areas and how everything needs to dovetail into a cohesive financing plan

The overoptimism and overcomplexity of projects require curbing oversanguinity and simplifying processes so that they can be managed effectively. Independent, critical, and objective evaluations, preferably by competent external advisors and consultants, can help a great deal. Project failures need to be seen from the individual project stakeholder's perspective and a project has failed if it does not meet that particular stakeholder's expectations. Hence, the need to monitor performance through all project stages and to manage stakeholder expectations to balanced and realistic levels using widely accepted performance measures and benchmarks.

In project financing, a major concern of the project manager and the PFO are organizational and participant competency, capability gaps, and less than due focus on evaluations connected with poorly:

1. Assessing megatrends and developments in the external environment and their impacts primarily on the industry and the project company

2. Helping to create, negotiate, validate, and manage a common assumption set to drive project feasibility studies and economic evaluations early on

3. Modeling the project structure, process, and operations and creating realistic scenarios to generate project revenue forecasts

4. Identifying, assessing, and allocating project risks, evaluating forecast implications, performing sanity checks, and validating project economics through independent, critical, and objective assessments

5. Coordinating activities and cooperating with internal planning groups and counterparts in the other project stakeholder organizations

One tool commonly used by external advisors and adopted by PFOs and project teams to identify gaps in their respective areas of responsibility is the enterprise model shown in Figure 3.3. The idea here is to identify gaps in areas that are crucial to project financeability success and determine approaches to fill those gaps in order to increase effectiveness and the chances of getting a competitive advantage through project finance.

A major benefit of using the enterprise model in project financing is that it helps to systematically assess each participant's internal organization dimensions from company culture, to competencies and capabilities, to ability to meet project needs and challenges and to deliver on required financial model input needs and evaluations. The second advantage of this model is that it helps in the efficient identification of the prerequisites for financing success. Namely, it helps to determine the key project and team focus areas, the scope of project participation, the most likely scenarios, and long-term forecast requirements. The comparison of the requirements for project effectiveness versus the internal organizations capabilities identifies gaps that need to be filled in order to obtain the objectives of each participant and ensure project success. Then, the measures needed to fill key identified gaps are determined and often negotiated between internal project participants.

The enterprise model is a mechanism to help transform and prioritize capabilities to remain competitive in changing markets. Why is this so important? Because it helps to:

1. Eliminate gaps in organizational structures, skills and competencies, and project management

2. Enhance coordination of processes and activities and project management efficiency

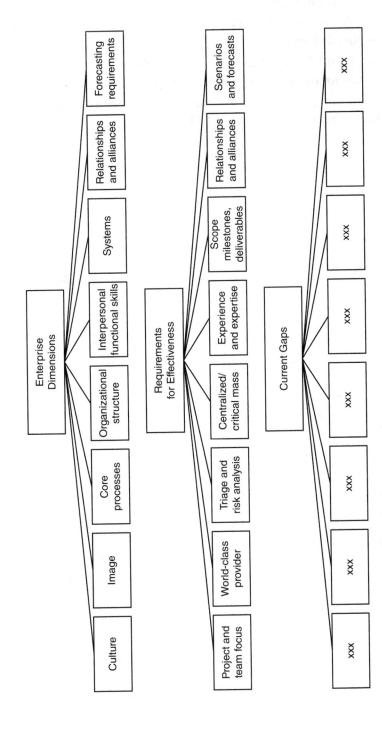

Figure 3.3 Enterprise Model for Project Financing
Source: Adapted from Triantis (1994).

3. Provide clarity on needed changes and assigning responsibilities to appropriate participants
4. Guide the approach to making changes to enhance PFO and project team effectiveness
5. Identify, prioritize, and create future capabilities to support new business development and project financings
6. Move a company towards obtaining a competitive advantage in project finance and win project bids

CHAPTER 4

Project Financing Processes

Roadmaps for Successful Financing

P roject finance processes are a key project sponsor company asset because they help build the capabilities and required infrastructure to support the PFO and the project team. They also provide a common platform for project stakeholder communication, coordination, cooperation, and collaboration. In the context of project financing, processes are designed, ordered, and interconnected in ways that align project objectives with deliverable results. That is, they are procedures that ensure judicious expansion of project team time and financial sources in order to produce expected deliverables efficiently.

Good project finance processes are those that are clearly understood by the PFO and the project team and are efficient and measurable. They provide needed analyses and assessments in an effective manner, and make recommendations to decision makers. They are needed to deal with the complexity of developing and financing this type of deal and they introduce discipline in the project team's undertakings and activities. Well-designed processes result in more reliable deliverables and are proven to be a major ingredient that increases the chances of project success. When project finance processes are consistently managed and executed well, they achieve superior results and may also lead to the project sponsor gaining a competitive advantage through project finance.

Project finance processes are the sequence of project structuring, developing, and financial structuring steps and actions directed to raising financing and closing. As such, they are a map or a blueprint for the project team to execute project financing efficiently. To do that, project finance processes should dictate when something needs to be done, why it needs to be done, in what context it takes place, how it should be done, and who performs a given activity. In practice, this happens rarely except in cases of highly skilled and experienced PFOs, but most project finance processes always include the what and by whom parts. For each step of the process, specific roles and responsibilities are assigned to project team members and expected deliverables specified. Thus, an efficient workflow record is created so it can be managed effectively.

The quality of project finance processes originates with organizational culture and is driven by corporate policies and practices, but not always by project strategy and objectives as they should. Since sound processes are designed to drive efficiency and realize project objectives most effectively, they require knowledge of the duties involved by each project team member. They also require controlling the different activities by the corresponding subteam heads. However, the function that brings the different project finance processes together and implements a project is that of project management. In the sections that follow, we present variants of project finance processes obtained from different sources, the nature of these processes, activities of participants in the processes, outputs of project finance processes, and characteristics of successful processes.

Section 4.1 shows how different sources familiar with project financing described the project finance process from their perspective. It demonstrates that there are no standard, common phases or processes to follow in every project. The nature of sound project finance processes is discussed in Section 4.2, which illustrate show each stakeholder's process is carried out separately, but in concert with the project team's processes, and eventually the outputs of the different stockholder processes are incorporated into a cohesive overall project process. Section 4.3 goes into the details of activities performed by the various stakeholders, while the milestones and outputs of the project finance process are presented in Section 4.4. The characteristics of successful project finance processes present in effective PFOs and project teams are enumerated in Section 4.5. Because of their importance, the discussion of project financing processes in this chapter is supplemented by material in subsequent chapters.

4.1 VARIANTS OF PROJECT FINANCING PROCESSES

There is a wide variation of views of project finance processes across projects that are due to differences in project size and complexity, core project team skills and competencies, sponsor organizational culture, and the experience of the project manager and each project stakeholder representative on the project team. Because each project has its own peculiarities and participant skills vary substantially, each participant has their own view of how things should get done. Following is a sample of the variety of highly abbreviated views. Some do not have a distinct project development stage or, in some instances, they include it in another stage and usually are not given the attention it deserves.

In addition to being treated as independent, the processes described by different participants are generic, very sketchy, and do not show many of the steps and activities involved. They are really stages and phases of the project finance process. However, more detailed project finance processes from the sponsors' perspective are shown in Section 4.3 and subsequent chapters. Many of the process activities performed by host government agencies, debt and equity investors, ECAs and multilateral agencies, and other project stakeholders are of a similar nature and are not treated separately. The views of project finance processes outlined by different participants are summarized below.

A. Project Financing Professional Perspective
1. Project award → Project viability assessment → Special purpose company creation → Offtake and supply agreements → Contractor

and equipment provider engaged → Construction completion → Sale or transfer (Slivker, 2011)

2. *Phase I Financial Structure*: Feasibility study → Contracts and risk management → Economic analysis and financing structure

  Phase II: Risk analysis

  Phase III: Financial closing, term sheet and contract negotiation → Financial closing (BBVA, 2006)

3. Create framework for private participation → Provide PPP project definition → Enter the bidding process (Klein, 1996)

4. Project origination → Financing the project → Project construction → Project operation (Kahn and Parra, 2003)

5. Project strategy → Stakeholder team → Integration → Benchmarking → Project development → Feedback (EFCA, 2001)

B. **Perspectives of Host Governments**

1. Internal host country assessment → Strategic planning → Project definition → Feasibility study → Project delivery planning

2. Project concept → Request for proposal → Proposal evaluation → Negotiations

3. Create conducive environment → Project definition → Project feasibility → Project packaging and marketing

4. Identify project objectives → Local market assessment → Feasibility study → Include stakeholders in decision making→ Ensure project is financially sustainable → Assign tasks to project participants (www.urbaninfrastructureindia.org/pdf/5-projdev_web.pdf)

5. Project description→ Financial and legal evaluation → Risk allocation → Issue of permits → Sponsor equity → Technical and financial feasibility → Issue a request for proposals→ Bidder selection and negotiation → Contract signing and financial closing

6. *Prefinance stage*: Project identification → Risk identification and minimization → technical and financial feasibility

  Financing stage: Arrangement of equity and debt investments → Negotiation and syndication of loan → Documentation and checking policies → Payment

  Post financing stage: Project monitoring and review → Project closure→ Repayment and monitoring (www.educba.com/project-financing-in-india/)

C. **Perspective of Sponsors and Advisors**

1. Project identification → Screening and definition → Feasibility study → Risk assessment, allocation, mitigation → Negotiations

2. Project identification and screening → Risk assessment and allocation → Project economic assessment → Commercial structuring → Closing and release

3. Project conception and early project screening→ Project development → Construction → Operation

4. Project development → Construction → Operation

5. Project definition → Prefeasibility study → Feasibility study → Due diligence → Raising financing → Implementation

6. Prebid → Development → Contract negotiation → Raising funding

7. Project development → Financeable project structuring → Project presentation → Implementation

8. Project identification → Consensus development → Creation of project objectives → Issue identification → Project plan preparation → Due diligence → Engage advisors → Project management structure creation

9. Project definition → Feasibility study → Project preparation planning → Contracts and documentation → Project implementation

D. **Development and Other Bank Perspective:**

1. Concept clearance → Due diligence → Term sheet → Final review → Board consideration → Financial close (Asian Development Bank)

2. Project identification and selection → Assessment of PPP option → Detailed project preparation → Procurement, bidding→ PPP contract and financial close → Project implementation (European Investment Bank)

3. Planning → Construction → Operations (Bank of International Settlements)

4. Strategic planning → Project definition → Feasibility study → Project delivery planning → Contracts and loan documentation → Project implementation (Asian Development Bank)

The common characteristic of the various perspectives is that they define stages of project finance and not processes and activities performed in each stage. The reasons that processes and specific activities are not described are:

1. Sensitivity about proprietary information disclosure considerations.

2. An unwillingness or inability of sources and discussion participants to share process details.

3. Incomplete knowledge of all the steps involved the project finance process.

4.2 NATURE OF PROJECT FINANCING PROCESSES

Due to the complexities and risks involved, project finance processes have to be highly coordinated and integrative because the outputs of a participant's activities are shared with the project team. The outputs serve as inputs to and are incorporated into other participants' processes and scheduled activities. They are interdependent and that requires a high level of communication, coordination, cooperation, and collaboration and, most importantly, skillful project management. By necessity, the complexity of projects and feedback effects of different process outputs render the project finance processes iterative. That is, data, information, analyses, evaluations, and validations are updated a number of times and in a recursive fashion. For that reason, project finance processes take a long time to complete. Individual stakeholder processes require patience and experience to integrate them into the main project process and build the web of negotiated agreements that support project financing.

Project finance processes can be sequential or performed concurrently, but in effective PFOs and project teams they are driven by purpose and sharp focus and have decision gates prior to moving to the next stage. Project finance process activities seek continuous updates of data, information, clarification, analyses, and evaluations because they have to attest to their validity and the reasonableness of assumptions and scenarios. Why? Because they help validate and support the project economic evaluation, the strength of project agreements, and the adequacy of the security package, which are major determinants of project bankability. Effective project finance processes are carried out in a manner that minimizes conflicts and seeks to accommodate participant needs in a balanced and fair approach. But, because of the number and complexity of subprocesses and segments within them, they are highly project management intensive. They are stewarded and brought together under the project manager's umbrella process as illustrated in Figure 4.2.

The overall project finance process of Figure 4.2 shows the integration of diverse functional processes of project stakeholder entities coming from different perspectives, objectives, interests, and constraints. The main functional processes that must dovetail and come together under the project management processes and procedures include the following:

1. The sponsor organization's regional sales and marketing plans, targets for the host country, and the processes used to manage customer relationships to bring forth projects

2. The host government ceding authority's bidding and procurement process and requirements

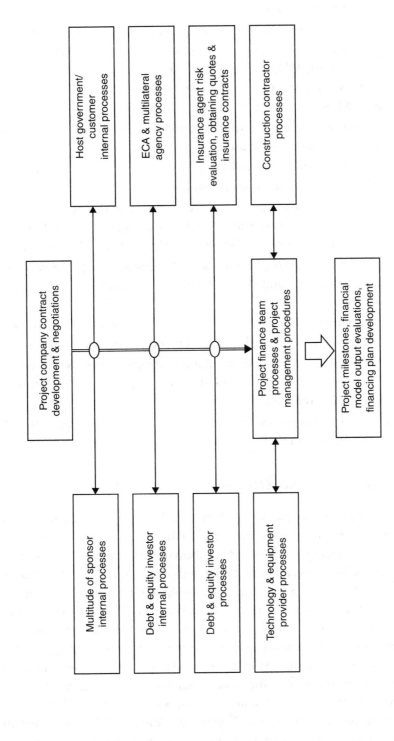

Figure 4.2 Amalgam of Project Finance Processes

3. The sponsor's PFO analytics and evaluation processes or, in its absence, the processes that external advisors and consultants use to perform assessments

4. The engineering and technology group's processes related to evaluating input and output requirements and equipment performance specifications and the project's technical feasibility

5. The project company structuring and project financing, implementation, and business plan execution processes

6. The technology and equipment provider(s) performance and warrantee certification processes

7. The construction contractor's processes for project delivery and performance tests on time and on budget

8. The sponsors' finance, tax, and accounting, and the treasury organizations' evaluations of project viability, tax efficiency, and finance-ability and the corresponding approval processes

9. The lender and equity providers' project assessment processes based on the feasibility and due diligence reports and internal approval processes

10. The insurance agent's project risk assessment and the insurance underwriters' project risk evaluation and remediation processes

11. The sponsor's legal and regulatory organization's assessment of project compliance requirements and drafting and negotiation of agreements processes

12. The review, evaluation, and approval processes of ECAs, unilateral, and multilateral institutions

4.3 ACTIVITIES IN PROJECT FINANCE PROCESSES

The nature of project financing involves a multitude of participants inside each project stakeholder organization and in the project team. The stages and phases of the project finance process are shown in Figure 4.3. The key stakeholders are the host government ceding authority, the sponsor, the funding entities, and the project team which is made up of representatives from each stakeholder. The sponsor core project team consists of the PFO and external advisors and consultants along with engineering and technology, marketing and sales, business development, legal and regulatory, and CFO agents. This team is supported by managers in the competitive analysis, market research, demand analysis and forecasting, and accounting and tax organizations.

Discussion of the project financing process is expanded in Chapter 7 dealing with participant roles and responsibilities, which shows that the quality of process execution is a major determinant of project financing success. One approach to describe the essence of the project financing process

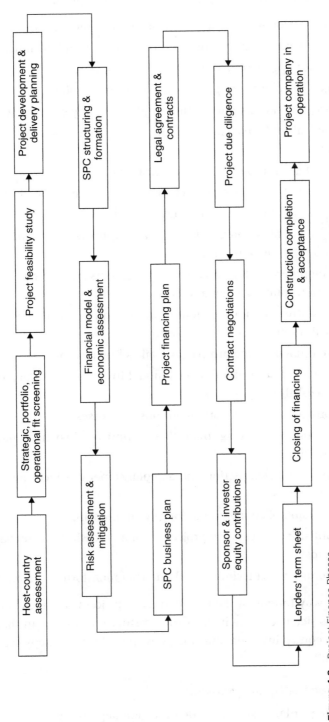

Figure 4.3 Project Finance Phases

is by showing its main phases, as illustrated in Figure 4.3, which is further defined by the group of activities in different phases. These process-defining activities are related to reaching the following milestones:

1. Project rationale, fit assessment, screening, and definition
2. Bidding and procurement event preparations and documentation
3. Issuance of government licenses, permits, concessions
4. Project development, planning, and setting of objectives
5. Partnership arrangements and project company structuring
6. Technical and financial feasibility study and report to the project team
7. Risk identification, assessment, and mitigation
8. Creation of the project financial model and evaluation of its outputs
9. Project due diligence and issue of report
10. Development of internal backing and approvals and political support on the customer side
11. Development and negotiation of agreements and customer and construction contract negotiations
12. Negotiation and documentation of equity and debt funding contributions
13. Development of the project company's business plan
14. Assessment of project financial model inputs and outputs to ensure financeability
15. Approvals of project participant business cases
16. Selecting a financing plan that optimizes financing and raises required funding
17. Construction completion and acceptance per contract time and cost requirements
18. Conversion of short-term to long-term financing
19. Establishing necessary project company cash flow management systems
20. Ongoing project technical and financial monitoring and reporting

Another way to look at the project finance process activities is through the sponsor's perspective, which in some respects is similar to that of the lenders and equity investors and includes the following steps segmented in four parts:

Part I: Setting Up and Screening

1. Strategic plan review and identification of gaps, needs, and competitive threats

2. Identification and cursory screening of current potential project opportunities

3. Selection and validation of best project by the strategic planning and business development groups

4. Clarity of project rationale, fit assessment, screening, definition, and other sponsor partner selection

5. Development of project objectives and assessment and management of participant expectations

6. Signing of an implementation or concession agreement or private contract

7. Creation of the special purpose vehicle and signing of shareholder agreement

8. Selection of the project manager and engagement of the PFO or external financing team and allocation of human and financial resources required for project development

9. Creation and meeting of the core project team with representatives from all stakeholders, development of key assumptions, and getting a consensus view

10. Screening and hiring of project advisors and consultants to supplement skills and experiences not available internally

11. Assignment of roles and responsibilities to project stakeholder representatives, the PFO, and its supporting core subteams

Part II: Project Evaluations

1. Sponsor organization and other project stakeholder SWOT analysis and external environment and trend assessments

2. Identification of project constraints, major issues, preliminary evaluation of engineering and technology issues, and project economic evaluations to determine funding needs

3. Refinement of current or development and validation of new assumptions to be used in forecasting and project financial models

4. Determination of project company financing needs and project economic viability evaluation

5. Preparation of inputs, development of the project financial model, and preliminary evaluation of its outputs

6. Risk identification, evaluation, and allocation based on a cost-benefit approach

7. Project feasibility study and creation of report to be used by decision makers to advance the project to the next stage

8. In depth megatrend and sub-trend analysis, industry analysis, and demand analysis of the project company's output

9. Project cost analysis and projections, revenue forecasts, and sponsor financial analysis

10. Development of project company cash flow estimates and ratios, sponsor cost-benefit and ratio evaluations, and lender evaluations and reconciliation

11. Internal sponsor organization due diligence at the start of the project development phase and joining the lenders' due diligence

12. Initiation of informal contacts and inquiries with potential private and official funding sources

13. Independent, critical, and objective validation of assumptions and scenario development and planning

Part III: Important Deliverables

1. Assessment of different project structure types and options acceptable to sponsors, financing parties, customers and suppliers, and validation of the project's economic viability

2. Examination of project risks from each stakeholder's perspective and if there are differences, various remedies evaluated

3. Leveraging of relationships with host government, lenders, and credit enhancement sources' personnel

4. Preparation and interim approval of project stakeholder internal business cases

5. Formation of the loan-financing syndicate and initiation of formal discussions

6. EPC contract signing and drawdown of debt procedures spelled out

7. Project review, final stakeholder approvals, and creation of internal project implementation processes

8. Core team re-assessment of risks and negotiation of political, technical, construction, legal, and economic risks allocation

9. Balance of project stakeholder interests and benefits with risks to be assumed, insured, or mitigated

10. Formal discussions with ECAs, unilateral, and multilateral institutions to obtain risk insurance and project funding support

11. Equity and human resource contributions of project stakeholders and accompanying requirements, conditions, and positions established

12. Development and negotiation of legal agreements with focus on enforceability of contracts, guarantees and insurance, offtake agreements, credit enhancements, and equity and in-kind contribution agreements

13. Creation of the project company's business plan to support development of a draft project information memorandum and make marketing presentations

14. Final project financing structuring, legal document reviews, and final due diligence report

Part IV: Financing Structuring

1. Financing implementation; that is, raising of equity and debt with negotiated tenors and terms and conditions

2. Project construction and drawdowns begin under close monitoring to ensure they are on budget and time to completion

3. Development of project company accounting and financial management and reporting systems and waterfall accounts

4. Preparation of project documentation which may include project rating as part of the information memorandum used in presentations to potential investors

5. Initiation of discussions with long term lenders such as insurance companies, pension plans, sovereign plans, etc. to convert a short term to a long-term loan

6. Acceptance of project completion and start of project company operations by the operations and management (O&M) company

7. Project technical and financial performance monitoring, reporting, and variance analysis

8. Loan repayment per cash flow waterfall arrangements and profit distributions to shareholders

9. Project review and post-mortem analysis and documentation of lessons learned to be used in future projects

4.4 MILESTONES OF PROJECT FINANCE PROCESSES

There are numerous project financing process outputs and the most important from a sponsor's perspective are shown in Figure 4.4. These are major milestones that form the foundation for other deliverables to be generated, such as a project sponsor-portfolio assessment taking place in the prefeasibility stage of a project to determine impacts on the portfolio's risk composition. Also project screening is performed to identify risks and issues, determine the transparency and fairness of the bidding process, gauge the level of political support in the host country, and report findings to the project team. In the project development phase, the project feasibility study report is issued and shared with all project team members to establish a

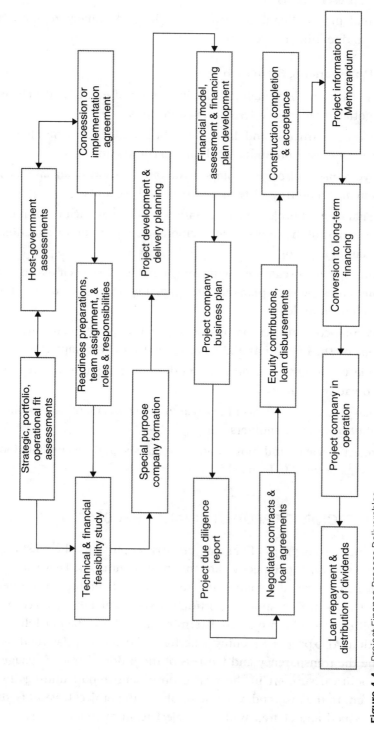

Figure 4.4 Project Finance Process Deliverables

common view of the project. Additionally, the risk identification, assessment, and allocation take form and create the basis for developing the project security package.

The formation and structuring of the project company is a major milestone of the project finance process. When completed, it allows the due diligence effort to move forward and produce the due diligence report; a critical document for all project stakeholder decisions. Legal contracts and agreements are drafted and the review, negotiation, and approval progression of these documents begins. A key part of these documents is the security package prepared to satisfy lender requirements. Once lenders are satisfied with the due diligence report's findings, especially with the adequacy of the security package, the term sheet with firm terms and conditions is released. But to get to this point, a project financing plan needs to be laid out and a project financial model, which was developed earlier, is updated to finalize and validate the project company's borrowing capacity, ability to repay debt, and make dividend distributions to equity investors. Also, a cash flow management system is developed and tested per waterfall account covenants, restrictions, and requirements.

Construction financing is secured and construction begins and debt and equity drawdowns start. In the meantime, the project company's business plan is fully developed. The O&M company is selected and prepares for start of operations upon acceptance of project completion. The conversion of short-term to long-term financing takes place once construction is underway and all debt and equity financing is complete. Upon satisfactory passing of project inspections and validation of performance specifications, project acceptance marks the startup of project company operations. In the event financing through public markets is contemplated, the information memorandum is prepared and a project rating is secured. As the project revenue stream flows in and cash flow accumulates, the repayment of debt and dividend distributions to sponsors and other equity participants begin.

4.5 SUCCESSFUL PROJECT FINANCE PROCESS CHARACTERISTICS

Successful project finance characteristics require all the elements of sound project finance processes and the most valuable benefit that flows out of them is avoiding project failure factors to increase the chances of project success. The project finance success factors that experienced advisors and consultants agree on include:

Part I:

1. Clear strategy and achievable project objectives along with exceptional relationship management

2. Independent, critical, and objective evaluation driven by facts that are checked and validated on an ongoing basis

3. Clearly marked maps with directions to navigate through the stages of project financing processes

4. Participants know well the scope of their assignment, their roles and responsibilities, and the deliverables expected of them

5. Project team members possess the required skills and experiences to implement processes effectively

6. High levels of all-around communication, coordination, cooperation, and collaboration among all project participants

7. Minimized duplication of effort in areas of responsibilities of project team members and advisors

8. Effective project development, due diligence, risk allocation, and project company and financing structures

9. Balanced, effective, and enforceable agreements that minimize time to negotiating contracts and obtaining funding and closing

10. Dovetailing of process outputs with the next process-input requirements and the outputs of other stakeholders' parallel processes

Part II:

1. Consistency, testing, and validation of financial model inputs, assumptions, and scenarios

2. Harmonizing project stakeholders' objectives and positions through ongoing and open communications and information sharing

3. Superior organizational and customer relationship management skills and tools to guide the progression of the various processes and address discontinuities effectively

4. Work plans marked by clearly defined deliverables, reasonable timelines, and achievable major check and decision points across all processes

5. Completeness, consistency, and thoroughness of processes with no gaps in coverage and in assigned roles and responsibilities to ensure working from a common information platform

6. Sound due diligence and project risk profiles that satisfy stakeholder objectives consistent with the sponsor company's corporate risk tolerance

7. A fair, balanced, and equitable allocation of risks on the basis of best-able-to-handle party and cost-benefit analysis

8. Project manager excellence and project advisor effectiveness to ensure that sponsor company, project company, PFO, and external processes

proceed as planned and come together in a timely, orderly, high quality, and on budget manner

9. Evaluation of project finance processes and participant performance, distilling lessons learned, and assessing changes needed to enhance processes and ensure project success

The characteristics of a successful project finance process can be fully operational when the project team has ample support from respective stakeholder decision makers. Also, superior project finance skills and competencies and agility are required to execute process steps effectively. Furthermore, a wide network of working business and personal relationships across internal organizations, other stakeholder groups, and funding sources, along with good customer relationship management skills and experience in conflict resolution are required. These skills are especially important in international projects.

The existence of success factors in the project processes is necessary evidence that a competitive advantage in project finance is present or in the process of being attained by the sponsor company. Other factors and conditions that must be satisfied to ensure sufficient evidence of competitive advantage are discussed in Chapter 16.

CHAPTER 5

Project Finance Organizations

Built for Competitive Advantage

The project team, the interweaving contract structure, and project and financing structures are key elements in project finance value creation. But, they do not happen in a vacuum instantaneously and do not come into existence on their own. They are developed over time in order to implement a project finance transaction successfully. Project finance organizations (PFOs) are part of the project team and are created to help the sponsor company's project manager manage information needs and flows, perform assessments and evaluate projects, and develop the right financing structures. Large firms in the infrastructure project business that specialize in project development, building, and financing have dedicated PFOs. Smaller companies usually assemble teams on an as-needed basis by drawing from internal disciplines and external advisors, or they outsource project financing in its entirety.

A key objective of PFOs is to ensure that efficient and effective project finance solutions are developed for customers and expected project value materializes according to project objectives and plans. Another key objective is to protect and advance the company's interests and image and ensure a coordinated and efficient management of company resources. The difference between dedicated, fulltime PFOs and ad-hoc PFOs is in the skills and qualifications, their commitment to project success, their standing with customers and funding entities, and the quality and results of solutions they develop.

Before discussing the PFOs business definition, let us see when PFOs are needed. This discussion takes place in Section 5.1, where instances of a need for PFOs are outlined.

> The business definition of an organization consists of its charter and scope of responsibilities, its vision and mission, its principles and values, its goals and objectives, its strategy, its stakeholders, its governance structure, and its internal functional links and external networks.

Section 5.2 deals with the components of the PFO business definition: Mission and vision, goals and objectives, governance structure, and scope of activities. The necessary skills and qualifications in general management, analytical competencies, and financing sources, techniques, and instruments are addressed in Section 5.3. Various challenges facing PFOs are discussed in Section 5.4. Section 5.5 presents some PFO performance-evaluation measures. Lastly, the attributes found to characterize successful PFOs are shown in Section 5.6.

Many of the PFO business definition parts apply to other functional groups and our arguments are extensive because they come from the idea that a good PFO definition and suitable skills and competencies are essential to obtain a competitive advantage. The discussion is based on the author's experiences, observations, and project notes, some of which are covered in Triantis (2013).

5.1 THE NEED FOR PFOs

Sales teams bring in projects and make unsolicited proposals. Business development organizations assess project fit, screen and evaluate projects, and make recommendations. Sponsors want value creation. Engineering groups respond to RFPs. Lawyers create and negotiate contracts and agreements. The project company wants management support from the sponsor organization. Host country governments want value for the money. PFOs work with all these groups to develop and finance projects that meet stakeholder requirements and are needed in the following cases:

1. Inexperienced sponsors or developers partnering or wishing to participate in international infrastructure project financing but experience difficulties structuring profitable projects like experienced competitors. In this case, a small but experienced PFO is the best option with some functions performed by advisors and consultants.

2. For equipment or technology suppliers, having their own PFO focusing in export credit agency financing and in project financing of ventures can be an effective approach to provide financing to customers to purchase their equipment or technology. These PFOs initially engage advisors to do financings that allow the group to develop needed expertise.

3. In cases where the sponsors' projects come in spaced out, certain functions should be performed by advisors, but appropriate-size PFOs can add value by ensuring best-project terms are obtained and company interests are advanced at every project stage.

4. For large sponsor companies, the likes of ABB, Raytheon, GE, Bechtel, etc., which have project critical mass, it is beneficial to have PFOs staffed with highly skilled and experienced project finance associates who perform the majority of required functions and provide a competitive advantage to those companies.

5. Due to large infrastructure needs, some developing countries want to attract infrastructure funding but realize their inability to manage project financings. When countries determine a need to create a PFO, it should be a small group to outsource functions requiring

highly skilled professionals but who retain control of the project and decision making until government employees develop sufficient skills and qualifications.

5.2 BUSINESS DEFINITION OF PFOs

The business definition of an organization usually consists of the following parts: The mission and vision, strategy, goals and objectives, scope of activities, and governance structure. A more complete business definition also includes the organization's principles and values, which are included under required skills and qualifications. The elements of the PFO definition are shown in Figure 5.2.1.1.

5.2.1 PFO Mission and Vision

The mission of dedicated PFOs is the reason for their existence; namely, to fill project finance needs and its purpose is to strive to achieve them with a competitive advantage. The reasons PFOs are established are to increase the success rates of infrastructure project financings through better project planning and preparation, screening and development, evaluation and execution. A PFO main objective is to identify and eliminate gaps and short-falls, provide better financing solutions, and support management decision-making needs. The mission of the PFO is one part of its business definition and to develop it, a company needs to answer the following questions:

1. Where are we today, how effective and credible and useful can be a PFO created on an ad-hoc basis?

2. What human and financial resources does the company have to work with?

3. Does the project volume and complexity warrant a dedicated organization in this area?

4. How willing is the company to establish and fund on an ongoing basis a dedicated, professionally staffed PFO?

5. How does the company get to the desired state of a competent PFO and how would it know if it has achieved that?

6. What characterizes a professional, effective PFO and what does it look like?

7. What criteria does one use to make judgments about competent PFOs?

To understand the underlying elements of how the PFO business definition is affected by various considerations that come together to produce project financing solutions, we draw attention to Figure 5.2.1.2. It shows what factors make that definition effective. Not surprisingly, the starting point is the corporate culture, followed by the company mindset, and then

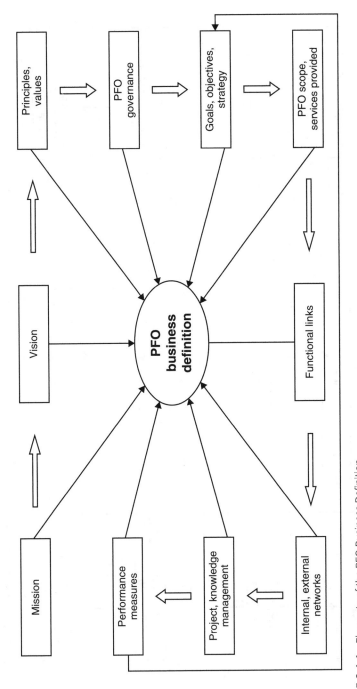

Figure 5.2.1.1 Elements of the PFO Business Definition

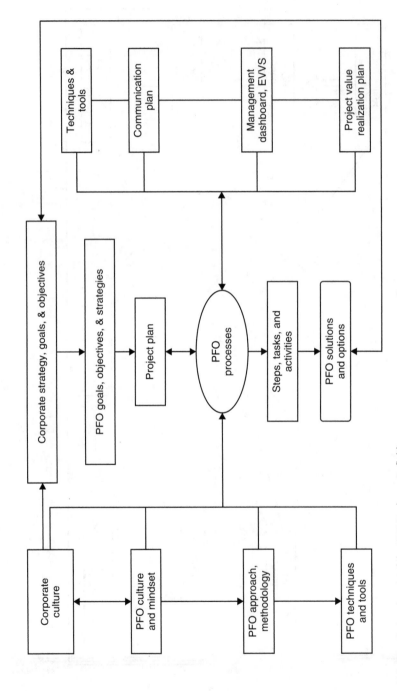

Figure 5.2.1.2 Determinants of the PFO Business Definition

comes the PFO's reporting structure. Notice how corporate strategy and objectives drive the PFO objectives which, in turn, affect the shaping of project objectives.

The vision of the PFO is an idealized statement that creates a clear picture of the desired state of this group. It is the first step in establishing its ultimate destination and determining ways by which the PFO team creates value and performs its functions successfully. The vision defines the purpose, often in terms of values, and communicates it to team members and clients. For team members, it provides a clear direction and inspiration to strive for competitive advantage; it also aids senior management and customer support, which helps to understand what the PFO function is all about and how they can benefit from it. The quality of the vision statement determines the innovation, creativity, and value of the team and it is most effective when it is consistent with senior management's views.

The PFO team's vision statement needs to resonate with customers and once a PFO is established and begins getting acceptance, the vision statement is updated to aim for even higher levels of service to project teams. As an example, the vision statement of a PFO of a European firm states that its vision is to become a trusted project finance advisor and valued partner to customers, decision makers, and project team members with high professional standards in accordance with its principles. A North American PFO states that its vision is to build strong financial market networks and alliances to provide consistent, efficient, and reliable project finance services and be a viable alternative to external advisors and project finance outsourcing. The vision of an Asia-based PFO is to help the company establish a competitive advantage and win project bids over competitors through project financing.

5.2.2 PFO Goals and Objectives

Goals are broad, general intentions that relate to purpose, vision, and aspirations while objectives are narrow, more specific attitudinal or behavioral propositions. Goals set direction for the organization; objectives are steps on the path to reaching the goals. To produce desired results, project objectives must be clear, challenging, and achievable and have PFO associate involvement in their creation. Client and senior management feedback to measure their effectiveness is also required.

Key goals and objectives that flow out of the PFO's core values and lead to sound project financing solutions are embraced by its associates, customers, and senior management and include:

1. Forming lasting global relationships and occasional alliances and being a source of reliable and trusted advice on major project decisions

2. Helping manage project risks and help management make better informed decisions

3. Making the project financing process less stressful and the jobs of clients and senior managers easier

4. Anticipating and meeting project, management, and customer needs and managing their expectations

5. Making realistic commitments of contributions and support to the success of a project

6. Reducing time to project financing and minimizing decision uncertainty

7. Sharing knowledge and insights and providing professional quality support

8. Making PFO associates business partners committed to the success of strategic investment decisions and winning project bids

9. Displacing external experts as the source of analyses and evaluations for strategic project finance decisions

10. Increasing customer satisfaction beyond expectations and ensuring resource availability and support to their decision makers throughout the project

The means used to achieve the stated PFO goals and objectives include several of the following common elements, such as:

1. Creating a cohesive PFO team and governance structure founded on stated vision and mission statements and on shared corporate values and principles

2. Establishing close business links with internal functional and external project stakeholder organizations and personal relationships with counterparts in funding sources

3. Customizing approaches, methods, applications, techniques and tools used in each project to fit the particulars of the situation and current needs

4. Benchmarking and adopting best-project financing practices, and learning from the best in the business and from competitor PFOs

5. Building effective processes and procedures to ensure consistency, discipline, and transparency and increase the productivity of PFO associates

6. Providing training and learning for project team members and government agency associates when needed

7. Ensuring that project financing solutions display consistency with financial principles and pass efficiency, balance, and fairness tests

8. Creating practical project finance options to offset or reduce the impact of project risks and uncertainty and develop options to manage risks when they materialize

9. Using all available internal and external expertise, insights, analyses, evaluations, and obtaining input from experts in scenario development and planning

10. Living up to PFO values and principles at all times, in all cases, under any circumstances, with no exceptions.

5.2.3 PFO Governance

The PFO governance structure deals with the organization and the system by which the team is managed. It is the relationships between the team members, the leader, and project stakeholders that define the way objectives are set and the means to reach them. A way of looking at the PFO's governance is the functions around customer relationships, knowledge, and project management; and the policies, contracts, financing techniques and instruments, and processes governing infrastructure project finance. Figure 5.2.3.1 shows one example of an effective PFO that has been in existence for several years and that provides a competitive advantage to its company.

The authority to establish and fund a centralized PFO team is derived from a clear need for competitive and reliable project financing to support successful project bids. The PFO's charter assigns responsibility for its activities to a supervisory body that sets the rules of engagement that include:

1. Specifying the distribution of roles and responsibilities among participants in project financing processes and laying down the rules and processes for decision making

2. Specifying the reporting arrangements, practices, policies, and rules affecting the way the PFO team is managed, and its goals and strategies

3. Providing a structure to set objectives consistent with corporate and business development strategy and focusing the group's efforts on major impact activities

4. Enhancing the team's productivity on an ongoing basis and increasing the likelihood of accomplishing efficient and effective project financing in every transaction

5. Reviewing, validating, and updating periodically the PFO team governance, policies, processes, rules, and relationships

6. Monitoring performance, establishing performance measures, and influencing how team members perceive themselves and how they communicate across the entire project team

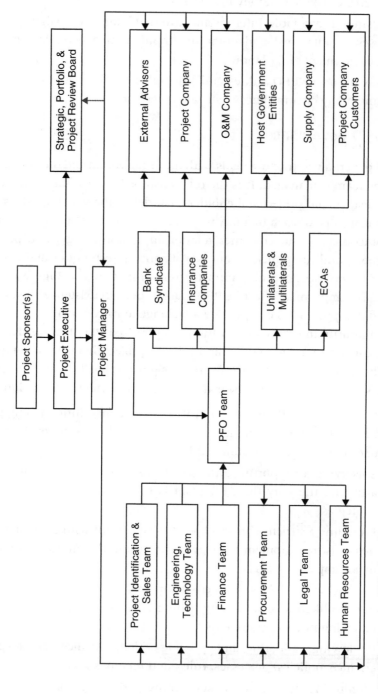

Figure 5.2.3.1 Example of Effective PFO Governance Structure

7. Sharpening the skills and competencies of PFO members and focusing innovation efforts on developing a source of competitive advantage for the company through project finance

8. Paying attention to structuring, operating, and managing the team to achieve its long-term objectives

9. Creating a culture of business ethics and professional conduct that supports the mission of the PFO and sets priorities aligned with team objectives

10. Aligning functions with new business development strategy and ensuring responsible and best use of human resources and corporate investments

PFO governance requires incorporating performance measures for project finance solutions and defining functional boundaries, responsibilities, and tasks, including PFO associate and project-team performance indicators. These elements require establishing specific PFO deliverables, educating customers about project finance, and building in checks and balances. Additional elements for effective PFO governance include stating clearly the activities that make the PFO accountable to organizations it supports, to customers, and to senior management, and being managed effectively. PFO accountability means:

1. Providing a clear understanding of project objectives, expectations, priorities, and issues

2. Assigning joint responsibility to project participants for executing parts of developing and implementing financing plans

3. Helping in project and commercial risk management through project realization planning

Good governance processes are critical in successful project financing and a sound structure helps the PFO supervisor effectively guide work activities. However, corporate culture, structure, and PFO strategy are also determining factors, along with the maturity of the PFO, and how stakeholders communicate and coordinate activities. Effective PFO governance structures are purposely designed and are revisited as the organization matures. PFOs usually have a simple configuration that is easily understood and minimizes confusion as to who does what, why, how, and when. Hence, sound PFO-governance structures produce clear, challenging, and achievable objectives, team-member involvement in setting goals and objectives, and obtaining ongoing team member and customer input and feedback.

The project executive has oversight responsibility for the project whereas the project manager has hands-on project responsibility. The project manager decides, with inputs from the PFO and functional groups, what needs to be done and provides direction and guidance to the project team. The project manager must be a highly motivated and effective manager with broad experience in the areas of 4Cs (unimpeded communication, coordination, cooperation, and collaboration) and relationship management, a team motivator, and uniquely qualified in project management, project finance, and project marketing. In some project teams, individual subteam members report to their functional area managers and to the PFO, who reports to the project manager on a dotted-line basis. The coordination of activities and the integration of the work done by the subteams are crucial and are often shared between the PFO and the project manager.

Ordinarily the PFO resides in the corporate CFO and it is self-contained, separate from but closely linked with subteams that provide support to it. Figure 5.2.3.2 shows the structure of the PFO reporting to the company CFO. There are other organizational structures that are well functioning and are shown in Figures 5.2.3.3, 5.2.3.4, and 5.2.3.5. In the first case, the PFO reports solid line to the CFO and dotted line to the project manager, and each subteam reports directly to their respective organizations and dotted line to the project manager. Here, the PFO has a central role and works closely with internal groups assigned to the project team. In its central position the PFO coordinates planning, external contacts, processes, analyses and evaluations with lender and equity investors, host government authorities involved in the project, unilateral and multilateral agencies, insurance agents, external advisors, and the project company.

Figure 5.2.3.3 shows a structure where the PFO and other subteams are assigned to the project manager for the duration of the project. Notice that in this project team structure, the PFO has all the important functions reporting to it on a dotted-line basis for the duration of the project and focus is placed on project participants and corresponding relationships. While the PFO, the regional sales and marketing, procurement, engineering, and legal subteams report to the project manager, the strategic forecasting, competitive analysis, tax and accounting, and external advisors engaged in the project report to the PFO on a dotted line basis. One important difference in this organizational structure is that because some of the subteams report to the PFO, efficiencies are obtained in the analyses and evaluations performed. This structure shows that the project manager and its support structure serve the needs of the project via their relationships with both internal and external project participants.

A third project team organizational structure is one where the other subteams report to the project manager for the duration of the project on a dotted-line basis as shown in Figure 5.2.3.4. Here, the PFO may report to the project manager on a solid-line basis. This tends to be an effective structure in small size, less complex projects and works well under a strong

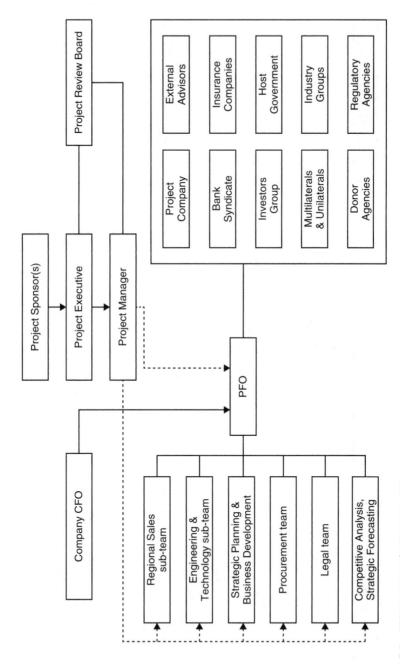

Figure 5.2.3.2 PFO Reports to the Company CFO

91

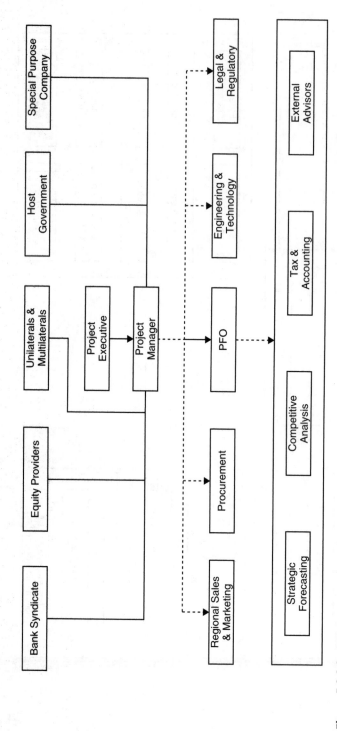

Figure 5.2.3.3 PFO Reports to the Project Manager

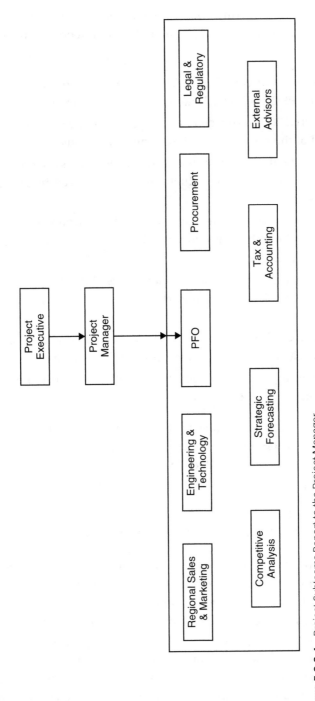

Figure 5.2.3.4 Project Subteams Report to the Project Manager

project management leadership. It also works well in cases where the PFO lacks the required skills and competencies and some project financing functions are outsourced.

All project team structures have advantages and weaknesses and what structure fits best a particular situation and project depends on a number of factors such as:

1. Project size and complexity. The higher the project complexity, the more the PFO is closely linked to the project manager
2. Managerial skill requirements on the part of the project manager and control of the quality of analyses and evaluations
3. Whether the flow of projects is slow or PFO skills are not fully developed and analyses and evaluations are outsourced in part or in their entirety
4. Perceived political influence issues and financial costs and benefits determine how the required activities are distributed and directed by the project executive
5. How easily a team structure can be established, altered to meet peak-load project needs, and dissolved when the project comes to completion
6. The degree of project team nimbleness and dexterity required for effective development of project financing solutions
7. How well a project management and PFO structure meet customer needs and serve their interests

A fifth PFO organizational structure is shown in Figure 5.2.3.5, where the PFO is part of the project management organization that reports to the project executive. This is an effective structure staffed with highly skilled and dedicated project finance and project management associates.

5.2.4 Scope of PFO Activities

The scope of the PFO charter describes the functions it performs and the activities necessary in order to accomplish them. The range of PFO activities is determined by its mission and vision, goals and objectives, and senior management's assessment of the requirements that are crucial for developing efficient project financings. It is also determined by PFO-associates' skills and competencies, the nature of internal alliances and external relations, and its financial market networks, contacts, and associations in the industry. It is also influenced and constrained by budgetary considerations and the size and composition of the organization.

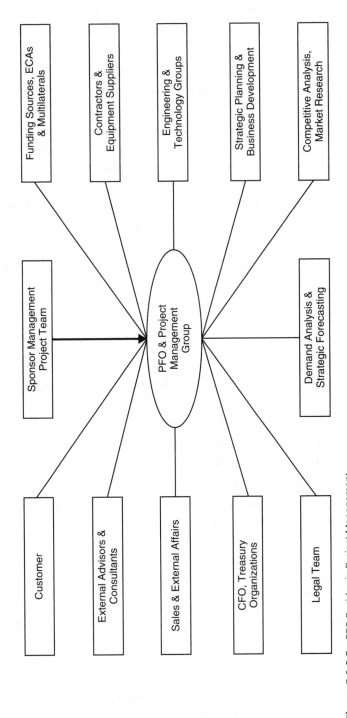

Figure 5.2.3.5 PFO Resides in Project Management

95

Depending on the resources available, associates' qualifications, and project needs, the PFO's scope of activities include:

1. Assessing internal human and financial resources available to undertake a project financing successfully
2. Participating in and coordinating processes, analyses, and evaluations around project structuring and development, due diligence, financial model development, and creating optimized project financing solutions
3. Determining and influencing the enabling factors to achieve project objectives, such as ensuring that realistic project objectives are adopted, participants' interests are harmonized, risk mitigation and the due diligence are thorough and complete, and the adequacy of project support and credit enhancements are beyond question
4. Providing support to senior management, the CFO, the project manager, the project team, and other project stakeholders
5. Dealing with funding sources, and working with host government agency personnel

Project financings developed by the PFO are a confluence of diverse experiences that make it a valued internal advisor. The services ordinarily provided by PFOs are:

1. Helping the project team define the project and its objectives, collaborate in strategic, technical, and operational-fit assessments; and support the project development effort
2. Providing data and information from current research and prior project experiences to help the project team avoid the problems and errors of past projects or competitors' mistakes
3. Leading a broad assessment of the project's external environment, megatrends and subtrends, and validating the findings of those assessments
4. Performing project risk analysis, assessment, and mitigation along with the project team and ensuring risk is fairly allocated to parties best able to handle
5. Developing, obtaining, or collaborating in creating and screening assumptions used in cost and revenue forecasts, and baseline and alternative plausible scenarios
6. Conducting independent, critical, and objective assessment of the project's economic viability through appropriate scrutiny and sanity checks of cost and revenue projections

7. Maintaining a repository of data, information, insights, and experiences that serve as acknowledge center for future project finance teams

Sharing knowledge and insights is an important task of the PFO charter and providing guidance on analyses, evaluations, and other required functions. Supporting the development of contracts and agreements and their negotiations, assessing the impact of proposals and counter proposals, and providing guidance to the investor relations and public affairs groups are part of the PFO's territory. PFO leadership in identifying influencing factors and determining their impact on project financeability, in order to shape the project's future by creating the conditions to make it happen, is also within the scope of its activities. This, however, is conditioned by corporate risk appetite vis-à-vis a project's risk profile and mitigation, other project participant support, and competitor activities.

The PFO helps the project manager in ensuring all-around communication, coordination, cooperation, and collaboration, as well as preparing project-status reports, and monitoring project performance by activities, such as:

1. Helping create project evaluation tools, usually in the form of a dashboard, which relates information to team members to determine progress on the project
2. Determining and defining what project parameters to include on the dashboard and the frequency of reporting
3. Developing early warning systems of risks about to materialize and to estimate their impact and inform the project team
4. Assisting the project team to develop a project value realization plan, adjustments to make, and actions to take to course correct, obtain additional support from the project parties, recreate the project company business plan, or restructure its operations
5. Explaining variances of actuals from projected costs and revenues and determining what changes in underlying factors are causing observed deviations
6. Performing a project post-mortem analysis to determine what went well and what went wrong, what was done right, what was done poorly, and the lessons learned and recording that information for project evaluation purposes and as reference material to improve team performance in future projects
7. Producing regular status reports for the project executive, the CFO, and the project team; discussing updates for issues that have come up, needed actions to address problems, and how problems have been solved

> Post-mortem analysis is a review performed at the end of a project to collect information and obtain feedback from project participants. It uses a survey of project participants to determine and analyze parts of the project that were successfully or unsuccessfully done for the purpose of continuous improvement and enhance project team effectiveness and what to do differently next time. Because results are published and distributed to the project team, it is also a knowledge-sharing tool.

5.3 PFO SKILLS AND QUALIFICATIONS

The many activities of PFOs require a multitude of high-level skills and qualifications to reside in these groups. However, not all competencies are present in every PFO and that is another reason project advisors and consultants are engaged to supplement the existing capabilities of PFOs. There are three major categories of skills and competencies: general management skills, analytical competencies, and knowledge of financing institutions, techniques, and instruments.

5.3.1 General Management Skills

The general management skills expected of PFO associates in order to be able to function in high visibility, intense activities include:

1. Knowledge of company operations and functioning of the industry globally and especially in the host country
2. Thorough understanding of corporate strategy, and business development and portfolio management objectives
3. Astuteness in identifying the true senior management interests and objectives, risk tolerance, and support for the project and the PFO
4. Strong internal functional links and personal relationships with CFO, strategic planning, and business development associates and ability to integrate their objectives in the project development stage
5. Ability to work with the sponsor's decision makers to structure and develop projects and usher them to completion
6. Thorough understanding of the procurement-management processes, requirements, and politics; and preparation of responses to requests for proposals
7. Adeptness in preparation of reports and senior management presentations with supporting documentation, data, and charts

8. Good appreciation of and ability to work with participants from different cultures and ways of doing business, and the capability to partner and collaborate with host agency personnel who lack project finance experience

9. Adeptness and appreciation of the project's physical and cybersecurity threats and issues to bring to discussions and address their resolution

10. Experience in determining project participant motives, needs, interests, and objectives, as well as personal gains and costs and benefits

11. Good understanding of Foreign Corruption Practices Act rules and the implications of their violation

12. Strong skills in large project management processes, tools and techniques, and project-team partnering and joint planning

13. Experience in integrating and managing project initiation, planning, implementing, and controlling and expertise in defining and assigning roles and responsibilities to the project team and other participants through the project manager

14. Effectiveness in ensuring the 4Cs within the project team and among other project participants, and an ability to implement projects successfully

15. Competency in developing the project company's business plan and influencing decisions around its operations planning

16. Skilled in knowledge gathering, evaluating, and disseminating and managing information in and out of the organization

17. Ability to manage project processes, human resources assigned to it, and advisors and consultants engaged in the project and help the project manager with quality, time, and cost-management issues

18. Capability in developing early warning systems, monitoring project performance, and understanding and explaining variances convincingly

19. Capability in relationship building and management along with persistence and experience to see the project to completion through a long and complex process

20. Ability to work in complex matrix organizational structures involving company and external organizations

21. Proficiency in educating host government agency personnel in the more significant aspects of project finance

22. Experience in leading or supporting teams to effective project financing and project marketing capabilities

5.3.2 Analytical Competencies

The analytical skills and competencies required of the PFO are an essential part for effective functioning and the other being experience in financing structuring and closing. The analytical skills and competencies cover a wide territory and require PFO associates to be:

1. Adept in situational analysis, industry structural analysis, and evaluations of project financeability and economic viability, especially in the presence of regulatory regime changes or changes in agreements

2. Critical thinking, but positive and objective in analyses and evaluations beyond any doubt

3. Thoroughly understanding of the project background, rationale, strategy, merits, and objectives as well as constraints present

4. Probing to determine key project influencing factors and perform reasonableness checks on an ongoing basis

5. Persistent in validating and verifying data, information, assumptions, and scenarios to ensure they pass sanity checks

6. Exceptionally perceptive in the evaluation of company strengths and weaknesses and external environmental factors influencing the project

7. Knowledgeable and experienced in assessing impacts of megatrends and sub-trends on the industry and the project itself

8. Astute in understanding basic concepts and premises of competitive analysis, market research, and forecasting techniques

9. Clever in developing, gathering, validating, and testing assumptions that drive cost and revenue projections and the project financial model

10. Adept in modeling project economics and assessing economic viability and able to evaluate critically, independently, and objectively project economics and develop effective reports

11. Experienced in commercial issues, familiar with project finance contracts, and able to dissect and evaluate every aspect of a deal

12. Skilled in supporting contract negotiations and evaluation of proposed terms and counterproposals

13. Competent in leading a team of professional associates in concurrent projects when the need arises

14. Proficient in project risk identification, evaluation, mitigation; and insurance contracts and programs, costs, and terms and conditions

15. Thorough in evaluation of project development areas, objective in review of the due diligence report, and in critical assessment of financial model findings

16. Adept in developing project feasibility studies, business cases, and project-company business plans and targets

17. Show penetrating thinking in the development of a baseline and alternative scenarios and the selection of the cost and revenue projections in simulation ranges

18. Proficiency in assessing all infrastructure project opportunities in its industry, including privatizations of public sector assets

5.3.3 Knowledge of Institutions, Techniques, and Instruments

Exceptional skills and competencies, knowledge, and networks and strong relationships with financial institutions, multilateral agencies, development banks, export credit agencies, and other financial intermediaries are a must. A deep understanding of customer financing needs as well as experience with project finance processes and rules, and ability to pick the right instruments must be part of the qualifications PFO associates bring to the table. The list of common PFO skills and competencies in this area includes:

1. Expert assessment of the host government ceding agency capabilities in project finance and its ability to deliver on future contributions and obligations

2. Recognized expertise, reputation, and acceptance internally and outside the company and proficiency in project finance practices and processes

3. Skilled in creating the project financing plan, developing and modeling project financials, testing and evaluating financial model inputs and outputs, and defining drawing and repayment parameters

4. Probing to understand global debt and equity market conditions and prevailing terms and conditions

5. Deep knowledge of the domestic, host country, and global financial markets; sources of short and long term financing, and relationships and access to decision makers

6. In-depth understanding of multilateral and unilateral agencies' functioning, programs, requirements, and approval processes

7. Knowledge of donor institutions' programs, requirements, criteria, and approval processes

8. Extensive networks and relationships with debt and equity sources around the world and knowledge of their processes and their way of doing business, documentation requirements, and thorough understanding of term-sheet terms and conditions

9. Expert in sound financial engineering processes and instruments and competency in project and financing structuring and implementation mechanics

10. Good understanding of the structure and content of project agreements and contracts and an ability to work closely with the legal team to develop the contractual framework and translate its structure into financial model inputs

11. Expertise in project finance principles, processes, prerequisites, guidelines, and channels and facilities available and experienced with the workings of credit enhancements and project support and their applications

12. Understanding of the implications of different structures and options for the SPC

13. Understanding of differences with the host country's models concerning bidding terms, concession grants, and financing

14. Structuring bids so they display transparency of the financing plan and influencing the negotiations framework and positions to ensure balance of participant interests and project sustainability

15. Skillful in addressing sponsor and host government agency project support and security issues

16. Expertise in managing project processes and coordinating other project participant contributions and deliverables in different stages and evaluating of financing structure implications

17. Competency in financial model building and analysis and understanding of how to influence key drivers to optimize the project financing structure

18. Knowing well the roles and responsibilities of financiers and getting their insights for successful financing

19. Experienced in developing and using project financing models, knowing the rules of negotiating project financing deals, and incorporating properly negotiated terms in project models

20. Ability to alter the project financing structure when condition warrant it and make changes to the project company business plan to achieve the desired state

5.4 PFO CHALLENGES

Each project has its own peculiarities and challenges and in every case the PFO's challenges are the project's challenges and vice versa, and those challenges often become the root causes of project failures. The reasons that projects fail to achieve initial objectives was the subject of Chapter 3. Here, the challenges PFOs commonly face are separated into six categories: internal project sponsor company, analytics and evaluations, host government agency, project stakeholder, project financing, and project company operational challenges.

A. **Project Sponsor Internal Challenges**

Challenges to the PFO's ability to structure optimal project financing solutions and attain a competitive advantage have their origin in the following internal factors:

1. Poor PFO business definition, a scope of activities beyond its ability to handle, and limited resources to carry out its activities as needed

2. Unclear PFO charter of responsibilities and an overlap of responsibilities among internal project participants

3. Inexperienced PFO associate performance, light project team preparation, and inadequate project planning

4. Inadequate internal SWOT analysis to determine the availability of skills and competencies to execute projects successfully

5. Organizational politics and competition for human and financial resources that contaminate projects and lead to inadequate communication and cooperation

6. Weak executive commitment and project support and misreading of the corporate risk appetite against project risk

7. Divergence of project objectives from corporate strategic objectives and deviation from project definition and project development planning

8. Inadequate project preparation and planning the entire project process execution, few evaluations and validations in each decision stage, and operating under tight schedules

9. Undue reliance on external advisors and leaks of proprietary material and valuable contract information to competitors

10. Long project duration using up a lot of resources and PFO and project team time, which causes fatigue and project budget overruns

11. The high cost of skilled internal resources to bring to the project and expensive project assessments and structuring by external consultants

B. **Project Analytics and Evaluations**

Several PFO challenges are present in project analytics and evaluations. Gaps, weaknesses, inaccuracies, and errors in project analyses and assessments are major challenges to the PFO and include:

1. Project complexity and no standardized templates to use for project evaluation require the creation of project-specific processes

2. An inconsistent project with stakeholder objectives and diffused focus that lead to inadequate planning and incomplete project plans

3. Convoluted processes due to ignorance of the right approach and means to perform the needed analyses and evaluations

4. Incomplete or faulty due diligence due to lack of data, erroneous information, untested knowledge, and conventions

5. Reliance on deterministic models and static scenarios to forecast project costs and revenues with erroneous, incomplete, baseless, and untested assumptions

6. Inability to define a realistic baseline scenario due to uncertainty not treated as project risk because it was considered controllable

7. Failure to accurately assess project-stakeholder expectations and manage overly optimistic cost projections and revenue forecasts

8. Concealed motives that cause overstating project benefits and understating project costs for internal and external project approval reasons

9. Lack of sanity checks of project model inputs and outputs due to project changes overload of rework, new analyses, more evaluations, additional negotiations, and contract changes

10. Failure to identify, assess, and allocate risks on a cost-benefit and balanced approach

11. Inability to integrate different project participant processes and deliverables with the main project team processes

C. **Host Government Agencies**

1. Poor assessment of the host country's challenging economic, social, and financial market conditions

2. Shifting emphasis from infrastructure to social projects and changing government positions on the project being considered

3. Multiple layers of decision making, absence of a single source of accountability, and unpredictability as to which agency approves what

4. Lack of knowledge and experience with project finance, the rules of international investments, and lender and investor expectations

5. Weak investment environment, unexpected changes to legal and regulatory frameworks, and an inability to enforce complete contract compliance

6. Lack of host government-decision criteria, evaluation process transparency, and rigged bidding and poor procurement practices mixed with corruption and fraud issues

7. Changing political conditions that contaminate and alter the bid selection criteria, as well as politically motivated interference in the project approval process

8. Inability of host government agencies to deliver on future obligations due to changes in government budgetary constraints and priorities

9. Long, convoluted, and intricate negotiations of project agreements, review processes, final approval, and changing expectations and objectives

D. **Other Project Participants**

1. Sponsor or developer short-term focus and unrealistic project expectations due to lack of clear project understanding and objectives dovetailing with corporate strategic objectives

2. Differing views and confusion about the common set of project objectives and assumptions, as well as each participant's roles and responsibilities

3. Multitude of project participants with not only diverse, but at times conflicting and shifting, interests and objectives

4. Unrealistic customer demands and failure to overcome dilution about the state of affairs in order to get a better deal than the particulars of the project dictate

5. Unforeseen or unexpected construction delays due to material and qualified labor shortages and technical design flaws and failures

6. Excessive cost overruns due to equipment delivery delays and underperformance large enough to warrant revisiting the construction contract

7. Ignorance or limited understanding of project finance processes and instruments and need for instruction and education by the PFO

8. Long project review and approval processes of funding sources, ECAs, and multilateral agencies

9. Stringent lender covenants and government restrictions requiring more difficult restructuring of project company operations

E. **Project Financing Structure**

1. Poor local financial market conditions and lack of local sources of funding other than the central host government agencies' budgets

2. Wrong assessment of the ceding agency's and the third-parties' ability to deliver on current and future obligations

3. Unreasonable host government expectations of high-level upfront sponsor equity contributions and future equity infusions, and low debt funding that leads to delays and increased costs

4. Multitude of project participants and agreements requiring lengthy contract negotiations and PFO support that may not always be timely and adequate

5. Incomplete accounts of negotiation implications included in the project financial model and their impact improperly evaluated

6. Need for refinancing if changing commercial conditions or regulatory interference require such intervention

7. Inability to maintain the negotiated project risk profile due to poor hedging arrangements and inadequate project-company operating performance

8. Faulty security packages, unexpected inadequacy of guarantees, and inability to control project risks

9. Poorly structured financing plan leading to inefficient project financing proposals

10. Surprise competitive actions or host government regulations requiring additional capital expenditures and project company operations

11. Exclusion of the PFO from active participation to ensure a thorough and complete project due diligence commonly conducted by advisors of funding sources

12. Misrepresentations leading to erroneous assessments of every project participant's ability to deliver on current and future commitments

13. Failure to balance project stakeholder interests that usually undermine project sustainability

F. **Project Company Operations**

Challenges originating with project company may not present problems to the PFO's ability to structure efficient project financing and bring the project to completion. They do however, impact the project's ability to achieve the projections that financing was based on. Hence, they may require revisiting the financing and make changes in the project company's operations. Some of the operational challenges are:

1. Lack of experience in host government, partnership, and customer relationship management

2. Inaccuracies in the assessment of the project company's industry and its operating environment, labor market conditions, and standard of living for expatriate managers

3. Inadequately prepared and evaluated project company business plan and lack of or optimistic performance targets

4. Poorly planned and executed project implementation, startup of operations problems, and lack of experienced and committed O&M team

5. Newly installed, inexperienced management team and inadequately trained labor force beyond initial expectations

6. Undue burden of cultural differences and business practices affecting the project company's operations and management performance

7. Inability to enforce full compliance of offtake and supply agreements and obtain regulatory relief

8. Inadequate long-term monitoring of operational performance and inability to restructure its operations in order to obtain additional financing

9. Resource shortages impacting the project company's ability to honor and deliver on its production commitments

10. Inability to mitigate unexpected commercial risks due to lack of early warning systems and business plan realization planning

5.5 PFO PERFORMANCE EVALUATION MEASURES

Assessment of PFO performance is undertaken to determine how well it met the objectives stated at the project development stage and assess whether benefits obtained from having a dedicated PFO justify costs of creating and maintaining that organization. However, PFO performance is closely linked with the overall project management performance evaluation. To assess the PFO performance in a project, one has to examine how well it performed its functions in terms of quality of analyses and evaluations, timeliness of the required tasks and activities, and effective cost management and controls. The reception of the project financing package by the customer, the strength of the financial ratios and related information evaluation, and the assistance the PFO provided to team members and project participants should also be assessed.

Some organizations want to see quantitative measures of performance, such as percent deviations of actual revenues from projected values, ratings of PFO performance by the project manager and the CFO, and efficiency of the financing raised in the project. Because driving a project from its inception to financing to completion involves the work of several different organizations and project participants, it is difficult to isolate exactly how and what the PFO should be measured on. Judging if the right financing plan was created depends on the individual project participant's perspective and because assessments are time consuming and difficult to do objectively, they are given a light treatment. Nevertheless, in the case of well-established PFOs, they are given proper attention in the post-mortem analysis.

A qualitative assessment of the PFO's performance entails obtaining survey responses from project participants to, at least, the following questions:

1. Under what constraints were the financing plan developed and how cooperative were PFO associates and other project participants?

2. How well was the project development phase managed in terms of validating project objectives, planning, and assigning responsibilities to associates?

3. How thorough were the analyses and evaluations leading to the definition of the baseline scenario and to cost and revenue projections?

4. How thorough and complete was the validation and testing of assumptions, analyses, and scenario evaluations?

5. How sound was the financial model created by the PFO, assessment of its inputs and outputs, and how effectively were they used to optimize project financing?

6. Were all the financial structuring options explored to the satisfaction of all project participants and justification provided for the one selected as most efficient?

7. How effectively were project stakeholder participation and expectations managed and their diverse interests and objectives harmonized?

8. How adequate was PFO monitoring of progress in all stages of the project to ensure due processes were followed, and how did PFO-relationship management contribute to it?

9. What type of support level and quality was provided to senior management, the CFO, the project manager, and foreign government officials?

10. How well did the PFO educate host government authorities and customers on project finance processes and requirements?

5.6 CHARACTERISTICS OF SUCCESSFUL PFOs

Characteristics of successful PFOs are a variant of the required skills and qualifications discussed in Section 5.3 or best practices observed in the project finance industry. PFO skills and qualifications affect project success to a significant extent, but how customers view and value the effectiveness of that group and the efficiency of the financing brought to the project are also important. Additionally, how well the dealings with sponsors went and how they valued the PFO's contributions to the project help define a PFO's success characteristics. Equally important are the factors that make its transactions with financial institutions smooth, efficient, and effective.

Objectivity in identifying successful PFO characteristics that lead to competitive advantage necessitates a long term, external advisor or consultant and customer perspective. The characteristics of importance to customers are listed below:

1. Listening attentively to understand the customer's situation, true needs, project objectives, and requirements
2. Knowing the criteria the customer will use to assess the quality of financing brought to the project
3. Showing sensitivity to the political and financial realities the ceding authority is facing and understanding that realities are always changing and require management
4. Focusing on providing excellent service to customers, seeking their input and feedback, and managing their expectations to reasonable levels
5. Demonstrating responsiveness to customer concerns and that their interests and objectives are considered and fairly balanced with those of other project participants
6. Being respectful, honest, and candid in all stakeholder communications when dealing with assessment of project viability and bankability
7. Offering willingly to educate customers on project finance and to make them more effective in conducting business and more cooperative and collaborative
8. Convincing customers of the PFO's ability to best handle project risk with fairness and balance is required to make projects financeable and viable most effectively

PFO dealings with financial institutions also determine project finance success. That is, how these dealings were conducted and what results they produced reveal the successful characteristics of PFOs. Some of the factors that come up repeatedly include:

1. PFO associates knowledgeable about the programs, processes, and requirements of the financial institutions involved in the project

2. Having extensive networks, contacts, and relations with financial institutions to leverage in order to get expedited, efficient responses from them

3. PFO offers to educate personnel of financial institutions on the particulars of the project's industry, selling the project to them effectively, and obtaining their support down the evaluation and approval processes

4. Leveraging expertise residing in financial institutions in the areas of risk identification and allocation, credit enhancements, and other types of support to structure financing efficiently

5. Introducing competition among funding sources to get better financing packages for the benefit of sponsors and customers

6. Agility, nimbleness, effectiveness in the 4Cs, and being knowledgeable so that customers feel that the PFO is easy to do business with

7. Collaboration with financial institution experts to conduct a thorough due diligence and leverage their expertise and influence to communicate to customers the fairness and balance of project risk allocation

8. Obtaining the best and timely debt and equity investor commitments with clearly spelled out terms and conditions to minimize time and the negotiations effort to closure

9. No gaps and issues in financing packages developed for the project, no surprises, and smooth closing and project completion

10. Effective long-term monitoring of the quality of the project company's business plan and operational performance and intervention when warranted

The third part that defines characteristics of successful PFOs is interaction with the sponsor group and the project manager. The characteristics that make a PFO successful are better described by the project managers' perspective as:

1. Guiding the project team through the entire project finance process and providing excellent support to the project team, the project manager, and senior executives

2. Demonstrating understanding of the sponsor(s) situation, needs, objectives, risk tolerance, and level of forthcoming support

3. Being mindful of sponsor-group dynamics and politics and remaining as neutral as situations and project interests require

4. Sharing knowledge, information, data, evidence, evaluations, and earlier project experiences to increase project-team understanding of current project issues

PROJECT FINANCE ORGANIZATIONS ◀ 111

5. Validating and adopting reasonable sponsor objectives as project objectives that are consistent with corporate and new business-development strategy

6. Seeking and incorporating project-team inputs and providing feedback and direct and honest assessments and evaluations

7. Maintaining close functional links and relations with all internal and external project participants

8. Supporting the project manager in all aspects that touch the financing phases and determining the best project and financing structures

9. Supporting project negotiations using a detailed and sound financial model to assess in real time the impacts of proposals and counterproposals on project value

10. Creating optimized financing structures and raising required funding efficiently with full support from key project stakeholders

11. Monitoring the long-term project-company performance, understanding and explaining deviations from projections, and providing feedback for performance improvements

12. Conducting, documenting, and sharing the results of a project post mortem showing the lessons learned to help future project teams avoid the mistakes made in the current project

One cannot omit the required PFO skills and qualifications from the characteristics of successful PFOs. Without them, there would be no basis for competitive advantage or project success. The required PFO skills and competencies were discussed earlier in Section 5.3, but here we look at some telling factors underlying PFO success, which are:

1. Fully trained PFO associates in project finance, with knowledge of global financial markets, and experienced in the use of project finance techniques and instruments

2. Successful raising of financing in earlier projects of different types, having learned from those experiences, and capable of applying that learning to new projects

3. Ability to understand behaviors of people from different cultures and backgrounds and work well toward achieving common objectives

4. Competency in assessing impacts of megatrends and subtrends on the industry, project performance, and ability to take advantage of them and create synergies

5. Aptitude in monitoring market research and evaluating results, leading the project development effort, and validating analyses and project evaluations

6. Experienced in selecting advisors and managing their roles and responsibilities, and their interactions with the project team and their activities

7. Ability to work in fluid environments to shape objectives, set targets, and achieve them in an efficient and timely manner

8. Expertise in translating qualitative information into testable hypotheses, assumptions, and alternative project scenarios

9. Experience in delegating less essential activities to subordinates, other project team members, and supporting organizations

10. Effective project management of process and activities and support of the project manager's responsibilities and superior customer relationship management

11. Continuous search for project finance innovations, improvement of PFO productivity, and knowledge management and sharing

12. Excellence in project marketing presentation skills, salesmanship, and ability to close a deal under pressures from different sources

13. Experience working with legal teams and external advisors to prepare and support the presentation of the information memorandum

14. Effectiveness in expectations, relationship, and conflict management within the project team and with other participants

CHAPTER 6

Project Development

Viability and Financeability Essentials

P roject development is where preparations, planning, analyses, evaluations, and decision events occur and activities that span project definition to creation of the project company's business plan take place. It is the preparation to manage complex, rigorous, and comprehensive processes that cultivates a conducive project environment in the host country and fair regulatory treatment. It is the stage where a balanced risk allocation, a bankable feasibility study, a thorough due diligence, and a sound project financing plan materialize. Project development is a lengthy process to assess, prepare for funding, and bring a project to completion. It is part of the project finance process, which has three main stages: The project prebid or development, contract development and negotiation, and raising the required funding.

The prerequisites of effective project finance are sound budgeting, comprehensive planning, financial modeling, and financial control and reporting systems and providing convincing evidence and clarity of project value creation. There are a multitude of activities in the project development phase which should meet those prerequisites and be guided by the following objectives:

1. Creation of a project plan with clear objectives, processes, and guidelines
2. Determination and assessment of the true project stakeholders' interests and objectives
3. Bringing in PFO and project associates who possess the right skills and qualifications
4. Determining stakeholders' abilities to deliver on financial, human resource, and credit enhancement support
5. Structuring the project effectively to ensure financeability and financial viability
6. Creating a foundation for decision making in each project phase whether executed in parallel or sequentially

The project development stage is important because what happens in this stage affects all subsequent stages and processes and the likelihood of getting expected results. It determines the financing of the project and value creation. It shapes the likelihood of project success when it meets prerequisites and delivers the proper execution of processes and activities described in following sections.

The key deliverables for the development stage are displayed in Figure 6.1, and a successful effort ordinarily produces the following results:

1. Project definition, screening, and selection among different opportunities and options

Figure 6.1 Project Development Stage Deliverables

2. Creation of the right project environment to harness sufficient political support internally and on the customer side

3. Appropriate strategic, portfolio, and operational fit assessments

4. Development of project objectives consistent with corporate strategy and new business development objectives

5. Harmonization of project stakeholder requirements and objectives and management of expectations

6. Identification and allocation of skills and resources required to execute the project successfully

7. The project team and subteams are established with specific roles and responsibilities assigned

8. Effective project management framework is established to ensure unimpeded, ongoing, 360 degree, unimpeded communication, coordination, cooperation, and collaboration (4Cs)

9. Completion of a thorough project economic analysis and timely feasibility study

10. Development of a project financial model to capture influencing factors, estimate relationships, and provide financeability measures

11. Comprehensive due diligence that validates the feasibility study results and reports on the project's financeability

The content of this chapter is an introduction to chapters dealing with the development-stage deliverables of project finance. Section 6.1 summarizes the prerequisites of project development that need to be satisfied to build a sound decision basis. Section 6.2 discusses the major undertakings necessary to determine whether to proceed with project development; that is, the activities around completing the project pre-feasibility study. Section 6.3 is dedicated to project definition activities where project rationale is articulated and project objectives are developed, while Section 6.4 discusses technical design and assessment preparatory activities. The effort required to complete the project feasibility study is crucial—it marks a major decision junction for a project—and it is discussed in Section 6.5.

The project due diligence considerations and report-related activities of vital importance to all project participants are the subject of Section 6.6 and the development of project and financial structure undertakings are discussed in Section 6.7. Project contract and agreement development and negotiations are the subject of Section 6.8. Section 6.9 presents the events that take place in preparation for marketing a project to investors to attract debt and equity financing. Section 6.10 presents project development cost estimates and success factors. The topics discussed in this chapter are primers to the activities, processes, analyses, evaluations, and decisions made in each phase of project development that are treated in more detail in subsequent chapters.

6.1 PROJECT DEVELOPMENT PREREQUISITES

For reviews and approvals to take place expeditiously, project team preparations and internal sponsor company and customer planning should be guided by funding source processes and requirements. There are some universal project development fundamentals and capability requirements that are necessary to develop projects successfully. Starting with experience and impartiality in selecting advisors, other project team and stakeholder skill prerequisites for successful project development include:

1. Expertise in bid preparation and evaluation, procurement experience, and skill in responding to requests for proposals and receiving a contract award

2. Experience in project assessment, structuring, and financial markets and instruments

3. Well versed in project risk identification and allocation and experienced in assessing adequacy of risk insurance coverage

4. Have established a global network of insurance providers with the ability to deliver on the contracted risk coverages in full

5. Expertise in macroeconomic country and industry analysis, cost estimation, competitive project company output pricing, cost–benefit analysis, and dealing with regulatory issues

6. Accurate assessment of the project's political environment and ability to obtain political support to take the project through the host government's evaluation

7. Strong civil, industrial, and environmental engineering, technical design and technology, and equipment evaluation capabilities

8. Experience managing the construction of projects and providing input and guidance concerning technical issues in the creation of contracts

9. Extensive knowledge of commercial and investment banking, unilateral and multilateral agencies, export credit agencies (ECAs), project credit rating, and in-depth understanding of lender and investor requirements, as well as those of the host government ceding authority

10. Experience in commercial lending, bond financing, insurance and pension fund investing, and private placements

11. Strong internal links with all project stakeholder organizations and an extensive network throughout the technology and engineering, legal, and financial communities

12. Skilled in developing sound project objectives and preparing project plans to drive the project through the development process

13. Competence in providing analysis and inputs and working with legal teams to draft and negotiate project agreements and contracts

14. Superior capabilities in managing complex processes and integrating outputs of different participants into the mainstream project process

15. Experience in presenting the work of the project development stage to senior management and the due diligence team and addressing issues and concerns

Regardless of how project development is defined or the order of activities, there are some key deliverables common to most infrastructure projects as shown in Figure 6.1. Common phases are the project prefeasibility, the project definition, the technical design, the feasibility study, the due diligence, the financial structure assessment, and the preparation for marketing and raising the financing phases.

6.2 PREFEASIBILITY ASSESSMENT

In this phase, needs are identified and ways to satisfy them are explored and focus is directed to project development. If more than one sponsor is interested in participating in the project, a project development agreement is signed. It spells out the project definition details, voting rights, and sharing of project predevelopment costs; confidentiality, and nondisclosure. It also defines functions to be performed, each partner's roles and responsibilities, and allowance for withdrawal from the project (Hoffman, 2008).

Contact is initiated with the host government and ceding authority to get consensus and political support, local partners are vetted to facilitate the response to request for proposal, and the sponsor or developer project team is established. A project design team is engaged to consider project design options, operational performance expectations, and preliminary project specifications to meet project requirements at competitive cost levels. Assessment of the political, economic, and investment environments takes place along with initial assessment of project risks. Also, the ability of the host government and the ceding authority to deliver on their obligations is evaluated. Then, a project briefing to the sponsor company's senior management team takes place.

A project financial model is developed with some initial assumptions and first cut estimates of capital costs, operational expenses and revenue estimates are produced. The planning, preparations, and assessments that come out of this phase are important because they provide initial estimates of project funding requirements and indications of financeability. These estimates form the basis for the decision to proceed with the project and move to the next phase; that is, project definition. Notice, however, that the project definition and the prefeasibility assessment may take place simultaneously or in some cases the order may be reversed.

6.3 PROJECT DEFINITION

The first step in defining a project is a clear statement of project rationale explaining the background and motives leading to considering the project. This is followed by a strategic, portfolio, and operational fit assessment where complementarity, consistency of objectives, sponsor company strengths and weaknesses, and competitor threats are considered vis-à-vis the project opportunity. It is important to determine how consistent the project being considered is with corporate goals and objectives and risk appetite, if it complements the company's portfolio and is operationally feasible, and how it fills current or expected gaps. In the process of doing the fit assessments, the company's situational analysis is revisited to determine if the company has the required resources for the project to be executed successfully. That is, if sufficient resources with the right skills and qualifications can be allocated to the project.

A key element of project definition is ensuring that project needs are correctly identified and determining objectively how and to what extent the project fills those needs. When proceeding to the project definition stage, all project participants are identified and additional skills are brought into the project team to conduct required analyses. Next, each participant's objectives and constraints are examined closely and stakeholder representatives are assigned roles and responsibilities. At this point, it is crucial that a common communication, coordination, cooperation, and collaboration plan is introduced to the project team. This plan is needed because of the complexity of project managing a large project financing; without it the likelihood of project success is diminished.

In the presence of more than one project option, a screening of related opportunities and selection of a most fitting project takes place. This provides the rationale of taking the project to the next phase after the opportunity costs of doing and not doing the project are considered. The activities mentioned so far are meaningful and valid only when project objectives are clearly defined and unambiguously stated. There should be no vagueness, implicit considerations around project objectives, and conflict with strategic, new business development, and corporate financial objectives. Objectives should be reasonable, realistic, and feasible, given the sponsor's resource constraints, and there is a high level of confidence that they can be achieved. However, in order for this to occur, the project team's scope needs to be specified and fixed; otherwise, project objectives become a moving target and so does the value created by the project.

6.4 TECHNICAL DESIGN AND ASSESSMENT

Some of the primary events of the project development phase involve the creation of a technical facility design consistent the performance requirements and initial specifications while capital requirements, timelines, and operational costs are firmed up. Physical and cyberspace security considerations and different options and costs are examined; then, a project design that satisfies the customer and key stakeholders is achieved. Feasible project parameters are determined, and technical project plans are crated along with a project technical implementation timetable. Detailed technical design and technical management plans are developed and the information created is then passed on for decisions and broader project planning and evaluations.

A preliminary technical assessment is performed to identify project design and specification strengths and weaknesses in the prefeasibility study, and a more in-depth assessment is conducted in the technical design and assessment phase before any proposal is created. Some of the activities involved in the project technical assessment include:

1. Project site and technology vendor visits and interviews of host government authorities to ensure there no problems, conflicts, or misunderstandings in the technical area

2. Collection and evaluation of technology, cost, reliability and other types of information and data to determine the useful life of the project

3. Estimation and evaluation of project costs and benefits of competing projects or project configurations, and selection of the project and configuration most appropriate given sponsor strategic objectives and customer needs

4. Identification of technology-related project risks and issues and making recommendations for project parameter variations that affect risk mitigation and costs

5. Providing inputs to the project financial model, the feasibility study, and the due diligence, and recommendations on how to optimize project value creation

6.5 FEASIBILITY STUDY

In this phase, more in-depth technical, economic, environmental, legal, and financial assessments take place to determine project financing needs, economic viability, and financeability. If advancing the project to the next phase is warranted, senior management approvals are obtained and additional required resources are allocated. This phase is important because it generates and validates data, information, and updates evaluations needed for senior management decisions. The feasibility study forms a basis for the due diligence phase, the sponsor and ceding authority business cases, the project company's business plans, and the project's risk assessment and mitigation. A sound feasibility study incorporates the findings of all project assessments, including physical and cyberspace security, into a report that serves as a guide to implement the project management plan.

The sequence of activities undertaken in the feasibility study fulfills a number of project team responsibilities, which include the following:

1. Revisiting the scope and objectives of the project in light of final project definition

2. Ensuring consistency of stakeholder interests and objectives, determining if additional participants should be added, and identifying and screening potential new participants

3. Understanding the true project-stakeholder needs and expectations and managing them to levels consistent with project facts and the reality of the project's environment

4. Engaging project advisors and consultants to assist in activities, briefings, and presentations to stakeholders' key decision makers

5. Probing deeper in the host country's legal, industry, and regulatory environment analysis. The industry analysis examines current versus needed capacity, costs and rates, market shares, and marketing, pricing, and sales aspects

6. Investigating project company accessibility to skilled labor and pricing of adequate production inputs to the project company and their availability

7. Conducting an updated technical options analysis and defining more precisely technical and operating performance specifications

8. Developing, updating, and testing a more complete set of assumptions and obtaining project stakeholder consensus and support

9. Evaluating the findings of the environmental impact study and assessing costs associated with needed remediation to include in the total project cost

A second set of project team activities in the feasibility study encompasses the following undertakings:

1. Setting up the project governance structure, which is the set of policies, functions, processes, roles, and responsibilities that guide management and control of the project

2. Performing political, economic, social, technical, legal, educational, and demographic (PESTLED), megatrend, and subtrend analyses to support a robust demand analysis of the project company's output and developing reasonable scenarios

3. Determining if required skills and capabilities are brought in the project and if not, ensuring that adequate resources and skills are allocated

4. Ensuring that in addition to project development, capex, and operational expenses, costs related to site preparation and physical and cyberspace security are included in funding requirements

5. Expanding the project financial model and incorporating new and updated assumptions, data, and information inputs to firm up project financing needs and financeability

6. Conducting additional reality checks on the assumptions, cost and revenue data, information compiled, and the results of the financial model

7. Identifying, evaluating, and allocating risks to parties best able to manage and obtain insurance and other project support needed

8. Verifying the robustness of the physical and cyberspace security package to protect the project from vandalism, sabotage, and terrorist attacks

9. Ensuring that the implementation agreement includes grants and project incentives, such as tax holidays, tax rate reductions, and payment and performance obligation guarantees and a waiver of host government immunity and import duties

An implementation agreement is a contract between the host government and the project company. In the case of PPP projects it is called a ceding agreement.

The sequence of project development activities can be changed or performed in parallel and the various feasibility study elements, timing, and evaluations are discussed in subsequent phases. The key elements of the feasibility study can be varied in order to satisfy information and evaluation requirements. Project feasibility study costs can be high, but entirely justified, because of the important elements that come out of it which include the following:

1. A technical design and engineering project plan with detailed specifications meeting customer requirements

2. The foundations for the project due diligence, which helps to identify shortcomings and adequacy of the risk management plan and address issues of concern and validate the evaluation results

3. Updated inputs for the project financial model and an outline of project structuring and financing plans with initial supporting material

4. A project schedule, inputs needed for the project management plan monitoring and controlling activities, and project milestones and deliverables

5. Assignment of clear objectives and deliverables to each project stakeholder and project team member

6. Required information, data, and guidance for drafting project agreements and contract negotiations

7. Preparation of inputs and guidance to draft agreements and produce and package tender documents and project public releases as needed

8. Creation of draft project company business plan, development of indicators of project performance, and draft plans for project course correction when necessary

9. Development of project viability and financeability evidence that creates a higher comfort level for senior management decisions

10. Recommendation to advance the project to the next phase and obtain senior management approvals

6.6 DUE DILIGENCE

In project financing, due diligence is an in-depth investigation focused on identifying issues of concern and confirming data, claims, and contract representations. It evaluates analyses and validates assessments before decisions are made and project agreements are signed. It also determines gaps in evidence, assumptions, and assessments; highlights problems, and investigates the extent to which risk assessment and mitigation have been achieved. Additionally, the due diligence does a thorough check on the participants' ability to meet current and future obligations and produces an independent assessment report of the project's funding needs and finance-ability potential. It also provides a common understanding to lenders and all project participants; that is, a common platform for decision making.

Ordinarily the due diligence is performed by advisors of lending institutions and it is paid for by the project sponsors; however, the project team is involved from the start of the project and plays an important role in it. The expertise of the lenders' advisors includes legal, environmental, technical, insurance, and economic and market analysis, demand forecasting, financial modeling, and other areas of expertise as needed. Additionally, it includes reviews and assessment of the host country investment environment, policies, and regulatory regime; technical and environmental issues, operational requirements, and expected commercial performance using a risk matrix approach.

> A risk matrix is used to characterize various levels of risk along columns and the likelihood of occurrence along rows that highlight areas and the degree of focus for risk mitigation.

The due diligence examination includes key items needed to validate technical feasibility, economic viability, and project financeability, such as:

1. Government and ceding authority project objectives and constraints in their ability to meet required contributions and contractual obligations
2. The project team's understanding and compliance with the public procurement process
3. Industry and market analysis, and pricing and tariff setting in the host country
4. Concessionaire obligations and property and land use rights
5. Risk insurance, other project support, and adequacy of the lenders' protection package
6. Dispute resolution and sovereign immunity
7. Default issues and termination compensation
8. Lender direct agreement and security package

The nature of due diligence varies by project type and stakeholder, but there are elements common to all due diligence efforts that include assessment of the following:

1. Project definition and screening details
2. Project design, technical specifications, scope of work, and schedule

3. Technology design and engineering and equipment assessment

4. Project risk identification, assessment, and allocation and mitigation

5. Project cost and revenue forecasts and the project company's business plan

6. The financial model structure and validated essential inputs and outputs

7. Construction specifics and commercial acceptance requirements

8. Operations and maintenance program over the project lifecycle

9. Draft project documentation and review of legal contractual agreements

10. The parties' ability to deliver on their obligations

11. Lender covenants and restrictions and systems to ensure repayment

Due to the limited recourse nature of project financing and risks associated with investing outside the sponsor's country, legal due diligence plays a key role in determining project bankability. Some practitioners maintain that project financing is contract financing and that contract review and negotiation includes assessment of applicable laws of the sponsor and host country and its legal framework and regulation. The review also includes laws concerning public procurement processes, environmental considerations, employment and labor practices, consumer protection, and taxation.

For PPP projects, the due diligence must also validate the best value for the money (BVM) principle in order to satisfy host government agency/ceding authority requirements. This principle seeks to validate project cost effectiveness; quality project design, technology, and construction that meets agreed-to specifications; and project sustainability. Sustainability means that the economic and social benefits shown in the business case support ceding authority and local government objectives and are equitably distributed. BVM is an accepted approach to evaluate the 4Es of the project; namely, its efficiency, economy, effectiveness, and equity.

6.7 PROJECT AND FINANCIAL STRUCTURES

The project ownership structure is a key determinant of the financing structure. It is determined by the customer or host country tender requirements, the debt and equity levels to be raised, control of the project, the tax laws of the host country, and accounting treatment of the project company considerations. A second key determinant of the financing structure is the project capital structure, which is determined by projections of revenue and capital and operational costs, operating cash flow, the risk allocation scheme and credit enhancements, debt service requirements versus debt service capacity, and net cash obtainable by sponsors.

The different key considerations in developing the project and financial structures include consideration of a number of factors, such as:

1. Defining a project company ownership structure; i.e. a corporate, joint venture, general partnership, or limited liability company structure
2. Ascertaining the amounts and timing of equity contributions, involvement and commitment of sponsors, and debt-funding requirements
3. Assessing the costs and benefits of different project delivery options, such as build, operate, and transfer of ownership at project completion(BOT), build, own, operate, and transfer (BOOT), design, build, operate, transfer DBOT, etc. to the host government's ceding authority
4. Performing in-depth project returns to sponsors and economic and ratio analysis to determine project viability

Infrastructure or other large project financings are collaborative and iterative efforts to balance participant interests, ensure project viability, and arrive at some optimal scheme of raising the required funding. Once the project feasibility study, the due diligence, and identification of the sources of funding for the project are completed, addressing risk allocation and credit enhancements needed in a manner acceptable to lenders comes into focus. In this phase, knowledge of financial markets and instruments along with extensive networks, close contacts with financial institutions, and a strategy for drawdowns and repayments are of paramount importance.

Financial structuring is determining the type and blend of funds used in financing the project, primarily the amount of debt to raise and its repayment schedule, intended to maximize the sponsors internal rate of return (IRR). Financial structuring also defines the financial support from different participants, drawdowns, their timing, and repayments to various sources of funds.

Parenthetically, the financial structure used in a project is also known as the project model and because of the variety of projects, there are numerous financial structures used, depending on the particulars of project definition.

In addition to the role of public sector involvement in the project, other project financial structure considerations are the parties involved in the project, their decision-making process, and their debt and equity contributions. Again, flow of money and contractual agreements, timing of drawdowns and repayments, project risks and their mitigation, and a credit-support package are prime concerns. The project financing structuring elements are addressed in the project financing plan discussion of Chapter 13.

The kind of project financing and the sources of funding are also dependent on the project stage. In the project development phase, funding comes from sponsors/developers and grants from governments or multilateral financing institutions, while construction financing comes primarily from short-term commercial bank debt. In the operational phase, refinancing with long-term maturity takes place. Notice that from the public participant perspective the essence of financial structure refers to the structure of the contractual agreements. From the project company's perspective, financial structure refers specifically to the project company's financial structure.

6.8 AGREEMENTS AND NEGOTIATIONS

Infrastructure project development is a lengthy process that, among other matters, addresses business and risk issues, documenting agreements, and drafting, preparing, and negotiating project contracts. In project finance, contracts are created when parties that have the capacity to deliver on contract terms reach agreements that define their rights and obligations. Contracts are legally binding and enforceable when the responsibilities and rights of the participants are stated in clear form and unambiguous language. For contracts to be valid and enforceable in the host country, they must be equitably made, balance the interests of the parties involved, and be consistent with the host country's laws, regulations, and policies that protect their integrity.

The purpose of project contracts is to allow stakeholders to tailor the contents of agreements, shape the participants' relationships, manage expectations, and define how negative project outcomes can be resolved. Also, well-structured contracts ensure that the parties involved understand the details of the agreements and their implications. Contracts are important because they guide processes that form the foundation for raising funding for a project. However, they are crucial in the case of disputes to ensure that not honoring their terms results in fair compensation for work done, products or services delivered, funds advanced, etc. Besides preparation for contract creation, contract management is important since it spans the initiation, planning, drafting, negotiating, and implementation of the project, and monitoring contract compliance in operations.

Infrastructure project finance contracts cover all key aspects of project ownership structure, the project company's structure, and the resulting financial structure. They also cover participant contributions and the procurement, project delivery, and payment parts such as, the duration of a project's concession, pricing, quality and performance, security packages, and costs. Contracts may cover many project aspects, but they cannot cover everything. Some things are best managed through relationships among the parties involved, such as flexibility, willingness to allow minor deviations from contract terms, and renegotiating contracts when it is necessary.

Project finance is considered contract finance by some project participants because the interweaving of contractual arrangements makes project financing possible. This is so because contracts are the venue and tool where risks are identified and mitigated or allocated through negotiations to entities best able to handle them. While the project type and its particulars determine what contracts are required, there are some elements common to most projects, such as the implementation or concession agreement, the offtake and supply agreements, the construction contract, and the operations and maintenance agreement. Other common contracts involved are the lenders' direct agreement between the government, the project company, and the lenders and the loan agreement. Also, performance bonds, collateral guarantees, and the loan term sheet are components of the project contractual framework.

Development and negotiation of contracts is a lengthy and strenuous activity that produces voluminous documentation. In one large infrastructure project financing in the mid-1990s, the contracts and related paperwork filled boxes that took up the entire space of a 20x20x12 room in the offices of a law firm in Washington, DC. Preparation for contract negotiations is essential because drafting agreements requires the engagement of the entire project team for:

1. Thorough review of the technical evaluation details, the feasibility study, and the due diligence report along with evaluation of financial model outputs
2. Briefings to the negotiations team with a package containing at least:
    a. Key issues and terms to be negotiated
    b. Data, analyses and evaluations, and reports to support the team's negotiating positions
    c. Opening, fallback, revised, and walk-away positions
    d. Assessment of impacts of contract variations and assumptions by the financial model

Important activities of the project team in preparation for contract creation and negotiation include the following activities and contributions:

1. Engaging legal counsel and expert advice early to manage participant expectations early
2. Developing a clear set of project objectives and contracts required to help achieve them
3. Conducting research on key project areas and planning according to those findings

4. Starting with a wish list, such as one of the term sheets, and creating a negotiation plan

5. Taking a reasonable and balanced approach to negotiations

6. Outlining reasonable negotiation positions and suggestions on how to move along positions

7. Being sensitive to cultural differences and different negotiating styles

8. Preparing for a long, tedious, going back and forth process ahead

9. Staying positive and seeking compromises and concessions to bring financing to closure

10. Learning from earlier experiences and introducing innovation along the negotiation process

6.9 PROJECT MARKETING AND RAISING FINANCING

The marketing of an infrastructure project is an integral part of raising financing and its foundations rest on the project economics of the feasibility study, the due diligence report, and the output of the project financial model. Various forms of project marketing are used to attract sponsor partners, lenders, and investors in different stages of a project. Nevertheless, the objectives of marketing an infrastructure project are to communicate effectively and convince potential participants of the value generated by the project and demonstrate how their interests and objectives are satisfied under a reasonable risk mitigation plan. Infrastructure marketing materials are not only lender and investor presentations, such as project prospectuses and information memorandums but, also, material information included in bid proposals or submissions to requests for proposals.

The project prospectus, or information memorandum, is a composite of the sponsor's business case and the business plan of the project company prepared for investors. Along with other marketing material they highlight the important aspects of the project investment opportunity. However, the information memorandum includes in a summary and succinct form for investor scrutiny with more analyses and evaluations than a prospectus does. The analyses and evaluations and supporting materials are prepared by the project team in conjunction with the legal team, project advisors, and consultants. The prospectus or information memorandum, marketing material, and presentations are packaged professionally and presented to different audiences by the sponsor's investor relations and public relations groups.

The project prospectus and the information memorandum contain synopses of work performed in the project development phase. They typically include the following required elements:

1. Market Review and Project Background and Rationale
2. Project description and the project schedule
3. Project technical design and performance specifications
4. Host country political, economic, and investment environment review
5. Assessment of the industry structure, competition issues, and industry trends
6. Appraisal of the host country's legal and regulatory framework
7. Evaluation of environmental, health and safety, and labor market issues
8. Project company structure, management team, objectives, and business plan
9. Project sponsors/developers and other participants involved and identified
10. Design, engineering, and technology partners participating in the project
11. Permits and approvals already secured, ceding authority support for the project, and compliance to the schedule and other requirements
12. Main assumptions underlying the revenue projections already validated
13. Costs and benefits of the project, both financial and social and environmental, and the project contributions to the local economy's development
14. Balanced and fair risk mitigation on a best able to handle and cost-benefit basis
15. Structure of the project agreements and all applicable contracts
16. Project financial plan showing funding requirements, capital structure, drawdowns and repayments
17. Results of the financial model analysis: project net present value (NPV), cash flow projections, investor IRR, and debt ratios
18. Risk factors and their mitigation and the insurance and credit support package
19. The project's long-term viability and the investment opportunity sustainability

20. The key success factors and the likelihood of achieving the project objectives
21. A summary of the value of the project and supporting appendices

The PFO's and the project team's responsibilities in the preparation of the information memorandum include:

1. Demonstrating to customers or the host government's ceding authority that the project as structured meets their needs and supports their objectives
2. Establishing that the project fully meets the requirements of the best value for money principle
3. Showing that the project is indeed producing adequate returns and is a long term economically viable investment
4. Confirming the reasonableness of assumptions underlying the financial model, the risk mitigation, and the credit support package
5. Establishing the transparency of project company governance and financial reporting
6. Creating, projecting, and maintaining a positive sponsor company image of the project throughout its lifecycle
7. Demonstrating the necessary efficiency of financing developed to support competitive bids

6.10 DEVELOPMENT COSTS AND SUCCESS FACTORS

Sources of funding for project development vary by type of project, but the most common sources of project development financing are:

1. The host government various agencies' project funding budgets
2. Assignment of host government human resources and in-kind contributions
3. Private capital, project developers, and sponsors
4. Sovereign loans and credits from development banks
5. US Agency for International Development
6. Sovereign loans and credits from development banks
7. Grants from trust funds and donor programs

Project development costs are high and vary not only by project type and size, but also by the skills of project participants, funding source, and host country economic development. High project development costs are due to acquisition of expertise residing in advisors and consultants, contacts with host government authorities, rigorous analyses and the due diligence effort, the identification of project risks and their effective mitigation, and the lengthy contract drafting and negotiation process of contracts. MacKinzie and Cusworth (2007) estimate project feasibility costs around 2.3% of total project costs. However, estimates of project preparation range from 5% to 10% depending on timing, definitions, and other project parameters. As an example, the Infrastructure Consortium for Africa (2014) reports the following estimates:

1. Average Africa regional projects: 7%
2. World Bank estimate: 5% to 10%
3. Ifraco Africa projects: 10%

Success factors for project development are factors that create a solid foundation for a project to achieve key project stakeholder expectations; that is, to satisfy everyone's interests and needs in an effective manner. Remember, the main objective of project development is to create the conditions for:

1. Accurate assessment of project characteristics via the technical evaluation and the feasibility study
2. Thorough identification, analysis, evaluation, risk allocation and mitigation
3. Ensuring the long-term project economic viability
4. Obtaining efficient project financing to allow timely and on-budget completion
5. Value creation and adequate returns to all project participants

From the host country perspective, the best project-development strategy is to plan and structure an infrastructure project that meets its needs with minimal environmental impacts and maximum social benefits. Successful project development also requires the principle of value for the money to be operative and that approvals, processes and procedures are closely followed. From the sponsor's perspective, project success is judged by close strategic, portfolio, and operational project fit; the NPV created, an acceptable IRR, strong debt ratios, and project company ability to make payment of dividends.

Value for the money (VFM) is a principle used by public entities to assess if they obtain maximum benefit from the goods and services they procure or provide given their resource constraints. It also evaluates the cost of goods and services and takes into account considerations of quality, cost, resources expanded, timeliness, and convenience to judge if they produce good value.

Effective project management is crucial for successful project development and in order for the objectives of successful project management to be realized, a number of pre-conditions need to be satisfied, such as:

1. Planning, organizing, and assigning a project team early on and staffing it with associates possessing the right skills and qualifications

2. Considering the opportunity costs of doing and not doing a project. These costs are often ignored, but are crucial in new business development decisions

3. Developing clear and effective processes that help form the project plan

4. Selecting an appropriate project-delivery strategy and vehicle

5. Scrutinizing cost and revenue forecast assumptions, models, and scenarios used and developing realistic project feasibility assessments

6. Objectively assessing project schedules, expected deliverables, critical paths, dependencies, and risks to the project

7. Creating participant consensus and obtaining buy-in and political support

8. Ensuring all around unimpeded communication, coordination, cooperation, and collaboration is prevalent

CHAPTER 7

Participants and Responsibilities

Activities and Deliverables

The stakeholders in project financings are the sponsor(s), the customer or host country government ceding agency, the debt and equity investors, the project company, the offtaker or user of the project company's output, and the supplier of production inputs to the project company. Other project participants are external advisors and consultants, the construction contractor, the technology and equipment provider, the export credit agency (ECA) of equipment origin and multilateral agencies, and the operations and management (O&M) company. The sponsor's or developer's project team usually consists of the project manager under a project executive and representatives from sales and marketing, the CFO and treasury, business development, engineering and technology, legal, and the project finance organization (PFO) that draws from internal and external groups to perform necessary functions.

In infrastructure projects there are numerous tasks that need to be performed, and several participants with different interests, objectives, and project finance skills and experiences; as well as an overlap of roles and responsibilities carried out over complex and lengthy processes. Different projects require different assignment of participant roles and responsibilities that vary by sponsor, host country government authority, and organizational and project finance capabilities. Hence, the need for clearly delineated roles and assigned responsibilities to the project core project team and other participants. Besides a clear specification of roles and responsibilities, a key requirement is coordination of tasks and cooperation and collaboration to produce required deliverables to move the project forward.

To appreciate the need for the project participants' roles to coalesce with the responsibilities of the core project team, Figure 7.1 helps to conceptualize the required coordination to incorporate their outputs and deliverables into the overall project finance process. A complete inventory of project participant roles and functions is lengthy and requires superior project management skills and a PFO capable of helping the project manager coordinate internal and external processes, activities, and deliverables.

In the sections that follow, the roles and responsibilities of participants are logged in sufficient detail to give a good picture of the effort involved in the monumental task of coordinating participant outputs into the project team main process. The undertakings, events, and activities associated with each participant's charter and how participants carry out their responsibilities are shown in the sections that follow: Section 7.1 deals with the project team and its roles; Section 7.2 discusses the roles of the host government; and Section 7.3 addresses the many roles of the project sponsor(s).

Section 7.4 reviews the roles of the project company while Section 7.5 describes the crucial roles of the project lenders, and Section 7.6 lists the roles of different external advisors and consultants. Section 7.7 shows the

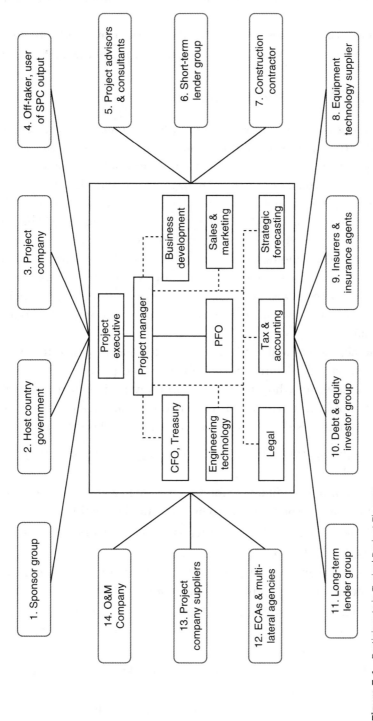

Figure 7.1 Participants in Typical Project Finance

roles of unilateral and multilateral institutions, Section 7.8 enumerates the roles of the engineering, procurement, and construction (EPC) contractor and Section 7.9 identifies the roles of the technology and equipment providers.

Section 7.10 discusses the roles of the project company's offtaker and suppliers and lastly, Section 7.11 deals with the roles of the O&M company.

7.1 ROLES OF THE PROJECT TEAM

Project leadership is usually vested to a sponsor company senior executive with industry experience, ability, and resources to complete a project successfully. The senior executive is usually the head of a business unit or a member of the company's senior management team. The project team is headed by the project manager who reports to the project executive and plays a key role in developing and seeing a project to its completion. The project team consists of the PFO and subteams with new business development, engineering and technology, sales and marketing, finance and accounting, legal, market research and competitive analysis, and strategic project forecasting experiences. It also includes representatives from other participants who perform activities and contribute outputs in coordination with the project team.

In the absence of a skilled PFO, the roles and responsibilities of the project team are to perform tasks defined in the project plan developed by external advisors who, in turn, perform key project finance functions. In reality, project team roles and responsibilities are determined by skills and competencies residing in the team, and major duties include:

1. Assigning specific roles and responsibilities to the core project team members
2. Assuming accountability for direction, management, and delivery of the project: scope, budget, schedule, and deliverables
3. Harmonizing participant interests and developing or clarifying project objectives
4. Engaging external advisors and consultants with skills and competencies not residing in the sponsor organization
5. Validating its own and coordinating delivery of timely and quality completed analyses, evaluations, and validations and external advisors and consultants
6. Managing core team, project participant, and customer expectations and relationships
7. Planning and managing project activities, schedules, costs, and quality of deliverables

8. Investigating, analyzing, and evaluating project issues, discovering gaps, and documenting unmet requirements

9. Overseeing and validating internal project analyses, evaluations, and recommendations

10. Ensuring sufficient skills, competencies, and training of project team associates and the project company management team

11. Making participant organizations aware of the need to address the adequacy of human resource contributions, timing issues, and skill deficiencies

12. Facilitating all-around, unimpeded communication, coordination, cooperation, and collaboration to develop project deliverables efficiently

13. Building, testing, managing, and maintaining and updating the project financial model

14. Handling project change requests and managing and resolving issues and conflicts

15. Managing and coordinating the development of project team documents and artifacts

16. Developing the financing plan and providing support to contract development and negotiations

17. Tracking and reporting project progress and project company performance on an ongoing basis

18. Following internal approval processes for the development of the project business case and the project company's business plan

7.2 ROLES OF THE HOST GOVERNMENT

The roles and responsibilities of the host government authority are determined by the nature of the project bid, type of project, public sector equity position, and government agency skills and competence in project finance. There is a tendency for the public sector to rely on the expertise of sponsors, multilateral institutions, and development agencies for management of the project financing process. Often, the public sector interests and objectives drive the agency's responsibilities to perform the following tasks:

1. Ensure transparent and proper project origination, bid, and procurement management

2. Prepare requests for project proposals and originate growth and social projects such as seaports, airports, railways, hospitals, schools, etc.

3. Ensure all project proposals meet value-for-money requirements and maintain political support across agencies involved

4. Meet urgent needs and maximize the economic and social benefits of projects

5. Retain as much control over the project as possible by acquiring project equity preferably through in-kind contributions instead debt or equity investment

6. Managing project costs and being an active, key party to commercial negotiations

7. Require compliance with local environmental, business, tax, and labor laws and demand safe and efficient project construction and operation

8. Provide input in the development and documentation of project agreements

9. Negotiate project finance documents and sign financing agreements and financial closing

10. Transfer risks to the private sector during project building and operations when feasible

11. Develop programs to attract new capital to increase the country's economic productivity

12. Obtain technological development assistance, transfer of knowledge, and training in new skills

13. Structure projects to help the country's economic growth and increase its competitiveness

14. Provide counter guarantees needed in order to satisfy lenders and multilaterals

15. Provide direct finance from tax revenues, issue bonds and guarantees, credit enhancements, insurance, hedging, and other financial instruments

7.3 ROLES OF PROJECT SPONSORS

The different types of sponsors are project developers making strategic investments, companies looking to increase their international presence and profits, industrial construction contractors, equipment providers, and others. Regardless of type, sponsors assume a good part of risks in infrastructure investments, especially in developing countries. Therefore, they have major responsibilities and play a key role in project structuring and financing. The sponsor tasks, roles, and responsibilities are carried out by the project manager and the project team are itemized below.

1. Decide on the composition of the sponsor group and define the terms of the agreement

2. Determine project company ownership structure, provide equity funding, and demonstrate commitment for future equity infusions to optimize the financing plan

3. Manage host government relations and public-sector expectations effectively through close relationships

4. Define strategic project objectives, provide policy direction, and assign operations and management responsibilities and personnel to the project company

5. Employ experienced managers for strategic expansion and portfolio diversification in infrastructure projects to satisfy new business development and financial objectives

6. Identify needs, originate projects, and determine project configuration characteristics, requirements, and specifications

7. Coordinate effective project development, obtain efficient financing, and price the project competitively in order to submit a competitive bid

8. Secure internal organizational backing and external political support for the project

9. Ensure proper project governance and make critical decisions

10. Outline project scope, objectives, deliverables, and success criteria and provide direction and coordination of project team processes and activities

11. Maintain oversight of project value integrity and resolve escalated business issues

12. Keep contract management responsibilities and review and approve key work, evaluations, and progress in each project phase

13. Select and approve project advisors, the EPC contractor, and local project partners or facilitators

14. Ensure participation in host government high-level consultations and decisions for project origination and development in different areas of sponsor expertise

15. Select reliable technology, equipment, and supplier partners to maximize profit and minimize development and production costs and project underperformance

16. Make available qualified people to help the project company start operations successfully and approve needed skills transfers to it

17. Decide the choice of contracts and project finance channels and facilities to be used in the project and lead project negotiations

18. Monitor and evaluate project company performance closely and initiate operational adjustments when necessary

7.4 ROLES OF THE PROJECT COMPANY

The special purpose company, or project company, is a shell entity created by sponsors to own the assets of the project, enter into contractual agreements, and manage the cash flow of the project. It is structured to maximize sponsor tax benefits and it has no obligations beyond the scope of the project. The responsibilities of the project company are concentrated around the following functions:

1. Enter into contractual agreements and ensure that its rights and obligations are clearly defined in commercial and finance documents and contracts

2. Negotiate all contracts in accordance with the project objectives set out by sponsors and the constraints of debt and equity investors

3. Pay close attention to the preparation of the construction contract to build the project facilities according to specifications and monitor construction progress

4. Enter into agreements and manage the offtaker or purchaser, supplier, and O&M contracts

5. Limit the scope of the project to that spelled out in the shareholder agreement

6. Obtain funds from debt and equity investors, collect revenues, royalties, or fees and manage project cash flows and disbursements

7. Comply with project finance covenants and restrictions and provide collateral assignment of project contracts, pledge stock, and grant of security interest

8. Implement the business plan, manage operations, and produce planned project output according to specified performance standards

9. Ensure availability, quantity, and quality supplier inputs and materials at agreed to pricing levels

10. Guarantee availability, quantity, and quality standards at predictable pricing to offtaker or purchaser of the project output

11. Transfer assets to the host government at the end of the concession period if it is part of the negotiated contractual agreements

7.5 ROLES OF THE LENDERS

Project lenders have a central role in project finance and influence the financing structure through loan requirements which are often considered stringent because their investments only have downside potential. Common roles assumed by project lenders are to perform the following functions:

1. Participate in or lead the loan syndication, perform functions of the lenders' trustee, and serve as the project company's account bank if they have a presence in the host country

2. Ensure a sound feasibility study through reasonableness tests of assumptions, rigorous economic evaluation of the project, and realistic, baseline scenario-revenue forecast

3. Review the project team's market assessment with the project market advisor and validate the cost and revenue projections

4. Facilitate the introduction of project sponsors to other lenders, potential investors, and insurance agents

5. Evaluate engineering, technical, and equipment specifications to ensure consistency with bid requirements and value for the money

6. Assess technical, market, political, construction, and other risks and ensure adequacy of the risk mitigation plan

7. Bring in trusted insurance agents and specialists to negotiate the best possible contract deals for the sponsors with insurance companies

8. Ensure completeness and adequacy of offtake agreements, supply and O&M contracts, and hedging contracts

9. Verify that the sponsor has solid industry experience to implement the project and provide technical and operational support to the project company

10. Make sure the lender's engineer, insurance agent, and other advisors liaison with sponsor and other project stakeholder counterparts

11. Lead the due diligence along with the sponsor's PFO and the legal team and act on the technical, engineering, and insurance recommendations of the due diligence report

12. Review and validate the final market assessment, baseline scenario, and project cost and revenue projections and any management adjustments made

13. Prepare and negotiate financing documents and define collateral and control positions

14. Have separate agreements with the project company to co-monitor construction progress and operations

15. Require sufficient sponsor equity contribution and ensure ability to provide support if the project has problems in the future

7.6 ROLES OF ADVISORS, CONSULTANTS, AND INSURERS

The roles and responsibilities of project advisors touch all aspects of project development, evaluation, construction, and financing as well as the risk assessment and mitigation and the due diligence parts. The discussion that follows assumes that internal skills and competencies are not available and that advisors are engaged to perform necessary functions. When a skilled PFO is in place, many of the advisors' roles and responsibilities are performed by that organization and the more specialized functions are left to external advisors. Project advisors are engaged either under a retainer fee or a success fee arrangement in the areas shown below and have corresponding responsibilities.

A. **Bid and Procurement Advisors**

These are experienced project facilitators who specialize in making contacts and smoothing out the entire project process. They manage customer relationships in the bidding process and their role is to:

1. Facilitate contacts and meetings with high-level, host country government decision makers and with local funding sources

2. Provide advice and guidance to sponsors and developers on bidding in the host country's public procurements

3. Provide advice and guidance to the host country contracting authority on dealing with private sector, highly skilled managers

4. Assess project output capability for local use, exporting, and generating income for public sector equity in the project

5. Ensure adequate project finance education in the sponsor and the host government ceding authority

6. Contribute inputs to the creation of the project prospectus or information memorandum and support in marketing efforts

B. **Engineering and Technology Advisors**

Engineering and technology advisors liaison and work closely with engineering and technology specialists of the sponsor and other project stakeholders. Their roles and responsibilities span across many areas and include the following functions:

1. Review and evaluate the project's engineering and technology bid specifications and performance requirements

2. Support the project team to manage the bidding and procurement process effectively

3. Conduct project site inspections to validate site preparation requirements and identify risks and issues

4. Provide detailed design specifications and conduct technology and equipment evaluations

5. Review and assess technology and equipment-related costs and conduct performance validation checks

6. Play a role in the project definition and development, cost estimates, feasibility study, due diligence, and the project post mortem analysis

7. Engage additional engineering, technology, and specialized advisors when needed and select the operations and management company

8. Monitor project engineering and construction progress to ensure contractor compliance with terms of the contract

9. Address engineering and technology issues around construction, project acceptance, and operations management

10. Identify and evaluate the impact of engineering and technology project risks and help in their allocation and mitigation

11. Help guide the engineering and technology segment of the due diligence and review and validate the findings of the due diligence report

12. Assist in drafting, reviewing, and evaluating the engineering and technical aspects of project contracts

13. Create the project company's operations plan and, if needed, supervise the O&M company's initial running of operations

14. Evaluate the production input needs and material supplies to ensure availability in order for the project company to achieve production requirements

15. Oversee and facilitate the project acceptance process and ensure that performance criteria are fully met

16. Contribute inputs to the creation of the project prospectus or information memorandum and support in marketing efforts

C. **Financial Advisors**

The main function of financing advisors is to liaison with the project team, funding sources, and counterparts in other project-stakeholder organizations. The sponsor company's financial advisors' roles and responsibilities overlap with those of the debt and equity advisors and each side's advisors are aiming to protect respective interests. The sponsor's financial advisor roles include:

1. Evaluate the host country's economic and investment environment and review business and tax laws affecting the project

2. Assess project definition; screen for strategic, portfolio, and operational fit; and identify possible alternatives to the proposed project

3. Evaluate the financial implications of the project concession, licensing, and permitting terms and conditions

4. Provide guidance on project company and financing structures and assist in maximizing project tax benefits

5. Estimate cost elements in each project stage and validate total project costs and produce or validate revenue projections

6. Play a major role in the feasibility study and lead the economic evaluation of the project

7. Review contracts and agreements and assess their financial implications

8. Assess and validate project-participants' ability to deliver on current and future obligations

9. Determine the project economic viability and the project's bankability early on and the potential to raise funding

10. Manage funding networks and alliances and facilitate development of personal relationships around the world for the sponsor's benefit

11. Introduce sponsors to potential funding sources, insurers, and to unilateral, bilateral, and multilateral institutions and educate them on their processes requirements

12. Identify potential sources of debt and equity financing, investigate terms and conditions, obtain and evaluate proposals, and negotiate final financing documents

13. Build a detailed project financial model, validate its inputs and assumptions, manage updates and reports, and assess model outputs

14. Identify alternative project finance structures and select the optimal debt-equity configuration

15. Educate the host government's agency personnel on project finance processes and requirements and their obligations to ensure successful financing

16. Participate in the project risk identification, analysis, and allocation and evaluate the adequacy requirement of the lender security package

17. Provide sponsor inputs to the due diligence and review and validate the findings of the due diligence report

18. Evaluate the loan, credit enhancement, insurance and potential for additional equity contributions

19. Manage debt finance disbursements in the construction period, monitor construction stage expenses, and evaluate construction progress and adherence to schedule and budget

20. Evaluate the project company's supply and offtake contracts to ensure the enforceability and availability of production inputs and demand for its production output according to set terms

21. Assist in the development of project financing documentation, negotiations, and evaluation of proposals and counterproposals

22. Help the project team develop the project company's business plan and validate the financial projections of the operations stage

23. Help develop project-company financial statements linked with the financial model and satisfy reporting requirements to project stakeholders and host government agencies

24. Provide analysis and input in the preparation and presentation of the project information memorandum

25. Provide objective assessments in the project post-mortem analysis, review findings, and help the sponsor company adopt recommendations for improving project team performance and increasing chances of future project success

D. **Insurance Advisors**

Insurance advisors play a major role in project risk management and their roles overlap those of advisors in other project areas, but they usually concentrate in the following:

1. Analyze the project definition and requirements in order to isolate insurable aspects of the project from those that cannot be insured

2. Help to identify, evaluate, assess, manage, mitigate, and insure the project risks that the project team deems necessary

3. Research various project risk types and help subdivide or allocate them among stakeholders who are best able to handle them

4. Work with sponsors and lenders to analyze insurance coverage issues to satisfy all project stakeholders affected by risks

5. Advise on project insurance that would be required to make the project financeable and help to arrange it

6. Obtain best insurance quotes from reputable global insurance companies for required coverages

7. Help the sponsor's legal experts to structure and negotiate appropriately priced, balanced, and enforceable and sustainable insurance contracts

E. **Legal advisors**

The roles and responsibilities of legal advisors vary by project stakeholders, are designed to protect respective stakeholder interests throughout the project, and include:

1. Liaison with legal teams of other stakeholders to draft, review, evaluate, and negotiate project agreements and contracts:
   (a) Sponsor group and interproject participant agreements
   (b) Shareholder agreement of sponsors with the project company
   (c) Implementation or concession agreement between the ceding authority and the sponsor
   (d) Inter-creditor agreement among lenders
2. Review host country procurement, environmental, construction, safety, labor, currency convertibility and repatriation of dividends laws, and tax laws and regulations
3. Assess bid requirements and stakeholder contribution commitment and ensure they are reflected in negotiated contracts
4. Review funding source, ECA, and multilateral and unilateral agency processes and requirements
5. Evaluate the host country's laws, rules, and regulations of the project industry structure and investment environment
6. Conduct thorough political and legal risk analysis and business law enforceability
7. Coordinate contacts with other stakeholder legal teams and counterparts in the host government agency
8. Validate the transparency and fairness of the host government's procurement process and requirements
9. Follow up, negotiate, and manage the project licensing and permitting process to completion
10. Represent the interests of the sponsor in the due diligence and review and validate the report prepared by the lenders' legal team
11. Interpret the implications of the due diligence findings and make recommendations to the project team on changes needed
12. Draft, review, evaluate, negotiate, approve, and manage the documentation of project agreements
13. Work with insurance agents to identify, evaluate, and recommend approaches to mitigate, manage, and allocate project risks
14. Provide advice and guidance to the project team on all legal issues and provide answers to questions as they come up
15. Review the project feasibility study report and provide feedback on additional support that may be needed

16. Communicate findings of the feasibility study to project participants, outline the project structure, and create the legal strategy to move forward

17. Review, prepare, negotiate, approve loan, credit agreements, security documents, contracts, and hedging agreements' terms and conditions to cover project risks

18. Monitor project finance activities and progress in the construction stage and resolve EPC contract compliance issues

19. Assist in the development of the financing plan, prepare and negotiate debt and equity finance agreements, and negotiate closing of permanent financing

20. Assess the adequacy of financial reports from the project company to appropriate project participants

21. Help in the preparation of the project information memorandum and its presentation to potential investors

F. **Market Assessment and Project Evaluation Consultants**

The roles and responsibilities of the market assessment and project evaluation consultants cover areas of project evaluation related to the host country's environment, megatrends, and subtrends, as well as the project's industry, market size, and growth potential. These roles include delivering on the following responsibilities:

1. Liaison with project team members and counterparts in other participant organizations to obtain and share information

2. Validate the project strategic, portfolio, and operational fit and the opportunity costs of doing and not doing the project

3. Assess the customer or user needs in the host country and how they are currently being satisfied and at what pricing and marketing levels

4. Perform a sponsor situational analysis followed by an internal strengths, weakness, opportunities, threats (SWOT) analysis to identify corporate risk tolerance and gaps in skills and competencies to execute the project

5. Perform industry analysis to determine current capacity, needs for structural changes, historical regulatory intervention and effects, and introduction of competition

6. Assess host country political, economic, social, technological, legal, educational, and demographic (PESTLED) trends

7. Develop data and information to quantify the project company's market opportunities in the feasibility study and project development phases

8. Perform market research and help estimate project development costs in cooperation with project team members

9. Identify what is needed to assess project economics, what is knowable, what is controllable, and key factors driving project value

10. Develop appropriate methods and techniques to conduct the project company's demand analysis

11. Create a baseline scenario, develop assumptions for the driving factors' future behavior, and produce a baseline set of cost and revenue forecasts

12. Establish project company demand and output requirements to determine project economic viability in the feasibility study

13. Validate demand related data and assumptions and provide input and information to the due diligence effort

14. Develop plausible alternative scenarios and perform sensitivity analysis and simulations

15. Assist in the development of the project company's business plan and develop its marketing and sales plans

16. Recommend a range of simulated project values for management to select for final decisions

17. Contribute inputs to the creation of the project prospectus or information memorandum and in support of marketing efforts

7.7 ROLES OF MULTILATERAL AND UNILATERAL INSTITUTIONS

There are several unilateral, bilateral, and multilateral financial institutions created to support different types of investments, programs, and countries around the world, and meet different project needs. Their roles vary by project and the scope of their activities is determined by their organizational charters which are discussed in more detail in Chapter12. Their responsibilities evolve around a variety of programs and support they provide.

A. **Multilateral Institutions**

They participate in projects globally and provide the majority of support to developing countries with a variety of instruments they offer and the functions they perform. In addition to economic growth and development initiatives, following are some functions these institutions perform:

1. Ensure projects contribute to economic growth or improve social infrastructure in the host country

2. Coordinate with sponsors and developers to deliver projects in countries the sponsors have no presence in or when bilateral aid is not available

3. Asses all project environmental issues and social considerations and ensure its sustainability

4. Help the host country through the process to manage project complexity and deliver timely approvals

5. Address voting rights and other intercreditor matters and provide lending when necessary

6. Provide quality partnership alternatives to sponsors and the host country's public sector

7. Use their influence with the host country's government to bring parties together, close gaps, and resolve issues

8. Educate public sector personnel involved on project approval processes and requirements

9. Provide options to balance different interests and add legitimacy and weight when challenging project development issues arise and need to be addressed

10. Bring unique expertise in project assessment, structuring, and financing and mobilize needed experience from around the world

11. Leverage their host government and global financial relationships to coordinate multicountry, multifinancial institution funding

B. **Unilateral Institutions**

The key players in this category are ECAs whose mandates and programs vary widely across countries. In general, their charter is to provide credit support in the form of equipment buyer credit or equipment supplier credit. Their programs include loans at subsidized interest rates, political and business risk coverage, and direct loans to exporters of goods and services produced in the ECA country. These government-sponsored agencies provide equivalent services to projects they participate in as multilaterals institutions do and coordinate programs and support to projects they participate jointly.

Other US federal or state agencies, such as Overseas Private Investment Corporation (OPIC), Marine Administration (MARAD) and Energy Research and Development Administration (ERDA) make programs available to projects and support that fit specific investor and project needs. State Infrastructure Banks (SIBs), and

Transportation Infrastructure Finance and Innovation Act (TIFIA) programs support only domestic US infrastructure projects. All advanced countries also have unilateral agencies that serve their country's economic interests and advancement of their foreign policies and image abroad. The programs provided by unilateral agencies include direct loans, loan guarantees, and insurance against risks. Additionally they provide guidance regarding economic, political, and business conditions; local partner selection, and other services that help assess the feasibility of projects.

C. **Bilateral Institutions**

These are regional banks and other financial institutions that provide programs and services for project development and financing, primarily in their region though, in some instances, in underdeveloped counties rich in natural resources too. In many respects, the programs and services offered by bilateral institutions mirror those of unilateral and multilateral institutions. Bilateral institutions are highly specialized in project evaluations, local and regional financial markets, and coordinating private investor and government activities in their regions.

7.8 ROLES OF THE EPC CONTRACTOR

The cost plus, fixed price, turnkey, and unit price are types of contracts used in international project finance, but the most commonly used ones are engineering, procurement, and construction (EPC) contracts. The usual roles of the EPC contractor include:

1. Liaison with the sponsor's engineering associates, host government engineers, and external advisors to clarify project specifications and requirements

2. Perform physical site inspections and environmental assessment to ensure access to and suitability of the project site

3. Obtain all required licenses and permits from the host government and technology providers

4. Conduct survey and report on physical and cybersecurity requirements of the planned project facilities

5. Oversee equipment and technology performance tests to ensure project requirements are fully met

6. Ensure availability and quality of materials and timely delivery access of utilities to the project site

7. Obtain attractive pricing and terms and conditions from subcontractors for turnkey projects

8. Be the single point of responsibility and satisfy all performance guarantees: provide performance and schedule guarantees, liquidated damages, and manage sub-contractor retainage

9. Ensure availability of acceptable housing and other amenities in the host country for its own and subcontractor employees

10. Coordinate all technical, equipment, and subcontractor activities and manage the risks of project cost changes

11. Design and build the project on a turnkey, fixed price contract on time and on budget, and assume liability for delay damages and for project performance that does not pass tests

12. Validate and support claims made in the information memorandum to increase customer and investor project confidence

7.9 ROLES OF TECHNOLOGY AND EQUIPMENT PROVIDERS

The technology and equipment providers are usually subcontractors to the EPC contractor and their roles and responsibilities are closely linked with those of the EPC contractor. Their roles are of particular importance in cases of new technology introductions to ensure that it works as designed. Their responsibilities of technology and equipment providers overlap and commonly include:

1. Procure suitable technology and equipment to meet project specifications at best pricing and terms and conditions

2. Ensure technology availability to the project and subsequent updates and upgrades

3. Obtain documentation of equipment and parts and service support agreements for the EPC contractor

4. Assess and address technical and equipment issues and provide technology and equipment reliability and performance guarantees

5. Oversee the quality inspection of equipment, proper installation, and technology delivery on time and budget

6. Resolve technical and equipment issues to the project company's and other project stakeholders' satisfaction

7. Provide ongoing assessment of equipment used and performance to ensure adherence to technology standards, processes, and schedules

8. Coordinate with EPC contractor and sponsor technical team activities and facilitate ECA documentation requirements and support for the project

9. Assume responsibility for technical tests and validation of performance to ensure project acceptance

7.10 ROLES OF PROJECT OFFTAKERS AND SUPPLIERS

Offtake and supply contracts are the glue that holds together infrastructure project financing. They are revenue and production guarantees provided by the customer and major supplier or the host government when appropriate; hence, the crucial role of these contracts.

A. **Purchaser or Offtaker**

The project company requires predictability and stability from the cash flow of its output revenue. Offtakers, on the other hand, insist on a balance of their obligations with requirements of the project company. The offtake or purchase agreement is a crucial part of project finance because it ensures predictability of the revenue stream on an ongoing basis for the duration of the project life cycle or concession. The offtaker's usual responsibilities include:

1. Provide unimpeded access of the project company's production delivery to the user or purchaser facilities

2. Negotiate and sign a sensible offtake agreement with the project company that makes the project financeable

3. Require limited variability in the project company's output, prices, and agreed to output quality levels

4. Make payment regardless of whether the project company production is generated on a take-or-pay or a take-and-pay contract

5. Provide assistance and support in resolving regulatory and unwarranted government intervention issues

B. **Project Suppliers**

The project company insists on adequate quantity, quality, and timely delivery of supplies and production inputs at stable and predictable prices. On the other hand, suppliers of production inputs to the project company want terms of the supply contract to be met with current market prices and timely payments. Supplier responsibilities evolve around meeting the following requirements of the project company:

1. Guarantee availability of adequate production inputs and supplies at predictable and stable prices

2. Treat the project company equitably and deliver raw materials and other production inputs to the project company at market prices

3. Honor delivery commitments in the provision of production inputs according to contract clauses

4. Ensure the quality of materials and other production input-specification requirements

7.11 ROLES OF THE O&M COMPANY

Last but not least are the roles and responsibilities of the O&M company that executes the project company business plan and ensures its long-term viability. The O&M company's primary responsibilities include:

1. Hire engineering, technical, and other specialized capabilities for operational management of the project company

2. Outsource functions not readily available in the project company or another O&M company

3. Provide strong operating guarantees and commitments to meet contractual obligations

4. Manage project company operations and provide management support and training

5. Monitor operating performance, conduct variance analysis, and provide regular reports to sponsors and other rightful parties

6. Generate and provide financial statements and manage the project company cash flow per agreed to covenants and restrictions

7. Make appropriate operational and business plan adjustments to offset the impacts of materializing commercial risks and ensure continued financial viability

8. Contribute inputs to the creation of the project prospectus or information memorandum and support marketing efforts

CHAPTER 8

Project Finance Forecasting

Ensuring Sound Decision Making

Forecasts are the foundation of all planning—whether implicit or explicit, qualitative or quantitative, objective or subjective, based on simple algorithms or complex statistical models—and are used in decision making. Because forecasts are used in planning and decision making they are of crucial importance in large capital investment projects to determine economic viability and project financeability. In Chapter 3 the record of project financing indicates that project failures are frequently due to forecast failures. To address this problem, we use strategic decision forecasting which is a method developed by Long Range Planning Associates to develop long-term forecasts for large capital investment project decisions.

Forecasting for infrastructure projects requires strategic-decision forecasts that are 15 to 30 years out, that are collaborative, and integrative of qualitative and quantitative methods. The focus of strategic forecasting is on modeling future project operations, uncertainty and risk identification and mitigation, and scenario development and planning to generate cost and revenue forecasts. Megatrend, industry trends, economic environmental-factor analysis, industry and competitive analysis, demand analysis, and forecast ownership and process management are of equal importance to generate the best possible forecasts.

In large project development, nobody knows with certainty what may happen 10 to 15 years hence. If we cannot say with certainty about future events and the outcome of the project value creation, then what is the purpose of an infrastructure project forecast? First and foremost, the process of developing a forecast entails an independent, critical, and objective assessment of the project company's operations. It introduces discipline and reduces uncertainty in decision making and helps identify sources of risks in planning for the project. Furthermore, it helps to identify enabling scenarios for project success and produces a more effective planning and decision making environment. More importantly, forecasts are used as flight simulators or a tool to create the future today.

The sections that follow describe the basics of strategic-decision forecasting for project finance starting with the definition of a forecast. Section 8.1 clears misconceptions about what is a good forecast. What needs to be forecasted for project finance deals and sources of forecasts outside of the sponsor organization are cited in Section 8.2. The important topics of ways of developing forecast assumptions and conducting sanity checks are treated in Section 8.3, while Section 8.4 introduces the intricacies of the project-forecasting process.

Section 8.4.1 discusses what is involved in situational analysis and the benefits from it, trailed by the function of environmental and host country assessment in Section 8.4.2. The importance of assessing the effects of megatrends and subtrends are discussed in Section 8.4.3, and Section 8.4.4 addresses the issue of forecast stewardship and accountability. The meaning, purpose, and use of project demand analysis and the selection of a forecasting approach are covered in Section 8.5. Some common forecasting methods and techniques are briefly mentioned in Section 8.6, and the value of sanity checks of assumptions and scenarios selected is presented in Section 8.7. The discussion of forecasting for infrastructure project finance would be incomplete without an examination of the causes and consequences of forecast failures and that is the subject matter of Section 8.8. This chapter ends with Section 8.9, which deals with forecast monitoring and forecast realization planning—the latter is missing from the majority of even professional forecasts.

8.1 WHAT IS A GOOD FORECAST?

A forecast has many definitions and its function depends on its use as well as the skills of forecasters. The following are some views of what is a forecast:

1. An estimate of future performance based on a systematic approach using data, quantitative and qualitative tools, past performance, industry knowledge, and analogs from similar experiences
2. A statement about the future that for decision-making purposes is a single number that is always wrong
3. A prognosis based on the process of identifying actions and events that affect a project
4. The art of translating qualitative and quantitative information used by models to predict future outcomes
5. The function that brings together data, business experience, and forecasting techniques to estimate what will happen at different future dates

Our definition of a forecast is all of the above, but more importantly, it is an independent, critical, and objective assessment of a project opportunity to guide decision making. It is, also, a tool to create reliable intelligence and the basis of sound decision-making to manage a project effectively. In the hands of professional strategic-decision forecasters, it is a way to create the future today and help run project development more effectively, thereby creating a competitive advantage for the project company.

Reality Check

Our research (Triantis, 2013) suggests that roughly:

a. 30% of business decisions are based on corporate strategy, policy, precedent, and established processes
b. 30% are based on people networks and personal relationships
c. 25% have foundations in analysis, assessment, and substance
d. 15% are based on senior management imperatives and external influences

Project revenue forecasts drive the calculation of benefits and along with cost estimates they form the basis of major-impact investment decisions. For that reason, revenue forecasts must be as reliable as possible. But what are good forecasts? Good forecasts are those that:

1. Incorporate external operating environment, market, industry, and trend evaluations and quantify their impact on project performance
2. Are derived from sound forecasting function ownership and management
3. Have clear, balanced, well-thought-out forecasting processes and are easy to explain
4. Create well considered, tested, and reasonable set of assumptions
5. They are based on the 4C principle of strategic decision forecasting: Unimpeded 360-degree communication, coordination, cooperation, and collaboration
6. Identify and evaluate key project risks through assessment of alternative future state scenarios
7. Are in line with similar project experiences and build confidence in using them to make management decisions
8. Come with instructions and guidance on their use, their shortcomings and limitations, and their implications
9. Have the support of the entire project team and the backing of senior managers responsible for project decision making
10. Are reality based and not influenced by optimistic and wishful thinking or personal agendas

Some revenue forecast users and decision makers judge the quality of forecasts based on measures such as mean absolute percent error. But such measures are of little use in the case of 20- to 30-year forecasts where the structure that generates the forecast changes. When forecasts include management adjustments or are numbers picked from a range of model simulations, subjective judgement enters the picture and then one cannot really talk about a forecast error or quality of the forecast; only about the quality of management judgement applied.

8.2 WHAT TO FORECAST AND SOURCES OF FORECASTS

The first activity in forecasting is to determine what needs to be forecasted followed by identifying what drives the forecasts of demand and what pricing driving factor data are available. Forecasts used in infrastructure development start to get created in the prefeasibility study and undergo updating and enhancement as the process moves through the project development stage and get finalized by the financing stage.

A. What to Forecast

The two forecasts that form the foundation for project evaluation are the cost and revenue forecasts. Cost forecasts involve predictions of project development costs, capital expenditures, financing costs, and operational costs made up of labor, materials, building and maintenance costs. Costs are calculated fairly accurately from stable engineering and accounting relationships. Revenue forecasts on the other hand, are based on changing environments and evolving customer and user behavior that require predictions about those changes and their impact on the demand and pricing of the company's output of goods or services.

Capital costs are the largest part of project costs and its main components are equipment costs, land, and construction costs. Equipment costs are obtained from technology and equipment providers; the land and building structure cost estimate comes from project advisors who are familiar with the host country's real estate market or from the host government authority involved in the project. Construction cost estimates come from engineering, procurement, and construction (EPC) construction companies or from expert project consultants. Operational and maintenance costs are calculated based on assumptions that concern the nature and size of facilities, scheduled and unscheduled plant service requirements, and the number of management personnel and skilled and unskilled labor employees. The cost estimation process starts with ballpark estimates and as the project goes through the project development, feasibility, and due diligence phases, the particulars of the project are fixed and cost projections firm up.

A specific forecast for the cost of developing a project depends on the nature of the project and requires a number of assumptions related to cost items such as:

1. Project definition, specifications and requirements, timing, and scope
2. Project team activities around bid preparations and delivery
3. Host country environmental assessment
4. Engagement of advisors, consultants, and project facilitators
5. Industry analysis and market studies
6. Engineering and environmental studies, and preparation of technical and project management plans
7. Feasibility study findings and preparation of the due diligence report
8. Length of project development and difficulty of negotiations
9. Cushion for unforeseen delays, risks, and cost overruns

When such assumptions prove difficult to make with some degree of certainty, the experience from earlier company or competitor projects is a good starting point. If there no such experiences or comparable project analogs, some benchmarks are the average cost of feasibility studies by MacKinzie and Cusworth (2007) and the estimate of average total cost of project development, which ranges from 5–10% of total project costs.

Financing costs are the fifth project cost component, estimates of which are acquired from funding sources and project advisors. The financing project cost components include the following elements:

1. Interest costs of loans and bonds
2. Various fees paid to lenders (arrangement, syndication, etc.)
3. Costs of insuring against different risks
4. Costs of hedging contracts
5. Project rating costs for bond issues and development of the information memorandum

Revenue forecasts require projections of demand for the project company's goods or services produced and projections of pricing over the project's time span. Assuming a stable operating environment, price forecasts for regulated project companies involve an assessment of the future regulatory regime and rulings, and the project company's ability to influence price changes. However, inflation factors should be included in future pricing. If competition is anticipated, price declines should be expected initially followed by a steady state of prices.

Cost forecasts are driven by project design, engineering, and performance requirements. Revenue forecasts are driven by a number of factors, such as the political, economic, technological, legal, educational and demographic environment, industry structure, competitor activities and pricing among a host of other factors to be discussed in sections that follow. Notice, however, that these forecasts are key inputs to the project financial model, which generates financial measures used to assess funding needs and financeability.

B. Sources of Forecasts

Infrastructure cost forecasts are usually obtained from technology and pricing quotes, engineering and construction estimates, and operations and maintenance contract quotes. Financing costs are derived from lender documents and from the output of financial model relationships. By the time the project goes through the feasibility study and due diligence phases, to some extent they are good projections. Project revenue forecasts are more often than not developed externally and, in most cases, with help from experts in the area of forecasting demand in the particular industry of the project.

There are sources that are useful to project teams in developing project revenue forecasts and include:

1. Internal company records of earlier project data, information, and experiences
2. Unilateral and multilateral institution project data, notes, and writeups
3. Interviews with professional organizations' experts in the industry of the project
4. Data sources of host government agencies and expertise in different industries
5. Industry research and the knowledge vaults of consulting companies

Help in forecasting project revenue also comes from earlier company and competitor project experiences that serve as analogs to build forecasts and to judge their reasonableness. Insights on forecast assumptions and predictions may be available from participating lender banks with experiences in the project's industry. Also, investment bank analyst research is often a good source of past project reviews, data, analyses, and the identification of errors in the sources of the revenue forecast.

8.3 FORECAST ASSUMPTIONS

The development of assumptions is a crucial activity in large project financings because assumptions underlie and drive project planning, forecasting, budgeting, decision making, and financing. Due to the particulars and complexity of infrastructure projects, the assumption set is project specific and an art based on:

1. Broad project team experience and understanding of the functioning of the industry

2. Review of the literature of business cases and on specific infrastructure project financing issues

3. The collection of expert opinions of project participants and market research information

4. Engineering studies of earlier and competitor projects and experiences

5. Review of assumptions negotiated and used in earlier project contracts

6. Shared knowledge of host country ceding authority personnel based on earlier projects

7. Management and key stakeholder judgment conditioned by the company's strategic objectives and financial priorities

8. Distilled learning from past project information memoranda and post mortem analyses

Once the project definition is done and the company's operating environment is evaluated, the development of the assumptions comes into focus and the key project-team activities then determine:

1. Impacts of megatrends and industry trends on the project company's consumer or user demand

2. What factors that impact pricing need to be known, what are knowable and unknowable, what are controllable and uncontrollable

3. The evolution of the original pricing of the project company's output over the project's lifetime

4. Current industry capacity and historical growth versus needed capacity

5. Numbers of consumers or users of the project company's output and their consumption patterns

6. Adequacy of project technology and efficiency to meet customer needs and expectations

7. Changes in user-demand patterns over the project lifetime

Assumption development is an evolutionary process that researches, evaluates, and selects information that is applicable to the project at hand and determines if there are variants of existing information to establish that are more verifiable and reasonable. The question now is: How does one go about creating well thought out and reasonable assumptions? The first and easy response is to rely on engaged advisors and consultants for help. The alternative is to research analogs and information from industry publications, to seek out the views of host government agencies' managers, and to obtain guidance from unilateral and multilateral institution publications and officials.

Another approach is to establish a basis through benchmarking by using publically available information, competitive analysis, and interviews with industry participants. These efforts lead to the development of the initial set of assumptions that are recorded with the name or source of the assumptions and the date associated with them. But, the analyses and evaluations of the feasibility study and the due diligence provide tips and guidance to update the initial assumption set. Also, it is a good idea to consolidate the inputs from different sources into one view of assumptions and subject those assumptions to scrutiny and sanity checks. In every case, when the assumption set is fairly stable, it is crucial to obtain project stakeholder consensus and buy-in on assumptions underlying the financial model and obtain political support.

8.4 PROJECT FORECASTING PROCESS

The work of Flyvbjerg, Garbuio, and Lovallo (2014) confirms that there are psychological biases that create cognitive delusion in forecasting for large capex infrastructure projects. They suggest that there is a sponsor/developer tendency to overstate completion times compounded by management bias originating with initial estimates and assumptions. They claim that there are misdirected incentives that result in different project outcomes than those preferred by senior management. Furthermore, there is evidence that in some industries inadequate cost forecasts are due to the behavior of some project participants and not due to lack of insight or forecasting techniques (VanWee, 2007).

A good starting point of the discussion of revenue forecasting for an infrastructure project financing is Figure 8.4. It begins with a situational analysis and ends with a final forecast used for funding decisions. In the subsections that follow we address the process components but focus on the situational analysis, the environmental and host country analysis, the effects of megatrends and subtrends on demand, and the issue of forecast stewardship and responsibility.

8.4.1 Situational Analysis

For infrastructure projects, situational analysis is an ongoing process of identifying and evaluating the current state of company operations and internal and external factors that impact the sponsor's or developer's ability

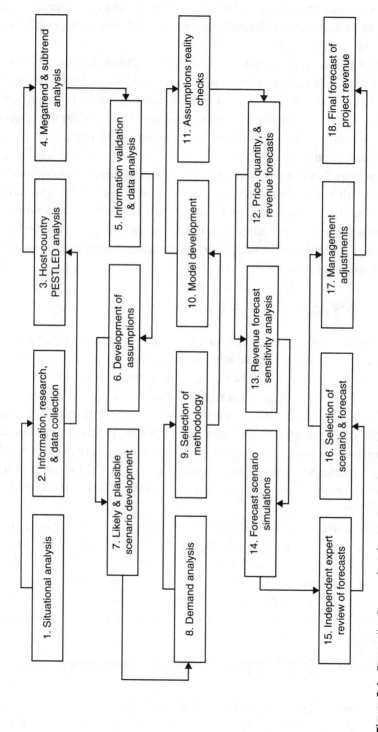

Figure 8.4 Forecasting Process for Infrastructure Project Decisions

to achieve their objectives. Usually, situational analysis is performed as part of project specific strengths, weakness, opportunities, threats (SWOT) analysis. Situational analysis begins with a review of the company's current operational and financial performance followed by a sufficiently detailed proposed project description to allow for its evaluation. A review of the corporate strategy of the sponsor company is conducted to assess its fit with the project and its objectives, followed by portfolio and operational fit assessments. The motivations and objectives of project participants are examined to ensure that there are no major conflicts of interest. Then, a competitive analysis is performed to identify and evaluate the competitors' strategy, interest in this and related projects, and their activities.

The project rationale, objectives, and cost estimates, are validated for consistency with the company's financial and human resources with the right skills and competencies available for the project. More importantly, project objectives must be consistent with corporate risk tolerance and the decision-makers' ability to deal with risks when they materialize. An objective assessment of internal project finance skills and experiences vis-à-vis the complexity of the project and the ability of the PFO to negotiate long periods of project development, financing, and implementation must also be evaluated. Additionally, the PFO's competencies in bid responses, contract closure, financing, and preparation for implementation need to be evaluated to determine areas of weakness to be strengthened by engaging the right external advisors and consultants.

A project selection among different investment options requires appropriate screening of these opportunities. To ensure that the selected project is the best option and the right decision is made, the costs and benefits of doing and not doing the project need to be evaluated. Once more, these activities are performed in the context of the company's current versus desired future state and the threats of competitive activities. But why is a situational analysis part of an infrastructure project forecast process? It is because it helps lay the foundation that helps define the assumptions used in the demand analysis and identify weaknesses in successful project development, financing, and implementation. That is, it provides reference points when conducting sanity checks and identifies the risk factors that underlie forecasts.

The purpose of a sponsor SWOT analysis is multidimensional and addresses factors that impact project success. The main factors in this type of analysis include:

1. Determining the availability of skilled and competent internal experiences to leverage in project development and financing

2. Identifying existing gaps and weaknesses in the resources brought to bear on the project and making appropriate changes

3. Exploring potential opportunities presented by the project and how to take advantage of them to the best of the company's abilities

4. Detecting and isolating current and future threats to the project and finding ways to avoid or mitigate them

The last part of the project specific SWOT analysis is basically project risk identification and mitigation, which is treated in Chapter 10.

8.4.2 Host Country Environmental Assessment

The host country environmental assessment is essential because it directly and indirectly impacts both the project cost and revenue forecasts, as well as their realization. Assessment of the host country's political environment is priority one and it involves an assessment of the political parties, the functioning of the government, the election process, and the stability of elected governments. It is followed by an evaluation of business practices and the degree of government officials' corruption. The second part of the host country's political, economic, social, technological, legal, educational, and demographic (PESTLED) analysis is assessment of the macroeconomic environment, which involves evaluation of GDP level and growth, per capita income, income distribution, government fiscal and central bank policies, unemployment statistics, exchange rates, and availability of foreign exchange among other variables.

> PESTLED stands for political, economic, social, technological, legal, educational, and demographic conditions in a country, and it always refers to analyses of those conditions.

The social conditions of the host country need to be understood beyond unemployment and per capita income by examining (1) the current state of the health and welfare of the population, (2) the population age distribution, and (3) the educational levels and availability of qualified labor force for the project company to draw from. Evaluation of living conditions in the host country is also important for ex-patriate employees and their families. Also, assessment of the technological advancement in the host country needs to be evaluated to determine availability of technical skills and local technology and equipment servicing capability.

Evaluation of the legal and regulatory environment is crucial and entails a thorough assessment of contract and business law, health and safety regulations, tax law, and foreign trade and exchange and remittance regulations. The differences between local laws and those of the sponsor's country are assessed not only in content but in enforceability as well. A thorough assessment of the regulatory environment is necessary to determine under what conditions the project company will operate, if it can operate effectively and profitably, and whether it can influence changes in the host country's environment. Here, reporting requirements, restrictions, obligations, pricing ability, and labor requirements are major factors to evaluate.

Industry analysis and market analysis are part of the host country environmental assessment and, beyond site environmental-conditions assessment, it includes evaluation of the current industry's structure, competitor presence, regulations, pricing and regulatory flexibility, current versus need capacity, and trends and changes in the project's industry. Industry analysis determines if a new competitor entry threat is likely, if privatization plans are being contemplated, if project company production inputs are available, and if labor trained in the industry is readily available.

Industry analysis defines the context of market analysis where consumer or user needs and tastes are identified and the willingness and ability to pay for the project company's goods and services is determined. Industry and market analysis, sometimes coupled with market research, are the foundations of demand analysis and forecasting, which then are used as inputs in the feasibility study and the due diligence phases.

The assessment of the host country's financial markets and investing environment are important for the project team to determine:

1. The extent of the local market development and its participants
2. Government policies and regulation of the financial markets to facilitate gaps in cash flow
3. Existence of local funding sources that are dependable and easy to do business with
4. Ability of local funding sources to deliver on future contributions
5. Availability of local credit facilities, guarantees, and other types of project support
6. Intricacies of financial contracts and their enforcement
7. Levels of government participation in the local financial markets
8. The views, positions, and support of unilateral, multilateral, and development agencies in similar projects in the host country
9. Costs of funding a project through local credit and its terms and conditions
10. Requirements and restrictions of dividend payments to foreign sponsors and investors

The host country environmental assessment is needed to determine the impacts of external factors on project costs and revenues and assess possible feedback effects on some of these factors as well.

8.4.3 Megatrends and Subtrends

Assessment of megatrends and subtrends is part of every environmental analysis regardless of project type and host country and the purpose of examining them is to better define the project context beyond the usual host country environmental analysis. A better defined project context enables the project team to:

1. Identify uncontrollable factors and demonstrate understanding of possible effects on the project forecasts
2. Create well-reasoned assumptions used in forecasting and simulations of scenarios
3. Develop more informed sensitivity analysis and selection of scenarios
4. Incorporate the assessment of megatrends and subtrends in the validation and sanity checks of the forecasts
5. Validate the reasonableness of assumptions and conduct sanity checks of the scenarios entertained
6. Determine impacts of megatrends and subtrends on the industry and the project
7. Support the due diligence effort and build a better foundation for management decisions

---

A megatrend is a worldwide, enduring change that affects operating environments, countries, economies, governments, and societies and which drive other trends that define the future of the world. A subtrend is a trend that is part of a larger trend which causes changes of a lesser degree to institutions, industries, businesses, and consumers.

For ease of exposition in this introduction to trend assessment for forecasting purposes, we consider trends in four major categories, but note that what are often called trends are really subtrends within the set of the megatrends: Generally well acknowledged megatrends, technological trends, socioeconomic and demographic trends, and infrastructure industry trends. The subject of megatrend and subtrend impact assessment on the host country, the industry, and the project company is a fascinating subject and it is treated in Chapter 15. Suffice it to say that for better cost and revenue forecasting purposes, the project team needs to determine if and how megatrends and subtrends impact project costs and revenues. The key is to determine how to incorporate those impacts in project forecasts and ride favorable trends profitably and avoid adverse trends.

8.4.4 Forecast Stewardship and Accountability

In the current project development paradigm, many infrastructure revenue forecasts used for management decisions do not exhibit much communication, coordination, cooperation, and collaboration among forecast stakeholders. Forecasters are by default accountable for the forecast and users own the forecast only because they subsidize the forecasting function. Also, in the prevailing state of the forecasting paradigm, forecast accountability is a diffused responsibility because forecasts use assumptions developed by different organizations and include management adjustments to the baseline forecasts.

In most project finance teams there is little, if any, expertise in the forecasting function over long horizons, which include several decision gates and project stages with different demand forecast needs. As a project moves across different phases, or when circumstances change, new players are introduced to the project, evaluations are updated by the project team, and assumptions are changed over time by forecast users. These circumstances make monitoring the performance of project forecasts developed years earlier meaningless. As a result, forecast users and decision makers change forecasts to fit the current situation and forecasters are not even involved in the process any more. That is to say that nobody is really accountable for the forecast, no meaningful performance measures are in place, nor can any in-depth and insightful variance analyses be performed in prevailing forecasting paradigms.

To avoid finger pointing and conflict among forecast stakeholders, corporate policies about forecast ownership, accountability, and project management of this function should be in place. Such policies save a tremendous amount of energy that is instead devoted to harmonizing different viewpoints and generating good long-term forecasts. Furthermore, forecast ownership policies help to plan at the start of a project and assign specific roles and responsibilities in all cases to avoid chaos being created where the most vocal interests dominate. Sound forecast project management provides an alternative to outsourcing forecasting to external consultants and to maintaining good relationships with all forecast supporting organizations.

We saw in Chapter 5 that effective project finance organizations either rely on internal professional forecasting capabilities or outsource the forecasting function to skilled consultants in the industry. However, after all is said and done, the PFO is accountable and owns the forecast, manages its evolution and updates through time, monitors its performance, and explains forecast variances. In these cases, the PFO evaluates not only the performance of the forecast, but the validity of actual data as well, and determines what assumptions and factors did not hold true.

8.5 PROJECT DEMAND ANALYSIS

Demand analysis is a multidimensional investigation that leads to ability to forecast demand and project revenue. A good demand analysis gives insights on how to shape the future levels of demand and what scenarios, assumptions, and project company business plan are appropriate, and what planning is needed for project development, inventory control, and corresponding costs and revenues. In infrastructure projects, demand analysis is also used to determine the required capacity to meet production of goods or services customers or users are willing to buy. The topics discussed in the forecasting process sections that follow are some key considerations of demand analysis and forecasting for infrastructure projects. Other key components of demand analysis are research, benchmarking and data collection, validation, and evaluation.

> In its simplest form, demand analysis is a study to determine the relationship of pricing and other factors with what quantities customers are willing to buy of a product or service to satisfy their needs while holding external influences constant. In more advanced forms of demand analysis, the influence of factors that were held constant is introduced through different scenarios and feedback effects and the impacts of those external factors are estimated.

The research and benchmarking part of demand analysis is a subset of the broader project development effort and it is primarily concerned with:

1. Reviewing the infrastructure forecasting literature, both scholarly and applied, for innovations in approach and forecasting techniques
2. Obtaining valuable data, project statistics, and other useful information
3. Examining case studies to identify comparable projects for applicability of analogy forecasting
4. Identifying best-forecasting practices well suited for different types of projects
5. Getting insights from earlier experiences on how to approach a project's forecasting problem and develop the right solutions
6. Determining what analyses may not yield good results and avoiding them
7. Finding out competitors' forecasting processes and methods and learning from them

8. Evaluating the findings, summarizing them, and creating a set of benchmarks to serve as guidelines to forecasting solutions for current projects

The data collection, validation, and evaluation part of demand analysis focuses on:

1. Determining what needs to be known and what does not and what is knowable and what is not

2. Identifying what specific qualitative and historical or cross-sectional quantitative information is needed

3. Determining the key driving factors of demand and pricing and the direction of influence

4. Separating out the uncontrollable factors and concentrating on controllable factors

5. Branding uncontrollable factors as potential sources of risk and make them known as such to the project team

6. Determining what can serve as proxies for important data that is missing or not available

7. Validating data collected for reasonableness, quality, and consistency with comparable project data using the tools of data analysis

8. Developing cross-sectional and historical data plots, understanding causes of outliers, calculating growth rates, checking for correlations, and identifying feedback effects

9. Assessing the extent to which the project company's products or services meet consumer and user desires and tastes

10. Evaluating the scale of consumers or users willingness and ability to pay for the project's output at planned pricing levels

11. Investigating if the demand and pricing driving factors are forecasted out and if their quality is acceptable to create reliable project revenue forecasts

12. Preparing data and information collected for use in modeling and forecasting demand along with a report summarizing the findings of data validation and evaluation

Different types of projects require different forecast solutions and have different data needs. However, a sample of commonly used data in-demand analysis, modeling, and forecasting includes:

1. Host country population data and historical growth rates

2. Educational levels and demographic data and distributions by age, region, etc.

3. Per capita income, disposable income, and income distribution

4. Host government subsidies, and credits for the project company's products or services

5. Industry capacity historical data and usage or purchase data, and pricing data for an existing own or competitor company or, at least, a comparable company

6. Market-size assessment, market research data, and observed market shifts

7. Historical data for project-company production inputs and materials and labor rates

8. Information on consumer or user needs and the extent to which they are currently met

9. Information about what factors may detract from future demand for the project company's output

10. Project equipment, technology attributes, and output quality and reliability versus those of competitors or other projects

11. Industry capacity gaps; that is, existing versus needed capacity to produce output to meet the projected demand

12. Evidence of past price change and ROI flexibility on the part of the industry's regulatory agency

The output of the project-demand analysis is used to decide what forecasting methodology to adopt, the kind of model specification that may be appropriate, and feed qualitative and quantitative information to models and scenarios in order to develop project forecasts. It is also used in the due diligence phase to validate funding needs and determine project financeability, in management forecast presentations, and in agreement negotiations. Just as importantly, it helps to identify the nature and sources of risks that underlie the forecast and quantify their impacts. Also, two important additional functions of demand analysis are to:

1. Develop ways to incorporate both qualitative and quantitative information from the country, industry, and trend analyses into predictive models

2. Help make adjustments to controllable driving factors and initiate actions to shape future project demand to reasonable expectations

8.6 FORECASTING METHODS AND TECHNIQUES

Generating revenue forecasts for project financing involves some kind of accepted qualitative or quantitative models or a combination of forecasts from both types of models. While forecasting models vary from simple deterministic relationships to qualitative and quantitative models to system dynamic models, our research findings suggest that roughly only a quarter of business decisions are based on analysis, evaluations, and substance (Triantis, 2013).This is a major factor in project failures to achieve expected performance and value creation.

Simple deterministic models are functions such as $y = a*x$ and are based on engineering studies, past experience, and financial/accounting relationships and are useful in developing cost component projections. Also, for small projects, deterministic models using good assumptions may be appropriate to forecast costs and revenues, but they are wholly inappropriate and inadequate to use for large, greenfield, complex infrastructure project revenue forecasting.

> Greenfield projects are new investments to construct new facilities for infrastructure projects. For our discussion, brownfield projects are projects outside a sponsor's or developer's home country; they are existing operational projects in need of investments to upgrade equipment and facilities to increase output.

Quantitative methods rely on sufficient past data to create relationships and models to forecast project revenue. They are statistical models based on internal company, industry association, and the host government authority's historical data and are appropriate to use in brownfield projects with adequate observations. Quantitative forecasting methods include the following types of models: Univariate time series, multivariate time series, various exponential smoothing models, and causal statistical models of high levels of complexity. Quantitative models do not use expert opinions and try to remove subjective judgement from forecasts.

For greenfield projects, the lack of historical data necessitates the use of qualitative methods, which includes:

1. Industry studies and market research
2. Delphi method and its variants
3. Sales force polling
4. Life cycle analogy
5. Panel of experts meeting face to face
6. Scenario building
7. System dynamics
8. Foresight maturity

The qualitative forecasting models of demand and project revenue use expert judgment for medium- and long-term planning purposes. Industry studies provide insights about upper demand limits and market research is conducted to identify consumer or user needs and preferences, their ability and willingness to pay, and yield additional data on the size of the market, potential demand, and project revenue. Sales force and regional company office personnel polling is another method of generating useful information and insights on demand and pricing developments and forecasts. Also, face-to-face expert discussions are used to create and validate assumptions and project revenue forecasts.

When a project team expects that demand and revenue of a PPP project is likely to follow the typical growth, maturity, and eventual decline, life-cycle analogy models are used, often with little consideration of underlying demand factors. Occasionally, these S-curve kind of models can have their basic structure modified to incorporate external influences and judgment to generate revenue forecasts. S-curve models are widely used in forecasting demand and revenue for new product or service introductions and do have some applicability in availability projects.

> Availability projects are private finance initiative (PFI) model projects under which the project company is paid for making the project available for the contracting authority's use and include seaports, airports, toll roads, bridges, etc.

The Delphi method was introduced in the 1950s and is a commonly used method to create assumptions, relationships, and forecasts and to build consensus. It is an interactive and iterative method of forecasting based on the views and opinions of panel experts. Panel participants can provide their individual inputs on data, assumptions, and forecasts and after each iteration, these experts revise their judgments toward the mean responses. The Delphi steps end when a process stopper is reached; usually when the responses converge to a consensus view.

The scenario building and planning method is related to contingency planning and is used when there is uncertainty concerning pricing and demand for a new infrastructure project. The purpose of scenario building is to identify a few possible scenarios for revenue outcomes and to plan and prepare for responding when negative cases materialize. This method of forecasting is used not only in the early stages of project development, but also when project risks are not fully identified and mitigated or when there is uncertainty about external factors impacting project revenue. Because of the importance of scenario building and planning in forecasting infrastructure project demand, this topic is discussed in more detail later in this section.

System dynamics models have been widely used in engineering, social sciences, and the military and recently in forecasting for infrastructure projects (Bala, Arshad, and Noh, 2016). But what are system dynamics models? They are a modeling technique that is capable of building a replica of the complex structure of a project's demand and revenue using assumptions, data, mathematical functions, and diagrams. Their structure allows for introducing quantitative and qualitative new factors, changes, and shocks to the project company operations and its revenue structure. In our judgment, they are well suited for large infrastructure project finance forecasting needs and evaluations.

System dynamics models are well suited for forecasting demand and revenue, especially in PPP projects because of their ability to integrate many different factors, external influences, assumptions, data, and relationships into one place. Their structure requires expertise in handling the interactions between the multitude of demand, pricing, and supply influence factors and the risks associated with these factors. The scenario development and simulation capabilities of system dynamics models shed light on the impact of each factor involved and their unique sensitivity analysis and simulation capabilities to generate project revenue forecast ranges for senior managers to have a higher comfort level in making decisions. They are also useful in determining the costs and benefits associated with a risk factor and whether to insure against it or absorb its impact.

The development of system dynamics involves the creation of conceptual representations of demand and revenue, which includes the following key elements:

1. Identifying the key influencing factors using any of the techniques mentioned earlier to anchor the model to a sound foundation
2. Creating causal loop diagrams that require knowledge of the host country's environment, the project's industry structure, and the project company's customers or users to assign direction of influence and feedbacks
3. Validating causal loop diagrams by expert analysis of the system dynamics model and forecasts generated by expert analysis and knowledge

Another approach to generate forecasts and make decisions in complex project structures that is beginning to get traction is foresight maturity models, which are particularly useful in guiding project teams when applied in the early stages of project development. Foresight maturity models help project teams to define desired, probable, planned, and creatable futures using data, qualitative inputs, and scenario building. In the presence of uncertainty, the foresight maturity technique helps to create strategies and plans to enhance project success rates by generating a baseline and plausible scenarios and limits.

In its simplest form, the basic structure of the foresight method consists of the following elements:

1. Gathering inputs from the situational analysis, expert views, and the project feasibility study

2. Assessing the inputs assembled, which helps in understanding what seems to be taking place and determines the project's future and the revenue stream

3. Interpreting the results of the assessment to determine what factors are indeed influencing project revenue

4. Exploring or prospecting what alternative project revenue outcomes may materialize

5. The actions the project team may need to be taking at this stage for the planned future revenues to be realized

6. Evaluating the outputs and conclusions and then developing a strategy and recommendations of what the project team needs to do and how to do it to ensure that revenue forecasts materialize

Companies with broad experience in strategic decision forecasting, which includes infrastructure revenue forecasting, usually employ more than one of the forecasting techniques and models discussed. However, better project revenue predictions are created by combining forecasts that come out of both qualitative and quantitative methods. The advantage of this practice is that it incorporates elements from different knowledgeable perspectives, which usually produce more easily accepted forecasts.

Every sound forecasting methodology, whether quantitative or qualitative, involves scenario building and the development of project forecasts. Scenarios are schemes, concepts, sketches, outlines, representations or plans of the sequence of events, their timing, and what happens when decisions are made and begin to get implemented. They are models of assumed or expected sequences of decisions, inputs, actions, reactions, and events constructed for the purpose of capturing their effect on a target variable. Namely, they show how a hypothesized chain of events leads to future states in a structured way of seeing beyond the current state, creating descriptions of future states, and describing how they unfold.

Scenarios are also used to explore wild card possibilities and black swans and quantify their impacts. In defining possible futures, scenarios help project-team members to understand the time-ordered events and causation from the current stage to the project implementation, and to create strategies and options to deal with uncertainties. They build "flight simulators" to create learning and sound project implementation strategies by clearly articulating the events and processes generating the future states, simulating them, and answering critical questions. Good scenarios are stories of plausible, divergent but deterministic futures, and they capture project-team biases and different points of view. Nevertheless, they can help to see vividly what drives the business and what is required to achieve the objectives of a project, to stimulate discussion, to question assumptions and the model of business operations, and to increase project-team effectiveness.

Scenario building is a structured approach to predict future project revenue by assuming a series of alternative possibilities instead of forecasting the future on the basis of extrapolated historical or analog data alone. Scenario planning, also called scenario thinking or scenario analysis, is a corporate planning method employed in making strategic decisions and long-term plans. It is an adaptation of the methods used by military intelligence and strategic planning that relies on model-simulation tools and controllable factors to manage the future.

When other methods of forecasting are not appropriate, scenario development and planning is a practical tool used to solve strategic-decision problems and create future-state forecasts. It is a method to learn about the future by understanding the impact of the most uncertain and important forces driving the business. Scenario development is based on the belief that strategic-decision forecasters are not at the mercy of fate; instead, they use this method of envisioning future states to incorporate them into scenario models to be simulated. The common steps involved in part one of scenario development include:

1. Starting with an accurate description of the project attributes and defining the project's environment, the context of the decision to be made, and its major objectives

2. Defining the scope of each scenario and brainstorming on the megatrends and the host country's external environment driving forces surrounding the project

3. Developing major assumptions about timing, causality, and the strength of relationships, gathering information, and evaluating industry and market trends and structural changes

4. Engaging an independent consultant to screen and provide suggestions on the driving forces and events and ensure objectivity and reasonableness of scenario building

5. Determining the extent to which scenario-driving forces can be predetermined, projected, and fixed and how steady their influence is on the projected project revenue

6. Creating distinct and convincing stories based on the effect of driving forces and critical uncertainties and eliminating competing narratives

7. Weaving hypotheses and plots to the stories to fit the identified events and forces and creating, at the most, three or four plausible scenarios

---

Key Takeaway

The most valuable application of scenario development, analysis, and planning is that scenarios can be used as a flight simulator that:

1. Enables project teams and senior management to visualize how to get to the desired future state of the project company and what is required to achieve it
2. Helps create the conditions, commitment, risk mitigation and support levels that have to be in place to obtain financing and achieve the desired project revenue objective
3. Allows the creation of the desired project state by influencing drivers and inputs in model form today before decisions are made and are implemented

---

In part two of scenario building, the forecasting team conducts sanity checks on the assumptions, actions, reactions, events and their timing, and on the processes that generate the future project states and their logic and performs the following activities:

1. Developing decision trees and influence diagrams based on modeling, simulations, and the Delphi technique and performing forecast analysis
2. Focusing on analysis of demand discontinuities of trends, cross-impact analysis, and analog experiences to identify unexpected driving factors and uncontrollable events
3. Assessing the financial, human resource, competitive, operational, and strategic implications of each scenario and evaluating differences with project expectations
4. Comparing the scenario generated forecasts against the baseline projection and estimating the contribution of each driving factor to the additional value created by the project
5. Creating a system of early warning indicators to monitor each scenario's performance as it unfolds through time and adapting the scenario to fit circumstances that approximate reality
6. Using the decision-selection matrix to identify, evaluate, and rate the economic value of each future state scenario and the likelihood of achieving them

8.7 FORECAST SANITY CHECKS

Forecasting infrastructure project revenue is an iterative and interactive process based on the considerations mentioned earlier. Forecast sanity checks are part of the process which entails reexamination, reevaluation, and revalidation of the following:

1. Project requirements and attributes, the extent to which it satisfies host government and consumer or user needs, and the political support it enjoys

2. Evaluation of the host country's PESTLED milieu and assessment of megatrend and industry trend impacts on the project

3. Information and data obtained from project participants and reliable external sources, advisors, and consultants

4. Checks of explicit and, sometimes, implicit assumptions about competition, the project company's output demand and pricing, and external future events

5. Input and guidance from industry experts, advisors, and international development institutions on project particulars

6. The conditioning effect of the risk tolerance of the project sponsor or developer and the host government ceding authority

7. The most likely scenario underlying the revenue forecast to validate its probability of occurrence and its applicability

8. Quantitative and qualitative models used to make revenue forecasts and their logical consistency compared with similar project experiences

9. Management or expert advisor adjustments to baseline forecasts to reflect their priorities

10. The strength of the negotiating position of the sponsor or the project originator in the project

Due to the vital importance of the revenue forecast to project valuation and its financeability, it is crucial that each of the above elements that affect the forecast be scrutinized, validated, and verified in an independent, objective, and balanced manner. Starting with project attributes and political support, and going down to the negotiating position of the project participants, the project team must determine whether the forecast foundations are sound and will withstand lender and investor scrutiny and the test of time. The second step in performing forecast sanity checks is comparison of forecast revenue growth rates with project-team expectations and those of similar projects to determine the reasonableness of the forecast. The third component of validating the forecast is the scrutiny of the project feasibility study and the due diligence phases where all data, assumptions, relationships, influences, analyses, and evaluations are subjected to sanity checks.

A fourth step in project revenue forecast validation is a thorough review by project advisors and consultants and other project participants to determine how forecast consensus was obtained and verification and validation of key models and forecasts. The next step is a forecast sensitivity analysis to see how variations in each key driver impact the revenue forecast due to deviations from their baseline specifications. However, the deciding activity of reality checks on the project revenue forecast is performed by the lending institutions, potential investors, entities providing credit support, and parties assuming business risks. The next question then is: What happens when a forecast fails one or more of the sanity checks? If the forecast validation fails for small infractions and has small impacts, a more conservative forecast may be picked from the range of forecast simulations. If on the other hand major objections are raised with respect to key assumptions, forecast adjustments, and the like, a revisiting of the issue and reexamination of risks should take place so that the remaining risks are managed effectively in order to satisfy all project participants. Appropriate adjustments are made to the forecast if warranted by evidence and convincing arguments.

8.8 CAUSES AND CONSEQUENCES OF FORECAST FAILURES

The causes of infrastructure project finance failures are several, but erroneous revenue forecasts are among the key culprits. Project forecast failures are instances where a forecast misses the mark by cumulative amounts in the range of 20–30% over the project's lifecycle. At the foundation of forecast failures is the wishful thinking produced by sponsor or host government project objectives that have superficial strategic, portfolio, and operational fit assessment, and minimal sanity checks. The prevalence of the groupthink problem related to optimistic views of a project's prospects is compounded by the poor or nonexistent forecast ownership and management function, which causes projections to be driven only by positive sentiments. A lack of qualified, strategic-decision forecasting skills and expertise, and late and restricted forecast organization participation in project evaluations are other causes of forecast failures.

Conflicting project participant views of future revenues sometimes lead to consensus views that are adopted so that the project can move forward. Inadequate preparations and planning for revenue forecasting, along with a lack of good data and expert advice, cause inappropriate assumptions to be created that, in turn, lead to erroneous forecasts. In some cases, an incomplete project environmental factor assessment and inadequate checking of facts and data lead to inadequacy and the failure of sanity checks, which allow the wrong model development and forecasting methods to be selected. Also, the lack of standardized infrastructure project revenue forecast processes and templates cause unnecessary iterations, often due to the inability to identify and quantify the driving factors and predict their future behavior.

Market research and other qualitative method data are often given undue weight but go unscrutinized and result in erroneous forecast adjustments. Inappropriate baseline scenario selection, no real sensitivity analysis, and ad-hoc forecast model simulations lead to the selection of forecasts on the optimistic side of the simulation range of values. In organizations with limited strategic decision forecasting capabilities, forecasts are taken as gospel. They are misused and not applied as intended to guide the overall value created by the project. In changing environments and industry structure, static forecast validity cannot be judged, but the absence of forecast realization planning is a major fault of most project revenue forecasts. The issue of project forecast realization is discussed in the next section.

Project revenue forecast failures are judged by forecast errors and are manifested in the project cash flow values coming in short of expectations. However, there are a number of forecast failure impacts to assess before looking at cash flow and beyond measuring actual versus projected value creation. Poor forecasts not only lead to wrong project selection but, also, to missed opportunities to invest in other projects. Regardless of the cause, project forecast revenue failures lead to miscalculations of costs and benefits, but the impact is much more severe if poor demand analysis has failed to identify and quantify correctly the risks that were thought easy to mitigate.

Another costly time, human resource, and money impact is the expansion of sizable resource allocation to a project's development phase, which should have been rejected in the first place, but because of erroneous forecasts it was not. Addressing the miscalculation of project risk failures caused by poor forecast impacts requires additional time, project team effort, and cost expenditures. There are increased debt financing and insurance costs, the risk of the project license being suspended, and termination in the case of large forecast failures. Poor project performance, repayment delays, and less than expected returns to investors leave many project participants very unhappy with the consequence of the snowballing effects on the sponsor company's reputation and future profitability.

In addition, project forecast failures cause funding sources to question the integrity of the project and require additional credit support and enhancements. Forecast failures eventually lead to rating agencies downgrading the project rating, which leads to additional financing costs. Also, a meager, actual project performance versus forecast expectations affects the credibility of the project team and the project originator, as well as that of the host government agencies that approved the project. Lastly, the project forecast failures lead to damaged reputation of the sponsor or developer companies among project financing circles, and this is a lasting and costly effect to remediate.

8.9 FORECAST MONITORING AND REALIZATION PLANNING

Forecast monitoring and reporting is done on a regular basis and usually involves a variance analysis of forecast versus actual revenues. Variance analysis reports on forecast errors and factors believed to be causing those errors. However, focusing on and rushing to judge forecast performance is incorrect without examining factors, such as:

1. Whether the initial project attributes are still factual in the forecast period

2. All project participants made timely required human, financial, and in-kind contributions

3. The quality of project implementation that was delivered met the required specifications

4. The validity of the project company's business plan, and its performance objectives and targets

5. The quality of the project company's operations management team

A proper forecast monitoring method first involves the creation of a forecast-monitoring dashboard that is usually a part of the overall project-monitoring system. The purpose of the forecast dashboard is to track in a systematic and effective manner the performance of the project-company operations and forecasts to get insights on how to correct problems as they appear. Then comes identification of the factors to include on the dashboard to monitor and how to do it, but it is necessary that only key factors be included in the variance analysis.

A number of questions need to be answered before blaming individual project finance team participants for forecast errors, such as:

- Were project forecasts done simply to satisfy baseless decisions despite objections to adopted forecasts?

- Were forecasts created by project participants or were they outsourced?

- Did forecasts have the benefit of expert reviews, inputs, and recommendations of independent consultants?

- Did the forecasting models identify all key drivers and did these drivers behave in the forecast period according to expectations?

- What changes in the project's host country and its operating environment take place that were not accounted for in the forecast scenario?

- Can forecast variances be attributed to overoptimism permeating all decisions?
- Is there a strategy to address forecast failures and what corrective actions were taken?

The discussion now leads us to the subject of forecast-realization management or adoptive-response planning, which stems from the belief that with appropriate structuring, evaluation, and implementation a project's future can be shaped well before actual operations. The forecast realization planning model consists of the following elements that are reviewed at each variance analysis session:

Adaptive Response Planning

It is the art of managing the sponsor project team and forecasting team behavior based on the action-reaction-action, etc. model of learning perceiving, planning, acting, and adjusting. It is a critical thinking approach that balances competitive response needs with the company's capabilities and resources and entails the following key elements:

1. Assessing uncertainty and risk and learning through experimenting and, sometimes, by trial and error
2. Creating organizational adaptation skills and capabilities to make sense of events as they occur and targeting project company responses to specific competitor or environmental conditions
3. Identifying competitive information quickly, interpreting it correctly, and applying it appropriately
4. Measuring how fast and to what degree the competitive response resulted in the desired response effects
5. Initiating process changes and project team motivation toward improved 4Cs

---

1. Environmental assessments which include industry, market, and PESTLED analysis
2. Independent verification and validation of processes, assumptions, models, and scenarios used to generate forecasts
3. Measuring project performance, which requires creation of a forecast dashboard and an early warning system, monitoring and understanding forecast variances, and determining how to prepare an updated risk management and contingency plan

4. Review and evaluation of the current state of the project company's operations and its initial business plan

5. Assessment of forecast error implications, which includes identification and quantification of new risks in the horizon and determining what preparation is needed to prepare a response plan

6. Preparation of a tactical response plan that involves assigning resources to coordinate the project company's response actions, make the7P adjustments defined below when necessary, and changing the project-company management team and providing support when warranted

7. Development of a strategic response plan that encompasses assessment of options to initiate, evaluation of restructuring and reorganizing the project company, undertaking new complementary support projects, revisiting corporate strategy and project objectives, and making adjustments where and when required

> 7Ps are a marketing tool used in new company operations and product or service introduction to help plan and create the conditions for successful company operations or delivery of new products of services by considering the place, people, product (or service), process, physical environment, price, and promotion factors involved.

Development of the forecast realization plan begins with determining what needs to be done to determine whether underperformance is due to forecast or actual data failures. This requires the right mindset, an appropriate and correct approach, employing tried and tested processes, and objectively assessing the results of the plans created. The process of creating the forecast realization plan requires a clear understanding of causes and the need for action and analytics to be performed in order to identify and evaluate the implications of the results. Following that activity, project uncertainty and forecast risks are reevaluated and adaptive remedial planning takes place to come up with a change plan. Changes may include initiatives such as sponsor, developer, or host government agency actions; industry regulator intervention, or key project participant or third-party additional credit support.

CHAPTER 9

Project Contracts and Agreements

Critical to Project Finance

The contracts and agreements part of project finance is a highly specialized field of legal expertise and this chapter aims only to introduce the basics of the types and nature of project documentation created by the sponsor's legal team. The intent of this chapter is to show the multitude and complexity of project contracts necessary to create the framework for project financing. To make the point, Figure 9.1 shows the signatories to and the commonly negotiated project finance contacts.

Having identified project risks and issues, the purpose of project contracts and security packages is to bring some certainty by addressing mitigation of potential future risks to the satisfaction of affected project stakeholders. Hence, familiarity with project contracts and their negotiations is a requirement of PFO and project team members. It is also a prerequisite for striving to obtain competitive advantage through project finance.

An agreement is one's commitment to deliver on an obligation that is accepted by another party. It is like a contract but it is not enforceable by law. A contract is a written and usually registered agreement supported by consideration and enforceable by law. Legally, an agreement binds neither party but a contract does and, hence, the need to document and negotiate agreements and create valid contracts. Contracts are a part of doing business and their importance derives from their use in legal systems to ensure compliance by all parties involved. They state the parties' expectations in terms and conditions, protect the confidentiality of project proposals, provide certainty for the parties involved, and create a basis to address disputes.

In project finance deals, contracts use standardized terms and conditions and deal with a lot of details in order to facilitate the project finance process. The type of contracts and their content vary by project, but in all cases they protect the parties from legal claims and counterclaims and reduce the likelihood of ending up in an international court of law. Because contracts hold all project finance participants accountable to written deliverables, project specifications, and performance expectations they hold the project together, enable project financing, and protect contract signatories from costly changes and surprises.

The structure, prerequisites, and costs of developing and negotiating project contracts are discussed in Section 9.1, and the process ordinarily followed by legal teams is presented in Section 9.2. The common types of project finance contracts that project teams encounter are briefly described in Section 9.3, and the challenges of project finance contract development and negotiation are the topic examined in Section 9.4. The last section, Section 9.5, addresses the factors that successfully complete contracts and projects.

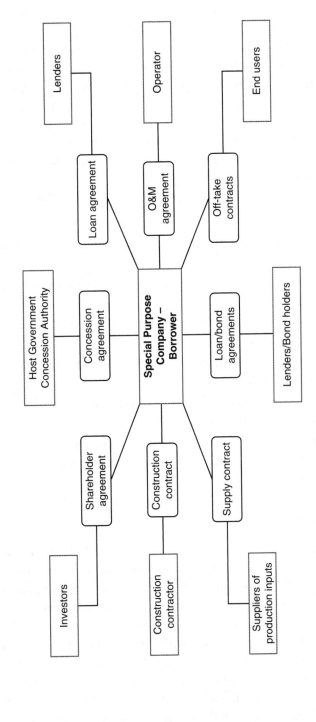

Figure 9.1 Signatories and Common Project Finance Contracts
Source: Adapted from Merna, Chu, and Al-Thani (2010).

9.1 STRUCTURE, PREREQUISITES, AND COSTS OF CONTRACTS

The role of the legal team is to provide answers to project-participant questions, organize the process of creating and negotiating project contracts, and provide a fair balance in the structure of the project's costs and benefits to make it sustainable. In the project finance literature, the terms contracts and agreements are used interchangeably, but in this chapter we will only use the term contract. Project finance contracts vary by size, type, and the parties involved but they all have similar structures and prerequisites, yet involve substantially different costs to create. The structure of contracts refers to the specific content used to lay out the participants' rights and obligations while contract prerequisites state what must be in place before contracts are drafted, negotiated, and approved.

The project prerequisites are the basis of contracts once they are satisfied and include the following:

1. Harmonized stakeholder interests and managed expectations to reasonable levels

2. Proper project screening and sound economic evaluation that validate project viability

3. Appropriate project specification and requirements evaluation to ensure technical feasibility

4. Comprehensive risk identification, assessment, mitigation, and balanced risk allocation

5. Thorough due diligence to verify project viability and stakeholder ability to deliver on obligations

6. Adequate sponsor equity, insurance coverage, and security packages

7. Sound project financial model structure with validated inputs and output evaluations

8. Reasonable and tested assumptions and scenarios used to generate financial forecasts

Project prerequisites also include the project stakeholder qualifications, eligibility, and ability to deliver on their human, physical resource, and financial obligations. A good part of the verification of project prerequisites takes place during the project development stage. International contracts are similar to domestic contracts but have some differences related to the rights of the signatories in different countries, so specifying the language and governing law used in project finance documents that control the transaction's dealings is crucial. Why? Because the enforceability of contracts requires that both the sponsor's and the host country's laws are stated in a common language, usually English, with the ability to enforce obligations.

The cost of developing project documentation and negotiating contracts is a significant project development cost component incurred over a period of several months or years and includes the following expenditure elements:

1. The salaries of legal personnel and wages of support and clerical staff
2. Travel-related expenses for fact-finding meetings and preparation of agreements
3. Acquisition of internal data and information from external providers and reviewers
4. Drafting of agreements, printing, distribution, and review
5. Updates and changes to contracts to include new information and lender requirements
6. Obtaining expert witness studies, reviews, opinion, and independent validation and verification
7. Storage and retrieval costs of legal documents and contracts produced for the project
8. Management and monitoring of contracts to ensure compliance in the host country
9. Expenses incurred to resolve legal issues outside the court system of the host country

Up until the mid-1990s, the storage of legal documents and contracts for large project financings could take the entire space of a large room, but now contracts and related documents are stored online and accessible by parties who have a need to know. It is commonly understood that because of the necessarily high legal team costs to create and negotiate contracts, projects under $75 million are difficult to prove profitable.

9.2 CONTRACT DEVELOPMENT AND NEGOTIATION PROCESS

The discussion of the project finance contract development and negotiation process herein is from the sponsor PFO's perspective. It is rather sketchy and lacking intermediate activities and steps performed by the legal team. It does, however, show the basic steps taken by the sponsor company's legal department that include:

1. Forming the contract development and negotiation team and linkages with the core project team, defining roles and responsibilities, and initiating contact with counterparts in other stakeholder organizations and potential funding sources
2. Identifying and assessing stakeholder expectations and contributions, verifying qualifications to enter into contracts and ability to deliver on current and future obligations

3. Developing a sponsor partnership agreement and forming the special purpose vehicle such as to maximizing the tax benefits to the sponsor(s)

4. Undertaking a host country fact-finding effort that involves legal and regulatory, environmental, and industry-structure evaluation; tax, labor, and environmental law review

5. Assessing the host government's competitive tender system, reviewing the business and industry environment, and obtaining contracting information and project requirement details

6. Reviewing the sponsor company's corporate strategy and risk tolerance, evaluating the feasibility study results, and defining contract needs and legal requirements in accordance with project objectives

7. Identifying project-critical success factors, links and dependencies, and project governance issues and determining key contract development and negotiation process objectives

8. Assessing project stakeholder organizations, values, and skills and competencies, and leading the due diligence effort jointly with the lender's legal team

9. Evaluating information assembled for decision making and developing a coordinated workflow and measurement and control system consistent with the project team's processes

10. Assessing the due diligence report, determining project risks, and evaluating the adequacy of risk mitigation and enhancement requirements

11. Creating a repository for management of contracts and their terms and conditions and identifying tools, systems, data, analyses, and evaluations needed

12. Assembling and cataloging all contracting information, beginning discussions with the host government's contracting authority and funding sources, and developing plans and schedules of events to take place

13. Reviewing financial model indicators and obtaining project-team inputs on contract needs and terms and conditions, insurance contracts, and other requirements

14. Drafting contracts and sharing with appropriate stakeholders and confirming participation of lenders, equity investors, and host government

15. Coordinating the development of a negotiation approach, plan, and process and ensuring that a correct financial model evaluation of contract new terms and conditions is performed in real time and results related back to the legal team

16. Negotiating contract terms, conditions, and deliverables with milestones on the scope of the project—pricing, budgets, performance specifications, contract language and compliance clauses, financial reporting requirements, construction costs and drawdown schedule, financing documents, approvals, and financial close

17. Creating a contract performance monitoring and control plan, overseeing project completion acceptance, incorporating change orders and resolving disputes, and performing compliance audits

9.3 COMMON PROJECT FINANCE CONTRACTS

The nature of project finance necessitates that contractual agreements form the basis of limited-recourse financing upon which funding for the project is raised. Some of the project contracts are developed or sourced from the sponsor group while others originate from the host government's ceding authority, debt and equity investors, and export credit agencies (ECAs), unilateral, and multilateral agencies. Many contracts are tailor-made to fit specific project needs and peculiarities, but our interest is on common project finance contracts which are the pillars supporting financing structures and include:

1. **The shareholder agreement**, between the sponsor(s) and the project company, defines the terms of participation and ownership interest in the project, the rights and obligations, and the roles and responsibilities of the signatories. Usually, this contractual agreement is preceded by a separate sponsor partnership agreement specifying their initial and subsequent equity and debt investments in the project company.

2. **The concession agreement**, also known as the implementation agreement, is a contract between the government and the project company that grants it the right to build and operate the project. It states the concession period, project company roles and responsibilities, eventual transfer of ownership, and project performance. Concession agreements include licensing, joint-venture contracts, production-sharing agreements, build, operate, and transfer of ownership (BOT) and public–private partnership (PPP) agreements, and offtake agreements. Concession agreements comply with host country laws and regulations and these contractual agreements usually include:

   a. The objectives, expectations, and support to the project by the host government

   b. Completion and termination dates

   c. The obligations of the concessionaire

    d. Direct lender agreements with the host government

    e. Security rights in the project company

    f. Force majeure clauses

    g. Liquidated damages and dispute resolution

    h. Changes in law and waiver of sovereign immunity

3. **The construction agreement**—one of the key contracts—spells out the scope of the project, the terms and conditions of a fixed price, date-certain turnkey engineering, procurement, and construction (EPC) contract, and the responsibilities of the contractor and the other project stakeholders. It covers items such as contractor responsibility for design flaws, extensions, and tests to determine completion of construction, payment procedures, and price changes. It also deals with issues such as contractor performance bond, performance guarantees, force majeure, and liquidated damages in the event of construction delays, security retainers, and dispute resolution measures.

4. **The intercreditor agreement is** a contractual agreement between project lenders that defines their position relative to each other and the project company, and what happens when problems arise, such as bankruptcy or default. It also spells out their lien positions and security interests and the rights and obligations of the parties involved and may include buy out provisions giving a lender the option to buy another lender's debt.

5. **The sponsor guarantees** is a form of credit support normally required by project senior lenders to reduce their risk in the project along with providing additional equity funding and cash infusions to handle cash flow shortfalls, secured interests over the project company's assets, guarantees related to project performance, and insurance against project risks

6. **The insurance contracts** can vary according to individual project risks and have a significant impact on risk mitigation and project negotiations and are covered in more detail in Chapter 10. Insurance contracts may include the following:

    a. Transportation insurance of materials and equipment to the project site

    b. Insurance of project assets before, during, and after construction

    c. Construction and erection of all-risk insurance that covers project assets and operations during construction

    d. Third-party liability insurance that provides third-party claims' coverage against omissions of the project company, contractors and subcontractors during construction and operation

    e. Consequential loss insurance for startup delays and business interruption

    f. Political risk insurance that includes partial risk guarantees, credit guarantees, and ECA or a multilateral agency guarantees

Political risk insurance provides coverage for revocation of permits and licenses, adverse regulatory changes, changes in tax and business laws, expropriation, currency inconvertibility, political violence and war, breach of contract, disruption of access to project company facilities, and asset transfer risks.

7. **The hedging contracts** are financial instrument contracts used in project finance to minimize interest rate and exchange rate risk with swaps when the parties agree to exchange floating rate to fixed rate loans and floating exchange rates to fixed exchange rates.

8. **The loan agreement** is an agreement between the project company and the lenders that provides loans for the project. The main parts of loan agreements include:

    a. The terms of the loan disbursement and repayment terms

    b. Conditions precedent

    c. Positive and negative covenants

    d. Representations and warrantees

    e. Remedies in the event of default

Additional project finance documentation involves an agreement on waterfall accounts, such as proceeds accounts, operating accounts, major maintenance reserve account, and debt payment and debt service accounts (Khan and Parra, 2003).

9. **The equity support agreement,** where the lenders shift completion and abandonment risks to the project sponsors by requiring equity commitments in the 20–40% range and in some cases even higher.

10. **The capital injection agreement** deals with a future sponsor's working capital contributions to cover cost overruns.

11. **The offtake agreement** is contract for the entire concession period that specifies the amounts the offtaker will purchase at a specific price adjusted for inflation. There are several types of offtake agreements for specific projects and financing requirements, the common ones being:

    a. Take or pay contracts where the purchaser pays for the project company's output even if they do not take it

    b. Take and pay contracts where the purchaser takes the project company's output and pays for it when the project company provides that output

From the project company and the lenders' perspective, the take-or-pay offtake contract is more advantageous because the project company's revenue is independent from the production of output. Other offtake agreements include:

a. Contracts for differences, when the project output is sold in the open market but the offtaker pays if the price goes below the agreed level and vice versa if the price goes above the agreed level

b. Long-term sales contracts of the project company's output

c. Throughput contracts used in pipeline projects where the user commits to carry at least a certain volume of a product and pays a minimum price

d. Input processing contracts used in waste incineration projects and sewage plants to agree to certain levels of inputs

Although project contracts form the basis for project financings, many of the problems encountered with them and project failures have to do with the terms and enforceability of offtake agreements.

12. **The supplier agreement** is a contract for the duration of the concession period between the project company and the supplier of the key production inputs and it is intended to ensure uninterrupted supply of key production inputs to the project company to meet its output requirements. It specifies the duration of the contract, conditions for price changes, and force majeure clauses. The supplier agreements in project finance are of the supply or pay, or put or pay type under which the supplier pays the entire cost of procuring alternative supply.

13. **The operations and maintenance agreement** defines the roles and responsibilities, the length of the agreement, performance expectations, and payments to the O&M company. This contract also includes incentives and penalties for the O&M company for meeting performance expectations.

Many of the risks associated with project finance deals are mitigated through the contracts mentioned above. However, the risks the debt investors bear beyond those contracts are mitigated with various project finance agreements, such as:

1. Each separate facility agreement, that is every debt and equity agreement entered to

2. The accounts agreement

3. Each security agreement

4. The equity support agreement

5. Each direct agreement, i.e., every lender's direct agreement with the host government

6. The drawdown request schedule

7. Each hedging agreement

In addition to the main project contracts, there are other contractual agreements and project documentation developed as part of the legal team's effort. They include ceding-authority collateral agreements, project-company performance bonds, collateral guarantees, bond and private placement financing documentation, and the project prospectus or information memorandum. Notice however, that there are a number of risks that cannot be mitigated through contracts and agreements such as misrepresentations, rigged procurement processes, corruption, and many others.

An important project finance document that is based on the feasibility study and the due diligence reports is the project prospectus or the information memorandum, which is prepared by the project team led by the legal group to market the project to potential debt and equity investors. It is a summary report of the project feasibility analyses and evaluations, the findings of the due diligence, and the project company's business plan to demonstrate the profitable value creation of the project.

9.4 CHALLENGES OF PROJECT FINANCE CONTRACTS

Some challenges of project finance contracts result in contracts that cannot prevent project failures and are caused by the following factors:

1. Lack of actual data from reliable sources, incorrect assumptions and methods used in cost and revenue forecasts and project evaluations

2. The feasibility study and due diligence reports leave project aspects partly investigated or reported incorrectly

3. Lack of skills and competencies in structuring effective project proposals and presenting convincingly analyses and evaluations

4. Unclear corporate strategy driving confused project objectives that translate into weak contracts, especially if the legal and financing processes are not properly aligned

5. Insufficient resources allocated to provide input and support in drafting project documents and contracts and assessing negotiations feedback

6. Time pressures resulting in ineffective contract reviews, merging of all contracts in a single package, and auditing and managing of contracts

7. Credit-impaired project stakeholder contract provisions for the currency governing the project transaction

8. Security agreements involving parties in different legal jurisdictions and disagreements among project stakeholders as to which country's courts should have jurisdiction and which country's laws should apply

9. Enforceability of force majeure clauses for project nonperformance

Additional project finance contract challenges are presented by the following individual factors and combinations thereof:

1. Contractual misunderstandings due to unclear contract provisions for dispute resolution

2. Insufficient front-end research and planning and inadequate contract development process

3. Complexity of multiparty, multifaceted contracts and multiparty reviews and approvals

4. Coordination issues between the legal team, the project team, and other project stakeholders' processes and deliverables

5. Errors related to multiple iterations of drafting, revising, reviewing, revising, and so on

6. Lengthy contract negotiations and renegotiations compounded by order changes, and schedule slippages

7. Lack of sufficient experience of project stakeholders in project finance contracts and, occasionally, lack of qualifications to enter into contracts

8. Language and cultural barriers and approach to negotiations focused on maximizing sponsor or host government benefits from the project at the expense of other stakeholders

9. Incomplete and unbalanced agreements, unconfirmed evaluations and unchecked assumptions, and faulty financial assessments entering into defective formal contracts

10. Contract enforceability issues in developing countries, contract failures, and inability to get remedies

11. Unmitigated risks passed into contracts due to weak third-party guarantees and insurance coverage

12. Reactive risk management and undue reliance on contracts to mitigate risks without proper attention to project economics and stakeholder qualifications, skills, and ability to manage to contractual requirements

13. Ethical issues and corrupt behavior that can never be managed effectively through contracts, but which must be dealt with at the early project phases

9.5 PROJECT CONTRACT SUCCESS FACTORS

Successful project financing relies on sound and effective contracts that are characterized by factors such as:

1. Clearly stated and reasonable project objectives and customer expectations managed to reasonable levels
2. Well-defined project scope and clarity of what needs to be done and clarity of participant obligations, roles, and responsibilities
3. Early participation of the PFO and the project team and all around, unimpeded communication, cooperation, coordination, and collaboration (4Cs) characterizing the contract development process, and sound vision and contract objectives
4. The prerequisites of drafting effective project contracts are satisfied
5. Early involvement of the PFO in contract preparation, structuring, and ensuring 360-degree 4Cs
6. Comprehensive contract planning, negotiation process, and assessment of negotiation results by the financial model
7. Balance of participant interests using unambiguous language and fair, balanced, and cost-benefit based risk allocation
8. Real commitment of the contract parties to project success throughout its lifecycle
9. Skilled and highly qualified legal staff and project team managers assigned to support the drafting of legal documents
10. Independent and critical review and evaluation of contracts by external legal experts
11. Creation of a project contract management system for contract administration, auditing, and control

CHAPTER 10

Project Risk Management

Crucial for Project Success

Project risk is the failure of a project to meet its objectives and the loss associated with it if a threat event materializes. For estimation purposes, it is the product of the probability of occurrence by the severity of the outcome. Risk is a part of business life and projects and when it happens it adversely impacts company strategies and project objectives. Project risks are not only of external but also of internal nature to both project sponsors and customers. Our focus is on external risks since the internal risks have already been identified by the sponsor and customer SWOT analysis and dealt with. International project finance deals entail a number of risks and a good deal of project success depends on effective risk management.

Risk management is an integral part of managing a project and the larger the project, the more attention is directed to risk management, which requires support from the project team and the decision makers of stakeholder organizations. Effective risk management is a prerequisite to striving to attain competitive advantage in project finance and create successful deals. Risk management is the progression of identifying, analyzing, prioritizing, and mitigating risks to minimize their impact on project value creation. To get a sense of the type and frequency of risks materializing and stress the importance of risk management, Table 10.1 shows occurrence percentages for various risk types.

Section 10.1 discusses the objectives and importance of project risk management and Section 10.2 presents a taxonomy of external risks. Understanding the origins or sources of project risks is necessary to develop appropriate risk management plans and Section 10.3 is dedicated to that subject. Section 10.4 provides a summary of the responsibilities and activities associated with risk management and the entities that are involved in it. The process of analysis, prioritization, and the mitigation of risks is presented in Section 10.5 and that helps to determine the activities involved in the sequence of the process steps. Section 10.6 presents some commonly used risk-management instruments and mitigants, and Section 10.7 closes the chapter with a discussion of risk-management benefits and costs, success factors, and regularly present challenges.

10.1 OBJECTIVES AND IMPORTANCE OF RISK MANAGEMENT

The purpose of risk management is to identify the sources of potential threats or problems in the project development stage so that risk mitigation steps are taken to minimize adverse impacts. That being said, the objectives of project risk management are to:

1. Clarify and assign ownership and specific responsibilities to project-team members with experience in the matter

Table 10.1 Statistics of Materialized Project Risks

Projects not completed on time	24%
Average time overrun	17%
Average of projects with disputes	11%
Average percent of projects with: ↓	
Budget overruns	19%
Change orders	15%
Projects with disputes	11%
Design change/scope creep	17%
Changes in schedules	49%*
Changes in costs	43%*
Design and engineering issues	51%*
Political environment risks	31%*
Contractual risks	31%*
Lack of cooperation	77%
Lack of risk mitigation knowledge	74%
Lack of project risk awareness	71%
Culture not embracing risk management	60%

*Figures for public projects.
Source: McGraw Hill, Construction; Mitigation of Risk in Construction: Strategies for Reducing Risk and Maximizing Profitability, *Smart Market Report* (2011).

2. Make project risk management a top priority, raise awareness of project participants, and provide a common understanding of actions and support needed to ensure project financeability

3. Use on an ongoing basis the sponsor-project team's risk management capabilities to ensure that projects are profitable and bids are competitively priced

4. Design and execute a project risk management process fully integrated with the strategic planning, new business development, and financial planning functions

5. Ensure consistency of risk mitigation with corporate risk tolerance and acceptance by the sponsor company and the customer

6. Communicate a common view of risks to all project stakeholders and an effective risk management strategy

7. Set out process rules to be followed by the project team and establish measures of risk management performance

8. Develop a system to monitor key risk components and assess gaps in the risk management plan and the team's ability to manage them

9. Effectively balance the sponsor's risk management objectives with the priorities of other project participants

10. Monitor the information given to decision makers to help them make the right decisions when risks are identified, how they are mitigated, and how to respond should they materialize

When project risk management is an integral part of the strategic planning, new business development, and financial planning functions its importance is derived from its ability to help the project team to:

1. Incorporate risk management in all planning and decision-making processes across all sponsor company participating organizations

2. Bring discipline and reality and reasonableness tests for scenarios, assumptions, objectives, and decisions

3. Use a cost-benefit approach to risk allocation to balance project stakeholder interests

4. Objectively determine the project's strengths, weaknesses, opportunities, and threats

5. Prepare responses for adverse events materializing and minimizing their impacts on the project's value

6. Protect the project's financial viability and the sponsor and customer reputations

7. Achieve project objectives through proper planning, preparation, and project plan execution

8. Share a common understanding and give clarity of the project's chances of success to all project participants and sound advice and recommendations to decision makers

9. Provide higher comfort levels to decision makers through satisfactory evidence of the adequacy of the risk management plan to avoid big disasters

10. Prevent cash flow surprises over the project's lifetime and ensure efficient project completion

11. Get a better understanding of the risk impacts on the sponsor company's competitive advantage position

12. Enable the sponsor company to allocate capital investments more efficiently

10.2 TYPES OF PROJECT RISKS

Project risks vary by the nature of project, the standing of the host country, project ownership, and the parties involved. They are usually classified by project phase or as precompletion, postcompletion, and political risks. Our taxonomy of project risks by type of risk is along ten major categories of risks related to the following areas and situations:

1. Project construction and completion
2. Host country macroeconomic conditions
3. Political situation in the host country
4. Host country social and environmental issues
5. Commercial or market conditions in the host country
6. Host country legal and regulatory environment
7. Structuring of project financing
8. Project company operating conditions
9. Project administrative issues
10. Force majeure

The various risks under each category are factors behind project failures discussed in Chapter 3. Because each risk category is easily understood, the risks in each category are identified without elaborating on their nature or their potential impact. Each of the categories above involves its own risk factors; the following is a register of corresponding risks:

A. **Project Construction and Completion**

1. Delays caused by project permit issues and additional license requirements
2. Poor project site conditions, or inadequately prepared access, and other construction site issues
3. Limited or no inspections of the project site allowed to sponsor and lender engineers
4. Technology, equipment, and construction contractor logistics problems
5. Project design and engineering defects and technology and equipment failures
6. Questionable reliability of the project cost component and time to completion estimates
7. Poor construction contractor procurement practices and time and cost overruns
8. Construction, labor, and materials costs that are above projected increases
9. Concealed construction defects requiring expensive equipment replacements and repairs

10. Project asset performance does not meet standards and specifications

11. Contractor failure to satisfy performance guarantees

12. Construction contractor company or counterparty business failure

B. **Host Country Macroeconomic Conditions**

1. Stagnant, low productivity host country economy

2. Deteriorating host country economic conditions

3. Wage, production inputs, and materials inflation beyond forecast ranges

4. Currency inconvertibility and an inability to transfer dividends outside the host country

5. Large local currency devaluation outside the assumed exchange rate range

6. Host country capital controls coupled with foreign exchange controls

7. Import and export controls of project company production inputs and outputs

C. **Host Country Political Situation**

1. Host government and subsovereign government frequent changes

2. Project interference and cancellation of agreements, permits, or licenses

3. Host government inability to fulfill contractual obligations

4. Expropriation of project company property and assets

5. Nationalization of the project company

6. Confiscation of project assets or creeping expropriation

7. Recurrent labor strikes and civil disturbance

8. Decentralization of host government project responsibility

9. Political force majeure

10. Corrupt host country central government practices

11. Partial-risk guarantees not honored

D. **Social and Environmental Issues**

1. Unexpected host country environmental law changes

2. Unreasonably high cost of compliance with environmental regulations

3. Project company equator principle violations

4. Negative impacts on the local population's quality of life

5. Corruption of local officials

6. Demands for delivery of essential services beyond the implementation agreement

7. Waste and carbon emissions and noise pollution

8. Local community opposition to the project

9. Changes in laws make the technology used in the project obsolete

---

The Equator Principles is a risk management approach originally developed by the World Bank and adopted by several international institutions to identify, evaluate, and mitigate environmental and social risks of infrastructure projects.

E. **Commercial or Market Conditions**

1. Worsening industry or local market conditions

2. Decreased demand for the project company's output

3. Reduced revenue growth prospects due to increased competition or customer changes

4. Unexpectedly high inflation resulting in increased operating costs

5. Less than expected social acceptance of the project company's output of product or service

6. Poor host government and customer relations

7. Default of counterparties

F. **Legal and Regulatory**

1. Arbitrary withdrawal of project company's permits and licenses

2. Changes to commercial and tax laws and regulations

3. Inability to enforce project contracts

4. Noncompliance with project approvals

5. New competitor entry allowed

6. Unfavorable tariff changes for the project company's production inputs or its output

7. Property ownership and ownership transfer issues

8. The host country's procurement law changes

9. Contract renegotiation with worse than initial terms and conditions

G. **Project Financing**

1. Limited availability and adequacy of sponsor's equity funding to develop the project

2. Lack of project finance skills and competencies in the sponsor organization

3. Inability of project stakeholders to deliver on equity requirements and future contributions

4. Reliability of project cost estimates and revenue forecasts

5. Inadequate assessment of project economics, funding needs, and financeability

6. Less than expected lender capacity to fund required debt and loan syndication difficulties

7. Insufficient cash flow and liquidity issues

8. Creditworthiness of project participants

9. Inability of lenders and other participants to identify and evaluate hidden project risks

10. Inadequate attention to risk mitigation and control over the project's life cycle

11. Lack of lender confidence in project stakeholder ability to control project risks

12. Unhedged interest rate increases during construction

13. Unfavorable exchange rate changes during construction

14. Host country changes of tax regulations and rate structure

15. Difficulties with refinancing the short-term debt of the project with long-term debt

16. Credit counterparty risk and partial risk guarantee issues

17. Rigid debt service requirements imposed on the project company

18. Project delays related to problems with raising financing

19. Cash flow shortages to support ongoing operations that cause project abandonment

20. Lower than expected termination value at project company asset transfer

H. **Project Company Operations**

1. Project company governance issues

2. Limited access to skilled human resources locally

3. Unreliable supply availability and shortages of production inputs and materials

4. Large, unprecedented increases in production input prices and supply quality issues

5. Host country's poor living conditions, culture, and way of life for expatriates

6. Poor management and execution of the project company's business plans

    7. Absence of the right project company management incentives

    8. Project company has output quality and performance shortcomings on several fronts

    9. Output purchase default by the offtaker

  10. Inadequate maintenance of project company assets

  11. Technology and equipment obsolescence

  12. Safety and work conditions

  13. Unexpectedly high labor wage inflation

  14. Large increases of project company operations and management (O&M) costs

  15. Labor strikes and work stoppages

  16. Project life is less than two times funding life

I. **Administrative Issues**

    1. Absence of effective processes to manage project stakeholder expectations

    2. Lack of sufficient buy-in and host country political support up and down the government bureaucracy

    3. Poor communication, coordination, cooperation, and collaboration among project stakeholders

    4. A poor risk management culture by the sponsor and lukewarm senior management support for the project

    5. Flaws in ongoing project risk monitoring, reporting, and responding

J. **Force Majeure = Project Frustration**

    1. Earthquake occurrences that cause catastrophic damage

    2. Severe project site flood events that shut down operations and cause repair delays

    3. A civil war or war with neighboring countries in the host country

10.3 SOURCES OF PROJECT RISKS

Every large infrastructure project involves risks. Some risks are identifiable and some are not; some are insurable and some uninsurable; and some are controllable while others are not. Unidentifiable risks, uninsurable risks, and uncontrollable risks are usually lumped together under project uncertainty and subject to contingency planning. The identifiable risks were mentioned in the section above, the sources of controllable and insurable risks are covered in this section. Notice that the origins of project risks are the same as the root causes of project failures, but worth revisiting.

Project risks have their origin in a multitude of diverse factors, but here we address only major sources. The first set of risk sources is when the sponsor's corporate culture and the host government's bureaucracy do not embrace sound, project lifecycle, risk management and dedicate inadequate resources to make risk management function effective. A lack of project finance skills and competencies and risk management expertise and experience are other sources of risks that are compounded by an unwillingness to hire highly skilled project advisors and qualified consultants. Misguided and misaligned project objectives and processes, and conflicting and unreconciled interests of stakeholders, are other source of project risks. These sources of risks are controllable and their impact limited with proper organizational cultures embracing lifecycle risk management and project financing and risk management skills and experience.

Inadequate bid and procurement practices and procedures in some stakeholder organizations lead to misinterpretation of requirements, and confusion among participants. So do erroneous bid or project selections and delays in developing a project and bringing it to conclusion efficiently. These are controllable risks, but can occur due to inability of project stakeholders to closely follow the requirements and guidelines of multilateral institutions and lenders. The risk of insufficient sponsor-equity contributions is a major delay factor and cause of project cost increases. It has its roots in uncertainty about a project's viability, less than full project sponsor commitment, and unwillingness to redirect resources and qualified management talent to the project.

Faulty project designs, engineering, technology, and equipment selection are risks originating in misunderstandings about project requirements, poor project assessment, highly compressed timelines, and cost savings. Sometimes the selection of new and untested technologies presents the same risk that is manifested in completion delays and cost increases. These risks are not as severe in impact as are project management failures to manage effectively the convergence of processes developed specifically for the current project to secure stakeholder buy in and commitment to bring the project to successful completion.

Inadequate contracts with gaps in issues covered and less than reasonable clauses originate in either the belief that it is not in every stakeholder's interest to cooperate in risk management or in the view that contracts are a zero sum game. In the first instance, risk management has taken second place after wishful thinking and in the second case it is an indication of ignorance of risk management principles. A weak legal framework and an inadequate regulatory regime in the host country are significant project risks, especially because of the contract enforceability issue, which is difficult in the case of inadequate contracts. Ineffective regulatory regimes and poor legal frameworks are rooted in a host country's low level of economic development, which multilateral and development institutions are trying to improve.

Unchecked facts and information and data are taken at face value and not subjected to scrutiny, and sanity checks are often due to a lack of understanding of project finance requirements and expediency to get the project done on time. More importantly, unfounded, unreasonable, untested, and erroneous assumptions drive the financial assessment of the project and are a major source of faulty feasibility studies, wrong decisions, and project failure. The sources of this type of risk are ignorance of forecasting principles, a poor understanding of the host country's market place, optimistic thinking, wrong motives, and misguided project objectives. Sometimes, senior management inputs and adjustments to assumptions and forecasts are responsible for infusing this risk.

Some decisions are made simply to satisfy senior management wishes to undertake and complete a project. Senior management enthusiasm about a project gets translated into excessive optimism of forecasts and scenarios selected for simulations. Excessively optimistic project revenue forecasts always lead to erroneous project economic evaluations and false expectations of project financeability. The reasons behind these risks are inadequate focus on the foundations of demand analysis and forecasting, poor feasibility studies, and weak due diligence due to a lack of skills and experience, appropriate processes, and sound project management. Lastly, spotty and ineffective monitoring of the project company's performance, inadequate variance analysis, lack of early warning systems, and no business plan realization explain an inability to control risks from materializing because they were thought to have been properly mitigated.

10.4 RISK MANAGEMENT UNDERTAKINGS

In most projects, the sponsor's risk management responsibility rests with the project manager. In companies where that responsibility is integrated with the strategic and financial planning and business development functions, risk management is effectively carried out by a risk management team across all projects. In both instances risk management responsibilities are practically the same and, besides creating and implementing the risk management plan, they include the following duties and activities:

1. Understand how project success depends on the risk management function's ability to recognize and manage all significant project risks
2. Follow industry practices and trends, establish and manage relationships with insurance advisors and brokers, and maintain a database of risk-related information

3. Develop and direct the project's risk management plan and assign appropriate responsibilities to the right people

4. Create actionable intelligence and coordinate risk management, contingency planning, and prevention activities

5. Create risk management plans tailored to the specific project, customer needs, and debt and equity investor requirements

6. Ensure that risk management plans are transparent, iterative and frequently updated, and responsive to change

7. Make recommendations to senior management after having identified and evaluated a project's risk exposure and prioritized risk mitigation

8. Serve as a risk management resource for the project and legal teams and provide answers to questions of project participants

9. Interview and select insurance brokers, negotiate hedging and insurance contacts, review and renew or change policies

10. Develop and manage risk management budgets and payments to insurance brokers and vendors as well as collecting insurance proceeds

11. Monitor on an ongoing basis loss control issues and develop risk prevention plans and processes consistent with those of the project team

12. Obtain external expertise to identify and address unknown risks and black swans and develop ways to deal with them

13. Determine the right controls and countermeasures in need of review and approval by senior management

14. Remain involved in the decision-making process to create value by systematically addressing explicitly uncertainty factors

10.5 RISK MANAGEMENT PROCESS

There are four basic kinds of risk management processes: reactionary, partial-project life risk, advanced planning up to project completion, and well-structured lifecycle risk management. What distinguishes sound from poor risk management processes are the following properties:

1. Effective communication, coordination, cooperation, and collaboration within the sponsor company and with host government agencies and other project stakeholders

2. Efficient entire project lifecycle versus partial and weak risk management

3. Depth of research, validation and verification, and analysis along with disciplined project economic evaluation

4. Deliberate, well balanced, and fair versus ad-hoc, unbalanced risk allocation or sharing

5. Risk management that is deeply embedded in project screening, feasibility study, due diligence, and financing processes

6. Skilled and experienced managers responsible for the execution of the business and risk management plans

7. Tracking closely, auditing, and reporting risk management developments

8. Ongoing, in-depth variance analysis to help understand causes of changes and assess project company performance

9. Creation of early warning systems, business plan revenue forecast realization plans, and threat response plans

10. Equal attention and weight given to sound project economic evaluation and risk management processes

The first step in the risk management process is the identification and description of all project risks by the project team in the early stages of project development; that is, in the screening and selection phase and then continues throughout the project lifecycle. A key to accurate risk identification is ensuring that the project feasibility study is based on accurate data and information that has been validated and the assumptions it is based on are tested for reasonableness. The feasibility study assessment determines which risks are induced by inadequacies within project development and may be manageable. This allows focus to be directed to other sources of risks.

Identified risks are then separated into five categories: Identifiable and knowable, unknowable, not identifiable, questionable, controllable, and uncontrollable risks. Risk factors considered unknowable or not identifiable are grouped together under uncertainty and subject to contingency planning. It is important that the identified events and factors are shared with all project stakeholders and external experts whose input is solicited on the completeness of the list of risks, the probability of their occurrence, and the severity of their impact which is recorded in the risk register.

The project register is a tool to describe project risks, identify their causes, and quantify their impacts along with handing out ownership of risks to parties best able to address. The project register updates and communicates periodic progress on the project.

It is always a good idea to break down the list of potential risk into parts that can be distributed to the rightful parties so that risk interactions can be better managed, such as along the taxonomy of risks in Section 10.2. The risk management and project teams are then in a position to develop a well considered, consensus type of probability ranges of occurrence for each risk, as shown in Table 10.5.1.

The next step in the risk management progression is to assess the potential impact of risks first in the ranges as shown in Table 10.5.2 and then in dollar-term estimates, if at all possible.

In order to rank the risks by likelihood and severity of impact and focus on the most critical risks we use the risk matrix, a prototype of which is shown in Table 10.5.3. In this matrix, the different risks are listed in their

Table 10.5.1 Likelihood Ranges of Project Risk Occurrence

Likelihood → Risk factor ↓	Very low; <10%; Unlikely	Low, 10–20%; Seldom	Medium; around 50%; Occasional	High; 60–80%; Likely to occur	Occurs; >80%; Definite
Risk #1					
Risk #2					
...					
Risk #N					

Table 10.5.2 Impact Severity of Potential Risk Occurrence

Impact → Risk factor ↓	Minor or insignificant	Marginal	Moderate	Serious	Disastrous
Risk #1					
Risk #2					
...					
Risk #N					

Table 10.5.3 Project Risk Matrix

Impact → Likelihood ↓	Minor or insignificant	Marginal	Moderate	Serious	Disastrous
Definite	Q	C	MC	MC	MC
Likely	SC	C	C	MC	MC
Occasional	NC	SC	C	MC	MC
Seldom	NC	NC	SC	C	MC
Unlikely	NC	NC	Q	C	C

impact category marked by levels of impact severity. Most critical (MC) labeled risks must be allocated or mitigated immediately and critical (C) risks need to have a good approach to deal with them. These two risk classifications have high priority and focus followed by risks designated as somewhat critical (SC). The remaining types of risks, designated as not critical (NC) and questionable (Q) have a lower likelihood of occurrence and lower priority, but still require some type action after higher priority risks have been addressed.

> Risk matrix, also known as probability and impact matrix, is a practical tool to assess the likelihood of occurrence and rate the impact of a risk event materializing. It is a table whose rows show risk events and columns show the probability of occurrence and their impact.

The risk prioritization analysis helps to order which risk factors and events need to be addressed first. This begins preparations and risk mitigation planning, which involves different options such as:

1. Avoiding risks by taking out their source upfront. This is the most effective option
2. Transferring risk to a project stakeholder best able to absorb the risk in question
3. Minimizing risks through creating ways to decrease the impact of somewhat critical risks
4. Accepting those risks that have a low likelihood of occurrence and small impact
5. Obtaining risk coverage from ECAs or multilateral funding institutions
6. Insuring risks that lend themselves most effectively to insurance coverage
7. Sharing risks with other project stakeholders in proportion to the benefit obtained from the project
8. Obtaining guarantees and security packages from project stakeholders for risks originating from their side

The next step in the risk management process involves monitoring, tracking, and reviewing the status of each risk on an ongoing basis. As a project moves along the development, construction, financing, and implementation stages the impact of some risks is eliminated or minimized. The opposite is true of other risks and of yet other risks that may appear further out on the horizon that need to be mitigated. Thus, the risk monitoring and tracking step becomes, again, a risk identification step, in addition to being a place where the outcome of threats is documented.

The last part of the risk management process is the response or mitigation strategy, which is developed by the project sponsor or in conjunction with the host's ceding authority, especially in public–private partnership (PPP) deals. Risk mitigation response options are often used in different combinations to address specific project situations.

Lessons Learned

a. Probabilities of risk occurrence are hard to estimate with a high degree of accuracy; instead, get help from expert advisors and the opinions of funding and insuring sources

b. Use the Delphi approach to assess the likelihood of risk occurrence and impact with industry experts and project finance professionals

c. Opinions about risk occurrence are unrealistic in the presence of excessive project optimism

d. Research and study the outcomes of risks in other projects or competitor experiences and learn how they were mitigated successfully

e. Risk-impact simulations over ranges of likelihood of occurrence are useful when realistic scenarios are selected to simulate

f. Unmitigated, high probability of occurrence risks always destroy project values and are the prime source of project failures

g. Try to avoid litigation when risks materialize as much as possible. Instead, get funding sources, ECAs, and multilateral agencies involved to get resolution

10.6 RISK MANAGEMENT INSTRUMENTS AND MITIGANTS

The first and best risk identifiers are an early and systematic project feasibility study followed by a sound project economic evaluation as project particulars become better defined. In the due diligence phase, risk mitigation gets a lot more attention and focus by the project potential lenders. For project risk mitigants to accomplish what they are intended for, the sponsor company needs to have risk management embedded in its corporate culture. In addition, a skilled and experienced project team supported by competent external advisors and consultants should be in place from the screening phase of the project down to recommending appropriate risk management solutions.

An abbreviated presentation of risk mitigants commonly used by risk management and project teams for the threats enumerated in Section 10.2 includes the following instruments according to type of risk:

A. Project Construction Completion

1. Independent validation and verification of project specifications and requirements by third-party experts
2. Preparation of a sound feasibility study based on assumptions tested for validity and reasonableness
3. Selection of a well-known, experienced, reputable, and trusted EPC construction company
4. Use of proven and tested equipment and technology that meets bid specifications and requirements
5. Turnkey engineering, procurement, and construction contracts
6. Technology and equipment warrantees by suppliers and vendors
7. Liquidated damages paid by the construction contractor
8. Project infrastructure failure risks are absorbed entirely by the host government

B. Host Country's Macroeconomic Conditions

1. Comprehensive, upfront macroeconomic analysis to establish host country's economic environment stability
2. Project output demand and price escalation clauses in contracts
3. Agreed wage and other labor-cost escalation provisions are included in contracts
4. Local currency hedging contracts against devaluation or currency depreciation
5. Local currency convertibility coverage is part of political insurance
6. Host government guarantees of free project company exports and imports
7. Contingency project-company accounts established outside the host country
8. Project company's business plan modifications to offset impacts of the host country's adverse economic conditions

C. Political Risks

1. Wide-ranging political, economic, social, technological, legal, educational, and demographic (PESTLED) evaluation and report of risk findings impacting other areas of risk management
2. Continuous alignment of sponsor and host governments' interests and objectives

3. Sufficient political support and good relationships with the host government at all levels

4. Host government's political risk assurances and counter-guarantees

5. Political risk insurance from multilateral funding sources and private insurance companies

6. ECA, OPIC, and other agency guarantees and insurance coverage

7. Building up adequate project company offshore escrow accounts

8. ECA and multilateral institution involvement and intervention to resolve issues

D. Environmental and Social Risks

1. Site inspections by professional environmental engineers and experts

2. In-depth environmental due diligence and site risk assessment

3. Upfront assessment of social and labor market conditions and labor unrest issues

4. Verification of adequate qualified labor and living conditions for expatriates as part of a sound project feasibility study

5. Ongoing monitoring of environmental and social conditions to ensure compliance with local and international laws and standards

6. Obtaining adequate insurance to cover adverse impacts of environmental problems

E. Commercial/Market Risks

1. Comprehensive industry, market, and competitor analysis to ensure operational adequacy of the project company's industry structure

2. Market studies to determine consumer or user needs, willingness and ability to buy and acceptance and absorption of the project company's capacity output

3. Adequate offtake contracts and long-term supply contracts with price protection clauses for both

4. Building up material inventories and input supply cushions to weather short-term disruptions

5. Futures contracts for project company production inputs and materials

6. Selection of appropriate technology to prevent obsolescence and discourage competitor entry

7. Close relationships with host government agencies and regulatory authorities to help offset adverse impacts on project company operations

F. **Legal and Regulatory Risks**

1. The host country's political support at the central government, ceding authority, and local government levels

2. Close cooperation with the ceding and regulatory authorities from project inception to transfer of ownership to the host government

3. Close evaluation of the feasibility study and the due diligence report findings to address outstanding issues in need of contract negotiations

4. Scrutiny of the due diligence and risk management reports to uncover risks addressed inadequately

5. Offtaker and supplier contractual obligations to pay compensation to the project company when there are adverse law changes

6. Adequate ECA and multilateral institution legal and regulatory risk insurance

7. ECA and multilateral institution involvement and intervention to ensure a level playing field

G. **Project Financing Risks**

1. Sound economic viability assessment with extensive data and information validation and testing of assumptions used in cost and revenue forecasts and reasonableness of forecasts

2. Consistency of project risk levels with sponsor company and investor risk tolerance

3. Validation of financial model inputs and outputs for consistency and reasonableness and adequacy of financial ratios

4. Monte Carlo simulations performed for a number of possible scenarios to determine forecast center of gravity

5. Insurance coverage for project delays that lead to renegotiation of contracts and agreements

6. Sponsor and host government guarantees backed by counter insurance

7. Lending institution letters of credit to cover working capital needs

8. Early negotiation for commitment to convert short-term to long-term debt at market rates

9. Building acceptable flexibility in the debt service obligations and waterfall accounts

10. ECA and multilateral institution credit guarantees and insurance coverage

11. Futures contracts, hedging, and interest rate and currency swaps

12. Setting up waterfall accounts with appropriate covenants and restrictions

---

Waterfall accounts area set of accounts created to separate and prioritize project company cash flow so that repayment of debt and interest is made in descending order of seniority and where low-tier creditors are paid after high-tier lenders have received full payment.

H. Operational Risks

1. Sound project company business plan, operational targets, and course correction options when threats materialize

2. Experienced management secondments from the sponsor to the project company to implement its business plan effectively

3. Selection of a reputable, experienced, and reliable O&M company

4. Sound O&M contracts with output quantity and quality performance requirements

5. Appropriate performance incentive-based O&M contracts with wage and benefit controls

6. Close cooperation and ongoing relationship management with the ceding and regulatory authorities

7. O&M company performance guarantees and insurance contracts

I. Organizational Risks

1. Skilled and effective project team, an outstanding project manager, and an experienced project company management team

2. All around unimpeded communication, coordination, cooperation, and collaboration

3. Congruence of sponsor corporate appetite with project risks and project lifecycle risk management embedded in its corporate culture

4. Complete and effective processes that assign clear roles and responsibilities to process owners in the sponsor and the project company

5. Close monitoring the implementation of both the project company business and the risk mitigation plans

J. **Force Majeure**

1. Obtain adequate force majeure insurance even though it is costly in developing countries

2. Allow some flexibility in schedules and extension of project timelines

3. Build up adequate debt service reserve funds, preferably outside the host country

4. Involve multilateral agencies to help resolve problems related to force majeure

5. Seek financial protection from insurance companies and re-negotiate debt payments

The following four key risk mitigants are worth elaborating on because they are useful in all risk categories and play a major role in project risk management, project financeability, and project viability. They are:

I. **Project economic evaluation.** After the project feasibility study, a sound economic assessment reduces the number and potential impact of risks, first through validation of contract specifications and requirements and project cost estimates. Validation of the demand and pricing models and the assumptions used for cost and revenue forecasts, along with verification of the reasonableness of scenarios used, are another avenue to reduce the number, likelihood of occurrence, and impact of risks. A sound project economic evaluation also requires development of a complete and well-structured financial model and thorough analysis of model inputs and outputs in order to minimize project risks.

II. **Project due diligence.** For all practical purposes, the project due diligence effort is an independent validation of the feasibility study and risk identification, assessment and mitigation. In the due diligence phase, all environmental, design, and technical aspects of the project are examined and expert advice is sought to minimize construction completion risks. Then, the project company structure and the legal aspects of the bid and procurement, licensing, and permitting are examined, as well as all the contractual agreements necessary to ensure a firm foundation for project financing. Required insurance and security packages are also evaluated and changes and additions are made to validate project financeability. The financial aspects of due diligence at a minimum involve validation of the project's economic evaluation, completeness of contracts, adequacy of the financial model, and sufficiency of the cash flow and the proposed financing structure.

III. **Host government guarantees.** These are guarantees that in most cases should span the lifecycle of the project and the majority of them are found in the implementation agreement. Starting with permitting and license duration, the host government guarantees should cover project site and environmental conditions and easy access to the project site and utilities. Additional host government guarantees can extend to project grants, local currency loans, and regulatory noninterference; certain operational aspects of the project company, and equity contributions and credit support when required.

IV. **ECA and multilateral institution involvement.** The participation of ECAs and multilateral institutions in a project finance deal is a major contributor to minimize project risks. This is so because these institutions bring discipline to project structuring, and temper host government expectations and sponsor optimism. They also dictate the processes to be followed and the required analyses and documentation that need to be in place in order to obtain loans, insurance, credit support, and final project approval from them and project funding. ECA and multilateral institution involvement helps to successfully and expeditiously resolve conflicts between stakeholders induced by project risks.

10.7 RISK MANAGEMENT BENEFITS, CHALLENGES AND SUCCESS FACTORS

The most basic benefit of project risk identification is that it informs project stakeholders of potential threats and subsequent losses if threats materialize. The analysis of risks identified goes deeper and examines the sources and causes of those risks and provides insights as to how they should be addressed effectively at the root-cause level. The benefit of the risk management evaluation process is that it uses the sponsor's internal expertise and external advice to assign ranges of likelihood of occurrence and it estimates the interaction and impact of different risks. The risk mitigation component is where all the benefits of the earlier risk management parts come together in effectively screening and prioritizing, avoiding, allocating, sharing, insuring, or absorbing risks in a fair and equitable manner among project stakeholders best able to handle. Only when risk mitigation is performed well does expected project value have reasonable chances of being realized.

The monitoring, tracking, auditing, and reporting aspect of the risk management progression is of equal importance because it helps detect risks as they begin to materialize. This helps understand the causes of events triggering risk occurrence, prepare effective responses, and make suitable changes to minimize risk impacts. Taken together, the benefits of effective risk management manifest themselves in reduced additional capital requirements, quicker contract negotiations and financing close, lower cost of funding, and achievement of project objectives. Another benefit that is often omitted in the discussion of risk management is the identification of opportunities to increase value creation through different project structures, financing, contracts, and business plan enhancements. Here, identification of new opportunities opens up additional avenues to augment expected project value and lessons to apply in subsequent projects.

Effective risk management is necessary to build a foundation for project financing, but it comes at significant costs. The reason costs need to be considered is because they can guide the decision of where to stop mitigation and prepare for risk absorption, project restructuring, or even abandonment of the project. The costs of project risk management evolve around the following cost elements:

1. Sponsor company's human resources from different departments are assigned risk management responsibilities
2. Fees and expenses of external advisors and consultants for research, data and information gathering, verification and validation, and preparation of expert opinion reports
3. Incremental cost for more in-depth project lifecycle analyses and evaluations undertaken to strengthen the project economic evaluation and the due diligence report
4. Various types of funding, institution, and private insurance contracts, and security packages
5. Development and negotiation of balanced and sustainable contracts supporting effective risk management
6. Creation of response plans, changes in project company operations, and options to mitigate risks appearing on the horizon
7. Contingency planning for risks determined to be unknowable or uncontrollable that could have severe, if not catastrophic, impacts on the project
8. Preparation of materials and convincing evidence of effective risk management used for project rating and in the project prospectus or information memorandum

A significant element usually overlooked in project finance is that of the opportunity cost. Namely, what other opportunities the sponsor company is foregoing by investing in the project. And, as is true with every other aspect of project finance, a well-considered balance of interests, costs, and benefits to different stakeholders in risk allocation goes a long way towards making contracts and agreements sustainable over the long run. It also helps in avoiding costly litigation and project value destruction.

Risk management is of high importance in project finance, but sometimes it is left to external advisors or legal experts to administer it because it involves contracts and agreements. We also observe that project teams undertaking this effort alone get lost in the process and end up giving that responsibility over to advisors, the lender group, and insurance agents. Often, data used in risk assessment do not always reflect the actual state of the project context, which is always evolving. This is true especially when the project context is not monitored properly. Additionally, risk tradeoffs are difficult to evaluate because of the many soft, qualitative types of information that are available and because they are not always subject to negotiations.

Risk management usually deals only with identified and known project risks while every other risk is lumped under contingency planning. Often, contingency planning is considered beyond the scope of project teams' responsibilities. Only in sponsor organizations does risk management include contingency planning, which is based on scenario simulation and scenario planning. Even in those instances, preparations for unforeseen events are mostly left to external experts or the project company's prospective management team to manage. Lastly, a lack of early warning systems and an ability and capability to respond are challenges to risk management, especially in the absence of forecast realization and response planning.

The sketch of a more effective risk management method is illustrated in Figure 10.7. The main features of this method are the following:

1. Project risks are a subset of uncertainty facing all stakeholders with different ambiguity levels. Collective assessment of uncertainty helps narrow the risk domain

2. Uncertainty may not involve all risks and risks may involve some uncertainty around sources and impacts

3. Communication is crucial and deals with disseminating information about the different parts of risk management to project participants at different times

4. Risk management is not only a sponsor's concern; it is shared by participants whose interests are better served by cooperating and coordinating individual risk management activities

5. Risk management is enhanced by soliciting and learning from the experiences of project participants and even from earlier competitor activities

6. Agreements on risk allocation and sharing are far quicker to reach and more effective when approached from a common platform

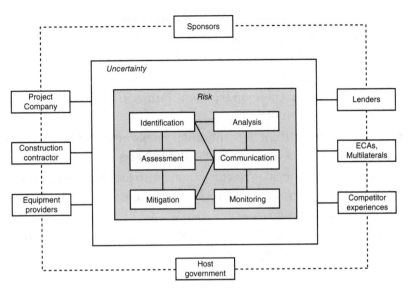

Figure 10.7 Broad Method to Project Risk Management

Risk management success factors are activities and undertakings that ensure a project reaches its objectives effectively. Experience and lessons learned in this area suggest that successful risk management is characterized by the following elements:

1. A risk management culture and mindset that permeates the project sponsor organization

2. The risk management function and its processes are integrated with those of the PFO, strategic planning, financial planning, and business development functions

3. Strong senior management support and funding to ensure organization-wide commitment to effective risk management, a prerequisite to obtaining competitive advantage

4. Sponsors build risk management capabilities with adequate resources allocated to team member training and development of a system to monitor risks on an ongoing basis

5. Project managers define the responsibilities assigned to risk management team members, pay attention to the processes used, and ensure knowledge to implement them

6. Undertaking risk management early, starting with an assessment of the RFP and the prefeasibility screening of the project and involving experts from appropriate functional areas to assess risks related to those areas

7. Risk management requires asking "what if," "why," and "why not" to understand the nature of risks and determine actions to take to mitigate their impact

8. Risk management builds on earlier internal project experiences and lessons learned as well as on the research and benchmarking of other companies with breadth and depth of experiences

9. Participation of all project stakeholders affected by risk management working from a common base to prioritize their activities and agree on the allocation of risks

10. Risks are prioritized after thorough assessment and based on a high probability of occurrence, high-impact basis

11. Sound project management judgment, trust, and reliance on risk management experts, and verifying if the right decisions are made and ensuing actions taken

12. Close monitoring of project development, financing, construction, and project company operations

CHAPTER 11

Project Due Diligence

A Pillar of Viability and Financeability

A good part of the project evaluation is done in the project development stage and summarized in the feasibility study. As a project moves along the assessment process, new data and information is obtained, additional analyses and evaluations are performed, and when the decision to move forward is made, the due diligence takes place. The due diligence is paid by the sponsor(s) and done primarily for the benefit of lenders, but sponsor(s) and other project stakeholders benefit from it and may be involved to some degree to ensure that the proposed project structure meets their objectives.

The intent of the feasibility study is to provide a common understanding of project particulars to participants and specify items they are committed to after financial close. The project due diligence is a thorough investigation to confirm data, information, and representations made before entering into project agreements leading to financial close. It is an extension of the feasibility study and its focus is on identifying missing information, validating analyses and evaluations performed, and establishing that the risk management and security package are complete and adequate to ensure project bankability.

The due diligence is performed to give the funding sources a critical, independent, and objective assessment of the project's viability and provide a reasonable comfort level concerning risk assessment and mitigation effectiveness. To do that, the due diligence first reassesses each stakeholder's ability to deliver on current and future requirements and, by extension, their qualification to share in the project benefits. The due diligence is thought of as a form of project risk management validation because it:

1. Confirms the accuracy of technical and financial data provided and the credibility of the engineering, technical, and economic aspects of the project

2. Validates the processes, analyses, methods, tools, and techniques used to evaluate the technical and financial project feasibility and project value creation

3. Tests and validates the assumptions and the baseline scenario underlying the cost and revenue projections and the project financial viability

4. Substantiates that a thorough and complete risk identification and mitigation are performed on a fair, reasonable, and the best-equipped party to bear remainder risks basis

5. Confirms that negotiated contracts adequately address all areas of concern to stakeholders and are enforceable in the host country

6. Validates and verifies that the project financial model is well structured and its inputs and outputs tested and found acceptable

The project due diligence is crucial to determine project funding needs and project viability and financeability. Its approach, depth, and requirements vary by project size, scope, and potential risk impacts; the nature of project finance due diligence is exhibited in Figure 11.1. It shows the many sides of due diligence and the functions it serves, which are discussed in ensuing sections. Section 11.1 tallies the main costs of project due diligence, which are fully justified by the many benefits derived from it. The first part is due diligence on the host country and industry to determine whether conditions are adequate to undertake a project. This is the subject of Section 11.2. Section 11.3 is a brief introduction to the technical due diligence that confirms if the engineering and design aspects meet project specifications and requirements.

Environmental due diligence is the topic of Section 11.4 to confirm that no adverse environmental and social effects are produced by the project, while Section 11.5 discusses the project's commercial aspect of due diligence. The validation of the adequacy of project contracts and agreements is the legal due diligence—an important part to confirm that project financing can reasonably be expected to develop—and this is dealt with in Section 11.6. The various financial considerations are enumerated in Section 11.7 and discussed in more detail in Chapters 13 and 14.

Operational aspects are verified and validated in the operational due diligence part, which is presented in Section 11.8 in order to provide assurances of continuity of operations. The crux of the project due diligence, however, is the risk management part that is discussed in Section 11.9. If its findings are unduly negative, the project is subject to restructure, additional support, or even termination. Other due diligence considerations that do not fit well in the above categories are presented in Section 11.10. Lastly, Section 11.11 discusses the due diligence report, its assessment, and quality characteristics.

11.1 DUE DILIGENCE COSTS AND BENEFITS

Project finance due diligence is usually performed by the lenders' advisors in cooperation with the sponsor's project team and is paid by the sponsor company. However, in companies possessing or wishing to get competitive advantage, project due diligence is undertaken by the project team starting at the concept stage and prefeasibility study to the end of the project development stage and completion of the project economic evaluation. It continues to the construction stage and then a different orientation for due diligence takes place in the operations and maintenance stage of the project.

When a good part of the due diligence is done by the sponsor's project team, the lender's advisor involvement and costs are reduced and its effectiveness is unquestionably superior. The upfront internal costs of the due

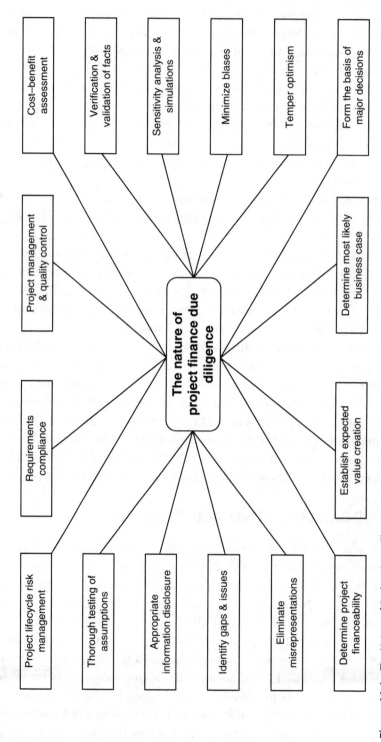

Figure 11.1 The Nature of Project Due Diligence

228

diligence include the development of systems and training for the project team on the due diligence process and associated activities. The external due diligence costs are recurring costs and consist of lender advisors' fees and expenses. Recurring sponsor costs are the cost of sponsor-project team members involved in the due diligence. The due diligence is a form of and an extension of risk management and despite all the effort that is expanded, it can be subject to errors due to misrepresentations, wrong impact estimates, and misinformed decisions whose costs cannot be estimated beforehand.

The benefits of a thorough project due diligence far outweigh its costs and limitations and includes the following paybacks:

1. Results in a better understanding of the sponsor company's operations and reduces exposure to high costs of damage control and remediation activities

2. Helps to set more realistic timeframes for project activities and processes as well as better stakeholder expectations

3. Enhances prospects for achieving better project outcomes and it is more effective when integrated with strategic and financial planning and new business development functions

4. Provides higher levels of comfort by focusing on the critical threats to sponsor, customer, construction contractor, and debt and equity investor concerns

5. Addresses project performance, economic viability, financeability and delivery issues, and communicates findings to participants from a common platform

6. Optimizes project scope evaluation and planning before decisions are made when all stakeholders are involved early in the process

7. Identifies and helps mitigate potential project threats to the stakeholders' satisfaction and minimizes cost, delivery time deviations, and unexpected problems

8. Uses a risk register and implements a risk-monitor system to create a better stakeholder communication, cooperation, coordination, and collaboration platform

9. Results in improved transparency of project economics, enhanced image and reputation of the sponsor company, and higher industry analyst recommendations and decreased capital costs (OECD, June 2016)

10. Improves project financeability efficiency and effectiveness and enhances chances of project success

11. Contributes to creation of competitive advantage in project development and financing for the sponsor company

11.2 HOST COUNTRY AND INDUSTRY DUE DILIGENCE

The first and early part of due diligence is the validation of findings about the host country's political, legal, economic, and investment environment evaluation because of the critical role the host government and ceding agency play in the structure, regulation, and support of the project. Hence, it is important that the due diligence provides sufficient comfort to decision makers concerning the following considerations:

1. The host country's macroeconomic environment assessment does not signal potential threat due to gross domestic product (GDP), inflation, income distribution concerns, and trade and foreign-exchange restrictions beyond those addressed by insurance coverage

2. The central and local host government's political environment is sufficiently stable and if there are outstanding threats, they are handled by political risk insurance

3. Local partners are vetted and have been determined to have the means to facilitate the bid submission properly and expeditiously

4. The host government and ceding authority have the ability to deliver on current financial and other commitments and future obligations

5. The transparency and fairness of the bid process and selection have sufficient political support in the host government agencies

6. Regulatory authority posture on the current industry structure, competition, pricing and regime flexibility is confirmed as not posing threats to project company operations

7. Megatrend and subtrend impacts on the industry and the project prospects are taken into account and included in the evaluation of the demand for project company's output

8. There are no reservations about the scope of the project as defined and that it meets host government and customer or user needs and fills the existing capacity gap in its industry

9. Political, economic, social, technological, legal, educational, and demographic (PESTLED) analyses and evaluations are correct and have been incorporated in the design, capacity, and performance requirements and the cost and demand and revenue forecasts

10. Key host government and sponsor interests and objectives are mostly harmonized and lesser, outstanding issues are identified to become part of negotiations

11. The likelihood that a host country's economic risk turns into a political risk is determined to be low, and how to deal with that outcome is addressed in legal documents

12. The relationship of the host country with export credit agencies (ECAs), multilaterals, and other funding sources is found to be acceptable based on past project history

11.3 TECHNICAL DUE DILIGENCE

Technical due diligence deals with issues starting from the request for a proposal to the project operations stage having to do with design, engineering, technology, and equipment used. Thus, it is intended to validate that risks originating in this area are identified and mitigated to the project stakeholders' satisfaction. Technical innovation and productivity enhancement considerations drive the introduction of new engineering, technology, and equipment as well as construction and operation processes. For that, it is important that the due diligence ensures the absence of problems, issues, and expensive fixes in this area by:

1. Confirming that contracts specify that proven technologies and well-tested equipment and engineering processes are used in the project
2. Validating that the design, technology, and engineering specifications of the project proposal meet the requirements of the project implementation or concession agreement
3. Confirming that the technical area processes and deliverables are fully integrated with the main project management processes
4. Validating projected capital expenditures and their reasonableness and ensuring project-company operating costs are included in the financial model evaluations
5. Ensuring that technical aspects of the engineering, procurement, and construction (EPC) contract are fully addressed and construction progress monitoring systems are in place
6. Verifying the project experience and competence as well as the financial strength of the EPC contractor are respectable
7. Ensuring the reasonableness and feasibility of the construction schedule and budget estimates and allowances for minor deviations and slippages
8. Making sure that the technical and engineering aspects of all project company agreements and contracts are reviewed and approved by the project stakeholders
9. Determining that there are no engineering, technical, or equipment issues foreseen in the construction and operations stages that may become risks

10. Validating the reasonableness of the project company's operating assumptions included in its business plan, such as input and output requirements, performance standards, etc.

11. Substantiating the operations and management (O&M) company's experience and reputation and validating the accuracy of the O&M cost estimates

12. Verifying that independent engineering and technical experts have approved the design, engineering, and equipment specifications and performance requirements

11.4 ENVIRONMENTAL DUE DILIGENCE

Major environmental pollution problems and the health, economic, and social effects associated with large industrial and infrastructure projects have increased public awareness that measures should be in place to ensure that they do not repeat themselves in new projects. Hence, the environmental due diligence is usually performed by specialized consultants in environmental issues, although some tasks are performed by the sponsor's technical and legal teams. To ensure that the project does not have adverse environmental impacts, the due diligence in this area must:

1. Verify that all permits have been issued and ownership rights and obligations are assigned to project sponsors and other equity providers according to their contributions

2. Confirm that visits to the project site have determined the suitability of the site, the terrain, and other pertinent factors

3. Ascertain that there is passable road access to the site and uninterrupted availability of power, communications, and other utilities

4. Show that environmental investigations by external experts found no adverse issues, defects, or wrong use by the site's previous occupants

5. Substantiate that every aspect of the project is in compliance with host country laws and Equator Principles

Equator Principles is a risk management approach to determine, assess, and manage environmental and social risks in project finance ventures that is used to provide a process for the due diligence to support responsible decision making.

6. Ensure that the project location is not a historical site and that there are no indications of archeological findings that could cause construction delays

7. Determine that there are no emissions, noise, and project company discharges affecting employees, polluting the environment, or impacting adversely the local economy

8. Confirm that environmental studies show that there are no adverse effects on the local population and neighboring communities' health and safety or other concerns

9. Ensure that stakeholders have reviewed, approved, and recognized as valid the findings of the independent expert's environmental assessment

10. Substantiate that there are host government processes to address future potential financial dislocation impacts due to construction of project facilities and its operations

11.5 COMMERCIAL DUE DILIGENCE

Commercial due diligence provides confirmation of the evidence produced concerning project economic viability and additional indications of bankability. It entails verification and validation of thorough analyses and evaluations of the project company's market, customer or user needs, industry structure and competition, rate and tariff regulation, and government subsidies. The purpose of the commercial due diligence is to:

1. Confirm the accuracy of the host government's identification and quantification of customer and user needs and that they are consistent with findings of the sponsor's market research

2. Validate the market research and industry studies' findings that there is a sufficiently large market and a growing need for the project company's output

3. Establish that the project investment in the host country enjoys sufficient political support in all agencies involved based on the project meeting their needs and value for money

4. Verify that the current industry and regulatory structures are favorable and do not adversely impact the project company's operations and prospects

5. Substantiate that, overall, contemplated industry and regulatory body changes and trends are advantageous to the project's success

6. Provide evidence of the existence of a substantial gap between current and needed capacity in the project's industry

7. Ensure that the issue of the operating license is on an exclusive basis and guarantees that if a second license needs to be issued, the project company will have first right of refusal

8. Confirm that past regulatory pricing rulings indicate a positive attitude of regulatory bodies towards price adjustments to ensure profitable project company operations

9. Establish that data, information, and assumptions used in demand and revenue projections are validated, are reasonable, and have passed stress and sanity checks

10. Demonstrate that the baseline and plausible scenarios entertained are realistic and convincing of their likelihood to occur, with black-swan events also considered

11. Ensure that influences of driving factors are well understood and project value realization plans are in place in the event assumptions and demand do not fully materialize

12. Establish that a reasonable project value realization plan is included in the project company's business plan

11.6 LEGAL DUE DILIGENCE

The legal due diligence is a collaborative effort among project stakeholders that helps establish validity of the big picture and processes of preparing and negotiating project documents. Its scope overlaps that of other due diligence areas, but it leads the process and provides solutions and suggestions to resolve stalemates and pending negotiation issues. The legal due diligence presents its findings, approvals, and disapprovals in relation to:

1. Protecting intellectual property rights concerning project design, engineering, operational processes and procedures, and information confidentiality of proprietary bid contents

2. Demonstrating that the project definition and specifications meet the terms and conditions of operating licenses and permits

3. Confirming that host government agencies are authorized by law and have the financial means to issue guarantees to sponsors and other private parties

4. Ensuring that project development, financing, and bid submission are in compliance with the Foreign Corrupt Practices Act and local laws, rules, and regulations

5. Identifying agencies involved and verifying the transparency and fairness of the host government's bidding, procurement, and selection process used in the contract award

6. Confirming that the project company's concession or license is issued on an exclusive basis for the duration of the project company's economic life

7. Ensuring that the scope of the license and permits issued provide adequate protection from unfavorable future regulatory rulings

8. Ascertaining that the terms and conditions of the license or concession provide host government guarantees of support for a profitable operating environment

9. Making sure that the no/limited recourse to the sponsors' condition is protected by the project contracts and agreements for the entire project life

10. Substantiating that government in-kind contributions are fairly valued and their delivery-timing commitments are included in project agreements

11. Verifying that sponsor and other participant debt or equity contribution commitments are backed by adequate guarantees

12. Ensuring that performance and price guarantees in project company contracts provide sufficient protection for future cash flows and return to investors

13. Demonstrating the suitability and adequacy of cost overrun, completion, and performance guarantees by the EPC contractor

14. Confirming that all environmental, technical, commercial, and operating risks have been identified and properly mitigated and contingent liabilities identified and recorded

15. Verifying the completeness of all contracts and the development of an insurance package powerful enough to ensure project profitability

16. Attesting to the balance and fairness of the project risk allocation to relevant project stakeholders on the best able to manage basis

17. Ensuring that the project company structure maximizes tax benefits and the optimized financing structure maximizes project value.

11.7 FINANCIAL DUE DILIGENCE

The focus of the project financial due diligence is primarily on the validation of the project economics, the evaluation and the project financial model and its output, and the adequacy of the security package and project support. Thus, the aim of the financial due diligence is to establish a solid factual foundation and determine whether the financial data and information coming out of the feasibility study and subsequent updates are true and consistent to use for project cost estimates and revenue forecasts. Because of the importance of financial due diligence, issues related to validation of financial data, analyses, and evaluations are further discussed in Chapters 13 and 14.

Project financial due diligence is generally based on four basic principles: Independence, prudence in using a professionally skeptical approach, comprehensiveness, and materiality according to levels of risk. Thus, the scope of the financial due diligence is to show adherence to those principles along the following areas of investigation:

1. Confirming the ability of project stakeholders to deliver on debt and equity requirements, guarantees, and other agreed to contributions
2. Ensuring that tax efficiencies are maximized and that the structure of the deal, based on the financial model parameters, is optimized
3. Verifying that the sponsor and other project participant equity contributions and contingency equity commitments are properly documented in contractual agreements
4. Double-checking the market size and industry growth estimates and validating the methods and techniques used to come up with project costs and revenue forecasts
5. Investigating, checking, testing, and validating data and assumptions for reasonableness, reliability, and consistency with industry norms, benchmarked practices, and earlier sponsor or competitor experiences
6. Validating, stress testing, and substantiating the reasonableness of results and scenarios used to forecast the project company's product or service demand and revenue
7. Confirming that sufficient and growing physical and cyberspace security protection asset and technology costs are included in the project company's business plan
8. Corroborating the adequacy of the project company's business plan and the implements needed to execute it successfully
9. Demonstrating the validity and accuracy of the project company's financial management and reporting systems and adherence of its financial statements to sponsor and host country accounting standards
10. Confirming the validity and inclusion of sufficient physical and cyberspace security expenses in the total project cost estimates
11. Ensuring thoroughness and completeness of the project risk identification, assessment, allocation, and mitigation

12. Determining the availability of options and adequacy of insurance packages to cover the entire spectrum of project risks

13. Showing how changes in factors driving project value affect the project's economic viability and financeability, and ways to affect positive changes through these factors

14. Demonstrating robust project company economics and that its prospects are not materially affected by less favorable scenarios materializing than the baseline scenario

15. Providing evidence that areas of synergies and improved project company performance have been investigated and included in its business plan

16. Demonstrating how well the project company's borrowing capacity is supported by the debt-cover ratios and other financial model measures

17. Ensuring that there are no omitted or improperly recorded contingent liabilities in the project company's business plan

18. Confirming that there are adequate internal project company controls to ensure sustainable operations for the duration of its license

19. Providing convincing evidence that the project's expected value creation is well within the conservative and achievable range of revenue simulations

11.8 OPERATIONAL DUE DILIGENCE

Operational due diligence includes review of a wide range of operational areas across the project company, including regulatory compliance, O&M company experience and qualifications. It is a complementary, detail-oriented effort to uncover unexpected weaknesses in the project company's business plan using personal interviews and sponsor company internal communications. Sponsors also look at this part of due diligence to uncover potential synergies not included in project financials, but which could be exploited with commencement of operations.

The operational due diligence requires that the following activities are performed in accordance of project processes and participant needs:

1. Confirming no risks are embedded in the project company's business plan and that opportunities for operational performance target enhancement are addressed

2. Showing the effectiveness of the sponsor's management control over the project company's operation and financial reporting systems

3. Validating the reasonableness and consistency of the project company business plan's components and financial performance targets from both the sponsor's and the project company's management perspective

4. Substantiating the presence of appropriate project company management skills and qualifications and adequately trained labor

5. Verifying that operational skills and capabilities are included in the human resource part of the business plan and adequate funding allocated to training

6. Establishing that key personnel contracts are prepared with market place remuneration packages for the duration of the contracts

7. Verifying that secondments and managerial talent infusion from the sponsor(s) takes place when needed are documented in the shareholder agreement

8. Ascertaining the O&M company's good past record and reputation and performance quality in earlier projects

9. Providing assurances that the project company's policies are in compliance with the Foreign Corrupt Practices Acts and with local health, labor, and safety laws

10. Confirming that sufficient and growing physical and cyberspace security protection asset and technology costs are included in the project company's business plan

11. Establishing evidence of ongoing sponsor support to the project company in terms of ability to deliver on debt and equity contributions obligations

12. Demonstrating that the project company's cash flow management plan satisfies stakeholder requirements, excess cash distributions, and reporting needs

13. Confirming the availability, delivery, and quality of project company production inputs and supplies are documented in the supply agreement

14. Verifying the strength of the offtake agreement under different operating, economic, and regulatory environments

15. Ensuring the adequacy of the project company's reporting requirements concerning operating performance measures, human resources, and financial data

16. Determining the project company's ability to course correct in the event business plan projections do not materialize as expected

17. Identifying potential synergies between the project company's operations and other project stakeholder operations in the host country or region

18. Verifying that O&M company processes and procedures are in place and that the project company retains adequate internal controls over key operational decisions

19. Ensuring proper alignment of the project company with equity contributor interests and creation of a conflict resolution process

20. Ensuring the adequacy of the project company relationship management plan with the ceding and regulatory agencies, the sponsor group, and the funding sources

11.9 RISK MANAGEMENT DUE DILIGENCE

The risk management due diligence refers to the effort of ensuring that all risk elements are identified, and their relationships defined, occurrence probabilities are estimated, and consequences critically assessed. It also refers to how risk events are prioritized using the project risk matrix technique and how risk mitigation is planned and implemented. It involves a review of the other due diligence parts and guaranteeing that there are no apparent omissions, miscalculations, and threats left uncovered. The risk management due diligence components involve the following confirmations:

> A project risk matrix is a commonly used risk management tool to define the different levels of risk by their probability of occurrence along rows and their impact along columns and to draw attention to high-probability, high-impact events and rank them by the product of these two elements.

1. Confirming that all identifiable project risks are assessed, ranked, and mitigated and risks that are identifiable but not measurable can be assumed with minor impacts

2. Ensuring that the project risk management stage had the benefit of input from all functional area experts, the project team, and external advisors

3. Showing which project threats require what collective action, when, and from which project stakeholder

4. Validating the findings of the risk matrix analysis and showing which risks are covered by contracts and insurance and which are not and their impact on project value

5. Demonstrating the effectiveness of decisions and response plans to adverse events and the response strategies to be used

6. Confirming how well the web of project contracts and agreements covers risks, provides enough assurances, and ensures project financeability

7. Confirming that independent external advisors and experts have reviewed and approved the risk management package for the project

8. Attesting to the validity of the due diligence findings included in its final report by a third, independent, and objective party

9. Establishing that the project company's employees integrity risks are recognized and insured against

10. Verifying the compliance of partners, intermediaries, agents, and counterparties to the Foreign Corruptions Practices Act and OECD and World Bank guidelines dealing with corruption and fraud issues

11.10 GENERAL AREAS OF DUE DILIGENCE

This is an area of due diligence where risk factors that do not fit well in other categories are included and may contain elements such as:

1. Establishing the objectivity and thoroughness of the sponsor and the project company SWOT analysis and ensuring project team ability to execute the project successfully

2. Ascertaining that the project is well positioned externally and the political support it has gathered in the host government and the local community is acceptable

3. Confirming the project's strong internal support and management commitment vis-à-vis the sponsor company's risk tolerance

4. Demonstrating that cyberspace threats are well understood and likely threats assessed as part of the security program delivery and crisis response

5. Verifying that cyberspace response plans are in place to detect and recognize a crisis, manage it effectively, and remediate cyberspace threats

6. Ensuring that a mature, risk-based information security program that mitigates unique project security risks is build, tested, and certified functioning as planned

7. Substantiating that training costs are included in the project company's operating costs for security management to crisis and kidnap response in addition to physical security costs

8. Validating the assessment of project participant skills and competencies in project development and project finance

9. Establishing participation and multilateral institution project support through contact facilitation and guidance of independent project finance advisors

10. Confirming that the project due diligence has included occurrence of black swans in the scenario simulation analysis and adequate thought has been given to managing occurrence of risks outside the risk matrix analysis with appropriate contingency planning

11.11 REPORT, ASSESSMENT, AND QUALITY CHARACTERISTICS

The information gathering and verifying aspect of due diligence is half of the work needed in order to benefit by it. The other half is evaluating its findings and developing recommendations on whether to proceed and do required changes to make the project company a better structured, run, and sustainable operation. This is a unique contribution of the due diligence effort and the more that is invested in it, the greater the ability to implement the project successfully, harness performance improvements, and create possible future synergies.

To be effectively communicated, the information and findings of the due diligence is organized by due diligence category. A good presentation approach to all project stakeholders is the due diligence report and assessment matrix of Table 11.1. For each due diligence area, the principal factors listed are: new data and information obtained, items verified and referenced, unusual transactions or events, positive and negative findings, guarantees and insurance, and action items. An important feature of the due diligence report and assessment matrix is that responsibilities are clearly

Table 11.1 Due Diligence Report and Assessment Matrix

Due Diligence Area	New Data and Information	Items Verified and Referenced	Unusual Practices and Events	Positive Findings	Negative Findings	Guarantees and Insurance	Action Items
Host country							
Technical							
Environmental							
Commercial							
Legal							
Financial							
Operational							
Risk management							
Customer or user							
Supplier							
Other							

delineated and assigned to associates with experience in the different functional areas.

The analysis of information, materials, and input obtained takes place in order for the due diligence to validate the project company's prospects in its entirety. Once the analysis is completed, the evaluation of impacts is summarized in the due diligence report, which brings together findings, analysis, and the implications of findings and provides a set of recommendations for decision makers. The due diligence report must be concise and show the assessment of findings and their impact on the project and all affected stakeholders and its recommendations should be specific and clearly articulated to the project team. Once the lender and project teams have digested the report and its recommendations, a briefing of other project stakeholders takes pace. At that point, the project team and the lender draw their own conclusions on how to proceed with the project based on their assessment of the findings. Reconciliation of views may be achieved through changes in project structuring and support required from different stakeholders.

The items included in the due diligence report vary according to project particulars, but should at least include the following items:

1. Summary listing of the due diligence findings concerning the project's technical feasibility, economic viability, and credit worthiness and security agreements

2. Show the lenders' review of the due diligence report and their assessment of the project's economic viability

3. Outline areas of additional analyses and evaluations needed to uncover more information and identify risks heretofore not identifiable

4. Recommend actions the project team needs to address and obtain additional support and insurance coverage

5. Make suggestions on changes needed to optimize the project financing structure and the project company's profitability

6. Raise questions and suggest additional plausible scenarios for project team members to investigate and prepare plans to address adverse eventualities

7. Opine on the project financial model architecture, assumptions, inputs, and outputs, and the validity of their evaluations

The due diligence phase is crucial in creating a sound basis for the decision to proceed with a project and contributes to project success. Experienced project teams begin the due diligence effort in the prefeasibility stage before full-blown project assessment begins, and use external experts and lenders to finalize it as negotiations are coming to an end. On the other hand, inexperienced project teams leave the due diligence effort until the negotiations stage. By that point, there is insufficient time to do a thorough investigation of project's risks or verify the representations of other stakeholders and generate the information needed to make right decisions.

Objectivity in analysis and interpretation of findings is another key quality characteristic of an effective due diligence, which requires experience and industry knowledge to assess issues properly. In acquisition and joint-venture projects, the due diligence covers many other elements, but any effective due diligence must be speedy and bring issues to conclusion rapidly. The due diligence report should also include recommendations concerning the ability to manage risks when they materialize and how to obtain potential synergies.

The last two elements of project due diligence quality are completeness of due diligence and effective communications during and after the report is issued. The due diligence recommendations must be supported by facts and communicated in such terms that the meaning is conveyed clearly and its language does not create overly negative impressions. That is, the basis of recommendations is included in a minimum-impact phrasing developed for the information memorandum and other external purposes. The internal communications are done by the project manager and the lead lender, while externally they are handled by experienced public affairs or investor relations personnel and external advisors (at appropriate times).

CHAPTER 12

Funding Sources and Programs

Essential Knowledge and Alliances

M ost large capital infrastructure projects are not pure project finance deals; instead, they involve the participation of several funding sources and the use of various facilities and instruments. Thus, the discussion of funding-source programs and instruments for international infrastructure projects is an introduction to pragmatic project finance. In the sections that follow, we present in summary the major funding institutions and facilities made available by official and private sources.

Multilateral and bilateral institutions play a major role in international project finance and their close relationships with governments enables them to manage difficult credit issues and coordinate financing for projects. In addition to help in project finance, funding institutions offer important nonfunding services, such as the knowledge and expertise they bring to project development and their influence on host governments to move projects forward.

The role of funding sources is to provide financing for viable projects, but in order to make funding available, they perform reasonableness checks and become drivers of processes and mobilize resources. These advantages, however, can result in extending project timelines because of the discipline introduced by their particular approval processes. Figure 12.1 gives a picture of the official funding sources that commonly participate in international project financings.

In Section 12.1 we preview multilateral, bilateral, and unilateral institution funding programs and instruments. Section 12.1.1 briefly explains the World Bank, International Monetary Fund (IMF), New Development

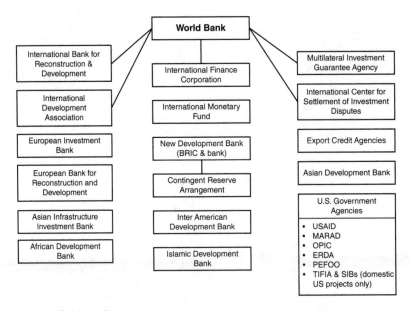

Figure 12.1 Official Funding Sources

246

Bank (NDB), and contingent reserve arrangement (CRA) programs and instruments, while Section 12.1.2 deals with those of regional development banks. The programs provided by the US EXIM Bank to exporters of capital goods and services or to importing customers are representative of those of developed countries and are addressed in Section 12.1.3. Many countries around the world have their own government programs to support economic development and infrastructure projects. However, the loan terms and support levels of ECAs vary widely from country to country. Hence, the discussion of Section 12.1.4 is limited to domestic US federal and state financing programs.

Section 12.2 deals with the variety of private-sector funding sources and instruments. First in this discussion are the private-equity channels and facilities discussed in Section 12.2.1. Project-debt channels and facilities are the topic of Section 12.2.2. Other private and public-sector project funding instruments that are often used are shown in Section 12.2.3. Due to the importance of multilateral institutions, ECAs, and regional development bank funding, Section 12.3 discusses their roles in funding infrastructure projects, their requirements, and the benefits of their participation that make a difference in projects.

12.1 OFFICIAL PROJECT FINANCE SOURCES

The official project finance sources of funding and facilities discussed in this section include the World Bank, the International Monetary Fund (IMF), the New Development Bank (NDB) and its Contingent Reserve Arrangement (CRA), regional development banks, export credit agencies, and other US government agencies. The discussion is based on the website materials of respective institutions and the OECD (2015); it should be noted that not all programs and instruments are available for all infrastructure projects in all countries.

12.1.1 World Bank and IMF

The World Bank and the IMF were created by the Bretton Woods Agreement to, among other major issues, promote economic development and support international monetary cooperation. Their role and participation in financings is changing in order to meet new economic challenges and development needs.

I. World Bank

The mandate of the World Bank is to promote long-term economic development and alleviate poverty. It provides technical and financial support to help low income countries implement infrastructure and social need projects with funding from member country contributions and issuance of bonds. The World Bank has played a major role in international project finance and roughly two thirds of World Bank financed projects provided support for private-sector development. World Bank support is provided through technical advice and financial backing via its three major arms:

A. **International Bank for Reconstruction and Development (IBRD).** This bank invests in economic development projects along with providing technical assistance and training to ensure adequate project support. IBRD provides loans at market rates for part of financing needed in a project and the rest is cofinanced by regional development banks (RDBs).

B. **International Finance Corporation (IFC).** This corporation provides advisory services, direct loans, and equity investments in profitable projects to fill private-sector financing gaps. IFC loans are cost based and at floating interest rates.

C. **The Multilateral Investment Guarantee Agency (MIGA).** This agency insures investments in developing countries against political risk and works closely with IBRD and IFC to provide financing packages for infrastructure projects.

The two other parts of the World Bank are the International Development Association (IDA) and the International Center for Settlement of Investment Disputes (ICSID). The former provides development aid to the poorest countries and the latter provides assistance to settle project issues and disputes effectively.

II. International Monetary Fund

The IMF's mandate is to promote international monetary cooperation and provide advice and technical assistance to build strong market economies. The IMF helps member countries with policy programs to address government deficits and balance-of-payments problems. It does not make loans directly to specific development programs or projects but it does help indirectly. IMF loans to governments help to manage their deficits, which may be due to borrowing accumulated from implementing vital infrastructure projects. However, IMF facilities are conditioned on the receiving country agreeing to implement economic policies and directives in order to obtain IMF loans.

The World Bank and the IMF work closely to ensure effective collaboration and coordination of programs through consultations on international economics, finance developments and trends, and resource requirements to fund low income country development.

12.1.2 New Development Bank and Contingent Reserve Account

The New Development Bank, also known as the BRICS Development Bank, and its Contingent Reserve Arrangement were established in 2016 by the five BRICS countries: Brazil, Russia, India, China, and South Africa to provide an alternative to the World Bank and the IMF. Led by China, it was created to counterbalance western financial institutions based in Washington, DC. However, the World Bank and other multilateral development institutions intend to collaborate with NDB in infrastructure projects.

I. New Development Bank

The NDB's mandate is to mobilize financial resources for private and public sustainable infrastructure projects in BRICS and other emerging and developing countries. Its primary focus is on renewable energy, telecommunications and transportation, irrigation, water treatment, and sanitation projects. NDB provides loans, guarantees, equity participation, and other financial instruments. In 2016 it approved loans of $1.5 billion and in 2017 it will approve loans of $2.5 billion.

II. Contingent Reserve Arrangement

NDB established the CRA to be its own version and a competitor to the IMF. Its mandate is to support short term balance of payments problems by providing liquidity and loan support and to strengthen financial stability of member countries. CRA functions and support programs mirror those of the IMF.

12.1.3 Regional Development Banks

Regional development banks (RDBs) are owned by member countries, have developed skills that are specialized to their respective region's needs, and they serve as trusted advisors and partners of member-country governments. They are well funded to finance economic development and social need projects through low-interest loans, and foster innovation and support for large infrastructure project needs.

    I. **European Bank for Reconstruction and Development (EBRD).** It was created to introduce private initiatives and stimulate market based economic systems in central and eastern Europe. Now, it also has presence in southeastern Europe, the south and eastern Mediterranean, and Russia. EBRD provides assistance to projects that have substantial amounts of sponsor equity, pass stringent criteria, and benefit the host country's economic development. Its investments in project sector projects include fixed rate senior, subordinated, and mezzanine loans with project company insurance against insurable risks. EBRD also makes minority equity investments in profitable projects, provides guarantees to secure payments of letters of credit, bid and performance bonds, and other instruments.

II. **European Investment Bank (EIB).** It is a European Union (EU) member country owned bank which provides expertise and financing for sustainable projects that are in line with EU objectives. It provides up to 20% first loss support, mezzanine debt, standby financing, loan guarantee instruments, and capital grants for availability projects. EIB acts as a catalyst for financial institutions to fund projects by developing EU country capital markets.

III. **Asian Infrastructure Investment Bank (AIIB).** It is a China sponsored and based infrastructure development bank created to influence the global financial architecture with focus on fostering economic development of Asian countries. It provides private and sovereign financing for sustainable infrastructure and economic development projects with programs similar to those of other RDBs.

IV. **China Development Bank (CDB).** It is a state-owned investment institution created to raise funds for large infrastructure projects and support Chinese companies going abroad. It provides medium and long term financing for foreign investment in cooperation with the China EXIM Bank. Its products include loans and bond issues and interest rate, commodity, and foreign exchange risk management.

V. **China Africa Development Fund.** It is a Chinese private equity fund sponsored by the China Development Bank to facilitate investment in Africa by Chinese companies in natural resources, manufacturing, power generation, and transportation. It makes direct investments in companies and projects and quasi-equity facilities; the likes of preferred shares and convertible bonds.

VI. **Silk Road Fund.** It is a Chinese, state-owned holding company designed to promote China development and prosperity for countries along the Silk Road Economic Belt. It is the land-based component that together with the oceanic Maritime Silk Road forms One Belt, One Road. The Chinese government created this economic development framework to integrate trade and investment in Eurasia. Its focus is on building ports, roads, and rail links, urban transportation, forestry, and energy efficiency projects along the Silk Road Economic Belt.

> Silk Road, also known as Silk Route, is an ancient trade route connecting China with the West that carried goods and ideas between the two great civilizations of Rome and China. Silk was exported from China and wools and precious metals were imported to China from the West.

VII. **Asian Development Bank (ADB).** This is an Asia-focused institution promoting development and cooperation in the poorest countries in the world. It works with governments and financial institutions to provide technical and financial assistance to infrastructure projects, financial market development, and education. ADB offers project development grants and loans in hard or local currency at LIBOR rates and co-financing with ECA and commercial credit sources. Its Asian Development Fund (ADF) provides grants at concessionary terms to financial intermediaries to fund development projects and credit enhancement products.

VIII. **African Development Bank (AfDB).** This is focused on improving economic conditions and provides technical assistance and policy advice to regional member countries. AfDB mobilizes resources to fund development projects and eliminate poverty through funding of both public and private sector projects. It offers flexible multi-currency enhanced variable spread loans to customize debt repayment and several risk management products such as indexed loans, commodity hedges, and interest rate swaps. It also offers loan guarantees for borrowers to access commercial funding.

IX. **Inter-American Development Bank (IDB).** This is focused on financing economic and social development projects in Latin America and the Caribbean and offers a number of financing products including flexible financing facility loans, local currency financing, and guarantees in local currency. IDB offers guarantees to public and private sector borrowers for political risk and partial credit risk guarantees. It also offers concessional financing through blended loans from its Fund for Special Operations and ordinary capital at 0.25% and LIBOR-based rates.

X. **Islamic Development Bank (IsDB).** This is an international Islamic financial institution fostering economic development and social progress of member Muslim countries. IsDB provides financing for infrastructure projects consistent with sharia law, which prohibits interest or fees on loans. Its debt-like instruments include Morabaha, a short-term working capital financing; Salam, a purchase of assets to be delivered in the future; and Sukuk, an ownership instrument with properties similar to ownership of a bond. The equity-like instruments of IsDB include Modaraba and Mosharaka, which are both very much like western general partnership arrangements.

12.1.4 Export Credit Agencies

Export credit agencies (ECAs) are mostly government institutions created to support exports of domestic producers of goods and services used in infrastructure projects whose participation in 2009–2010 amounted to 5% of total project finance loans. During the 2011 to 2014 period, US Exim Bank new export support was $79.3 billion. In comparison, 2011 project-finance loans from OECD country ECAs were $213.5 billion. All developed countries have their own ECAs and their mandates vary widely between countries, but OECD member ECAs operate under the OECD Consensus Agreement. That agreement provides for a level playing field where competition is based on the price and quality of exported goods and services and not on the financial terms provided.

The US Export–Import Bank (US EXIM) is a major player in export financing of goods and services used in infrastructure projects and offers a number of support products typical of other ECAs' offerings. It offers several different programs to support project finance deals, which include the following:

1. Competitive, direct fixed-rate loans up to 12 and 18 years to foreign buyers of at least 50% US export contents, covering up to 85% of project value (which includes principal and interest)

2. Medium and long-term loan guarantees of 85% of exports plus 30% of local costs with a 15% buyer down payment

3. Working capital loan guarantees that are 90% loan-backing guarantees to banks issuing standby letters of credit or bid and performance bonds

4. Export credit insurance policies for foreign accounts receivable protection against buyer nonpayment risk

5. Protection against political risk at 100% and commercial default at 95%

The major commercial default risk factors are deteriorating economic conditions, drops in demand, adverse tariff changes, unexpected competition, technical obsolescence, and import–export restrictions.

In the project finance area, US EXIM provides loans and guarantees for new projects above $50 million in structures of 25% equity and 75% debt with the option of financing loans of 85% of export value to private borrowers with the following options:

a. Political risk coverage only in the pre-completion period

b. Political risk coverage only in pre-completion and comprehensive coverage post-completion

c. Political risk guarantee in pre-completion or no pre-completion coverage but only post-completion political risk coverage

One of the other US EXIM programs is the Engineering Multiplier Program, which involves support for architectural, industrial design, and engineering services in international projects. Also, the medical initiative program is helping the export of medical equipment from US-based companies to borrowers who are unable to obtain financing without US EXIM support. Another program is tied-aid financing, a government to government-based program, which is a mix of a large grant with a standard export credit of up to 10 years, or a credit with a repayment term of 20 to 30 years and interest rates lower than market rates.

12.1.5 Other US and State Government Agencies

There are several private and US government agencies created to provide long-term funding for projects within the United States and overseas. The funding and support of these agencies is of a relatively small scale with the exception of the US Agency for International Development (USAID) and the Overseas Private Investment Corporation (OPIC).

I. **US Agency for International Development (USAID).** Its focus is on eliminating poverty and promoting the development of democratic societies abroad. The USAID's Development Credit Authority made $4.0 billion in private finance available in the 1999 to 2016 period using risk-sharing agreements to mobilize local private capital to fill financing needs. First, it offers a 50% guarantee on loan principal backed by the US Treasury and guarantees on private-sector debt capital for up to 20 years. Additionally, the USAID provides grants to identify project requirements and for market research, business forecasts, bid solicitations and evaluations, and negotiation; that is, for project development.

II. **Overseas Private Investment Corporation (OPIC).** This US government agency works with financial institutions and mobilizes private capital to support development projects. OPIC provides long-term financing and guarantees to investments in developing and emerging market countries and cooperates with private funding sources to increase their lending capacity with commitments from one third for equity or debt to two thirds of total fund capitalizations. OPIC is also known for offering several types of political risk insurance; namely, currency inconvertibility, expropriation, political violence, regulatory risks, and other host government interference.

III. **Private Export Funding Corporation (PEFCO).** This is a US, privately owned institution; owned by commercial banks, industrial companies, and financial services companies. It makes medium and long-term fixed rate loans to foreign borrowers when such loans are not available from private-sector lenders; these loans have long disbursement and repayment periods. It is included with government funding entities because it supports commercial bank securitizations of US EXIM guarantee obligations

IV. **Maritime Administration (MARAD).** This US government agency is an arm of the US Department of Transportation that is responsible for ensuring the adequacy of the merchant marines to handle domestic and foreign waterborne commerce. MARAD and US EXIM bank have an arrangement to provide EXIM-guaranteed working capital loans for shipping, logistics, and other companies involved in the ocean transportation of US exports to foreign countries. Under this agreement, US EXIM increases its working capital guarantee to 95% of exported goods that ship on US flagged vessels.

V. **Energy Research and Development Administration (ERDA).** This is an agency of the US Department of Energy (DOE) that supports energy commercialization projects of DOE technologies and project management to deliver projects on schedule, within budget, and required performance. ERDA support to projects also requires compliance with environmental and health and safety standards. It performs independent reviews and cost estimates of projects and helps in the acquisition of capital assets for energy related projects. Furthermore, ERDA provides guarantees, assists investors in demonstrating the commercial viability of energy projects, and promotes the development of such projects.

VI. **Transportation Infrastructure Finance and Innovation Act (TIFIA).** The programs of this agency of the US Department of Transportation support only large domestic transportation infrastructure projects including highway, passenger rail, ports and airports, intelligent transportation systems, and other related projects. TIFIA invests in PPPs along with private investors in terms of direct loans, loan guarantees, and standby letters of credit to projects of national and regional importance. Credit assistance is usually capped at 33% of reasonably estimated project costs and senior debt and TIFIA loans must have investment grade ratings.

VII. **State Infrastructure Banks (SIBs).** Established by the US Department of Transportation, these are revolving infrastructure investment funds for surface-transportation projects that are created and managed by individual states. A SIB, much like a private bank, can offer a range of loans and credit assistance enhancement products to public and private sponsors of highway construction projects, transit capital projects, and railroad projects. SIBs offer loans for all or part of the cost of a project with flexible terms and at market or below market rates and short term construction funding or long term financing. They also provide letters of credit, bond insurance and loan guarantees, and security for bond or debt financing instruments.

12.2 PRIVATE SOURCES AND INSTRUMENTS

There is a large variety of private funding sources and instruments, but we concentrate on the most commonly used sources and instruments. This section also draws from OECD (2015) and Dewar (2010); Figure 12.2 is a pictorial summary of the private sources and instruments used in project finance. However, not all funding channels and facilities are open to all projects and host countries.

All project finance deals involve some sponsor or developer group equity in order to attract private debt investments and the debt/equity ratio is commonly viewed as a proxy for sponsor commitment to a project. Sponsors want high debt/equity ratios which mean high return on equity investments while lenders prefer lower debt/equity ratios to confirm sponsor commitment and provide some protection in the event of poor project company performance.

12.2.1 Project Equity

Equity in the form of ordinary share capital in project finance deals comes primarily from project sponsors or developers but, also, from construction and operation contractors, equipment providers, and financial institutions. Usually, project sponsor equity ranges between 20% and 30% of project value, but the higher the project risk, the larger the share of the sponsor or developer equity required to get lenders willing to lend to the project.

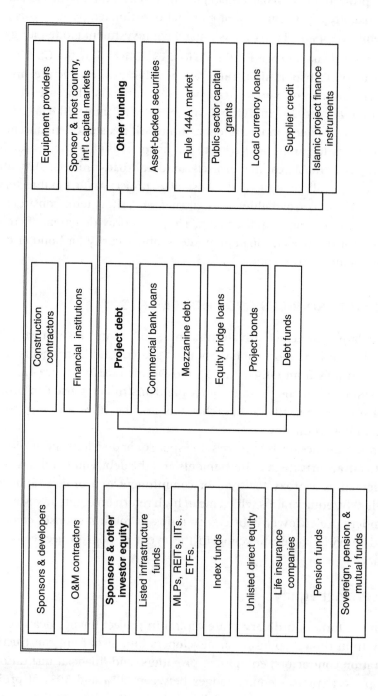

Figure 12.2 Private Financing Channels and Facilities

I. **Sponsor equity.** By their nature, project finance deals require some sponsor equity contribution for ownership of project company shares. Sponsor project equity takes the form of ordinary capital, which is long-term capital, and debt that is temporary equity or quasi-equity, which is a shareholder subordinated debt. Sometimes, equity is provided by the host government and, in some PPP projects, may take the form of in-kind contributions. In other cases, project construction contractors or O&M contractors make equity investments in the project company. Shareholder subordinated debt or junior debt ranks below commercial bank debt that is senior debt.

II. **Other investor equity.** The broadening of the project finance market has increased equity investments by other investors who have long-term horizons and are interested in stable cash flows. This group of equity investors is made up of participants who have the skills and experience to evaluate the potential of infrastructure project investments and includes the following funding channels:

1. **Listed infrastructure funds.** These are funds that invest in companies that generate stable cash flows from infrastructure assets usually diversified by infrastructure sector and geographic region.

2. **Master Limited Partnerships (MLPs).** These are entities structured as partnerships whose shares are traded in equity markets and yield income taxed only at the shareholder level. They invest in infrastructure projects and give investors dividends and liquidity similar to those of corporations.

3. **Real Estate Investment Trusts (REITs).** Infrastructure REITs are companies that own mostly, but not exclusively, the real estate assets of projects and distribute at least 90% of their income to their equity holders.

4. **Infrastructure Investment Trusts (IITs).** IITs are similar to mutual funds that invest in infrastructure projects to earn stable income and in some cases they are a modified version of REITs.

5. **Index Funds.** They are a type of mutual fund whose portfolio consists of stocks of companies owning or investing in infrastructure assets weighted by their capitalizations and are designed to track the performance of the project infrastructure market.

6. **Exchange-Traded Funds (ETFs).** ETFs are passive management funds that trade in stock exchanges like ordinary shares and they are similar to index funds in that they track a group of infrastructure companies' assets they own.

7. **Unlisted direct equity.** These are investments in shares of new infrastructure projects not traded in open public markets and because of the nature of their structures they are considered risky investments. For that reason, they are the purview of large, sophisticated investors who avoid the costs of funds and fund managers.

8. **Life insurance companies.** Life insurance companies are subject to some strict equity investment restrictions and corporate bond investments and limits. However, life insurance companies with large reserves that have long payout horizons, as do some property and casualty insurance companies, are looking for higher than Treasury bond returns and invest in sound infrastructure projects. In general, insurance companies hold a significant part of all outstanding credit market instruments in the United States and invest the majority of their assets in stable and liquid instruments.

9. **Sovereign funds.** There are several types of sovereign wealth funds which are national government funds coming from taxation and trade surpluses and which due to differences in their objectives they invest in different proportions and asset classes. Because of currently low interest rates globally, they have begun investing in promising infrastructure projects that have predictable cash flows and instruments and consistently pay dividends.

10. **Pension funds.** These are government and private company funded, benefit defined, retirement plans for employees that make payments out of the returns on invested pools of funds. Much like sovereign wealth funds, most pension funds make conservative investments although their asset allocations and appetite in infrastructure projects vary widely across countries.

12.2.2 Project Debt

Project debt is a crucial component of project finance and it takes the form of loans, bonds, and subordinated shareholder debt. Project debt is the largest share of funding, usually in the neighborhood of 70–80% of the project's value, with a good part of it coming from commercial banks.

I. **Commercial bank debt.** Commercial bank loans for project finance deals are facilities that take the form of revolving credit for construction financing, term loans drawn during construction, standby letters of credit to support issue of commercial paper, and bridge loans up to four years. They also provide comprehensive credit facilities covering a project's entire loan requirements and, for large projects, they involve different lenders providing different portions of a loan. Syndicated loans and senior debt instruments are secured by project company asset collateral and cash flow.

II. **Mezzanine debt.** This is a subordinated debt or preferred equity instrument that is often a desired channel to raise project funding that is senior only to common shares. These loans are unsecured bank loans that, in the event of project company asset liquidation, can only be repaid after all claims of secured creditors have been met. Mezzanine debt is a hybrid instrument that gives a lender the right to convert debt into equity in the event of a default and because of higher risk, mezzanine debt carries higher interest rates than commercial bank loans. The most important lender requirement for mezzanine financing is the project company's ability to generate sufficient cash flow.

III. **Equity bridge loans.** These are short-term loans—also known as capital call facilities—that are often offered as revolving credit while permanent financing is secured, at which point bridge loans are repaid. This type of loan is backed by project company asset collateral and carries higher interest rates and origination fees.

IV. **Project bonds.** These are privately placed or issued in public markets and are used to finance specific infrastructure projects. They are a source of long-term funding, particularly for brownfield projects. Institutional investors are the majority buyers of project bonds, which carry superior risk-adjusted returns. A specific type of tax-exempt bond, called green bonds, are issued by government agencies and are used to develop brownfield sites that are abandoned or underdeveloped.

12.2.3 Other Funding Sources and Instruments

There are private and public channels and facilities available to finance profitable projects in addition to the sources of funding and instruments mentioned earlier. The most important channels are the Rule 144A market, asset-backed securities, and Islamic financing. The latter is a large player in project financings in Moslem countries.

I. **Asset-backed securities.** These project finance instruments are bonds sold to investors in public markets and are backed by infrastructure loans pooled together and issued in tranches.

II. **Rule 144A market.** This is a Securities and Exchange Commission regulated market that specifies the rules for privately placed securities and was planned to facilitate trading among institutional investors. Internal Revenue Service Rule 144A is the basis on which project finance bonds are issued. These are restricted securities in private sales from an issuing infrastructure project company and may not be sold to the public.

III. **Supplier credit.** It is also known as supplier financing and it is an extension of credit, with repayment over a 7 to 10 years, to project companies buying equipment, goods, and technology and other services. It is credit extended from a bank in the supplier's country that takes the form of letter of credit. Supplier credit is usually supplemented with export credit for equipment, goods, and services produced in the supplier's country.

IV. **Public sector assistance.** A significant part of public sector assistance comes from local currency loans to infrastructure projects for purchase of local resources and to fill gaps in the financing of a project. Often, public sector assistance comes in the form of in-kind contributions, tax incentives, export support, subsidies, and other assistance programs.

V. **Capital grants.** These are contributions from public sector entities or from bilateral and multilateral institutions supporting economic development, often with concessionary terms or not repayable. They are used to fund development for badly needed infrastructure projects or to establish the viability of commercializing new technologies. Capital grants, however, require strict compliance to requirements of grading agencies assigned to rate the project.

VI. **Islamic financing.** Project finance facilities from Islamic institutions are instruments compliant with Sharia law that are structured instruments for infrastructure project investors to obtain income. One of the most common debt-finance instruments is the *sukuk*, whose structure resembles a conventional bond, and the other being the equity-like instrument *modaraba*, which is very similar to a western limited partnership arrangement.

12.3   BENEFITS OF OFFICIAL FUNDING SOURCE PARTICIPATION

A key element of project finance is selecting a mix of instruments from various funding sources to maximize the value created by the project once other appropriate decisions are made to optimize project financing. The selection of funding facilities is affected significantly by the participation of ECAs, regional development banks, and multilateral institutions in a project. ECAs support domestic businesses by guaranteeing or lending to overseas projects and that support comes with discipline on the supplier of capital assets' documentation, price, and the quality of goods and services delivered. On the other hand, regional development bank loans are paired with technical assistance, project oversight, and guidance on the approval process to ensure successful project implementation.

The primary roles of multilateral agencies are to support development infrastructure project financing, affect technology transfers, develop the experience of host countries in aspects of project finance, and assist host country governments to develop and manage projects. The participation of these institutions in projects requires that a number of conditions are met, such as:

1. Good relations with the host country's government and positive working experiences with the authorities responsible for infrastructure projects

2. Sufficient political support for the project up and down the central and local government bureaucracies

3. Appropriate screening of project economics and validations of sufficient project development financial resources

4. Adequacy of required project finance skills and competencies of the host country's ceding authority personnel

5. Transparency of the bidding and procurement processes and project selection criteria

6. Sufficient private sector equity in the project to ensure sponsor or developer commitment to the project

7. Positive project feasibility study, balanced risk allocation and effective mitigation, and favorable due diligence findings and recommendations

The World Bank and the IMF—and now the NDB and the CRA—are working to strengthen the financial sector of member countries with appropriate tax policies and regulation. Along with ECAs and regional development banks they create effective partnerships with governments. They help them achieve sustainable growth objectives through the funding of sound economic and social infrastructure projects. But why should sponsors or developers invite these institutions to participate in projects? Because they bring many benefits to project financings that are worth the delays their engagement may cause, such as:

1. Adding weight and legitimacy with their participation in projects and unique ability to address challenging issues

2. Influencing host governments in developing regulatory regimes favorable to foreign investments in infrastructure and in resolving project problems and conflicts

3. Bringing high levels of expertise, corporate knowledge, and the ability to mobilize resources from around the world

4. Providing independent, critical, and objective project assessments that make their approvals carry a trusted endorsement for governments and investors

5. Offering programs in countries where sponsors have no presence and where there is no governmental or bilateral aid or financing support for a project

6. Coordinating programs with other funding sources to improve financing efficiency and sharing knowledge and lessons learned from other projects they participated in

7. Leveraging relationships with advisors for technical support and financing, which increases project credibility and participant commitment

8. Introducing innovative approaches, helping with request for proposal (RFP) preparation, and mobilizing global funding

9. Stewarding the project through the processes of each stage down to final approval of financing

10. Providing experienced resources and guidance to resolve issues when conflicts arise or risks materialize

CHAPTER 13

Structuring Project Finance

How Everything Comes Together

The structuring of project financing is a framework in which ownership structure, project structure, risk structure, and financial structure decisions are made and tied together in the project's legal structure which, in turn, forms a foundation for funding the project on a limited recourse basis. The ownership structure is how the special purpose company (SPC) is organized; that is, as a corporation, unincorporated joint venture, limited liability partnership, etc. Project structure on the other hand refers to the agreements defining responsibilities and transfer of rights and/or ownership of the SPC such as build, operate, and transfer of ownership (BOT), build, own, operate, and transfer (BOOT), build, lease, and transfer (BLT), etc.

Risk structure is the prioritization and mitigation of risks after the identification, assessment, and allocation process is completed. The project's legal structure is the web of contracts and agreements negotiated to make financing possible. Financial structure refers to the mix of financing used to fund a project, which includes equity, short- and long-term loans, bonds, trade credits, etc. and the cash flows to equity providers and the lenders.

> Note: Financial structure and capital structure are used interchangeably, but there is a difference: Capital structure = Financial structure – Short-term liabilities.

An example of a financing structure is presented in Figure 13.1, which is a simplified version of a plant project financing structure. Its key elements are the participants, the agreements that hold it together, and the money flows indicated by arrows. The structuring of project financing is done in a recursive manner, in a fluid environment, and in the context of decision interrelationships, which require skills and experience to arrive at a balanced solution that satisfies all project stakeholders. Many of the processes, evaluations, and decisions made in public–private partnership (PPP) or private finance initiative (PFI) projects are the same as those performed in all private project finance deals around the world. The differences of entirely private-sector funded projects are the following:

1. The absence of a host government as a project stakeholder
2. No multilateral agency involvement or funding by regional development banks
3. Reliance not on offtake agreements for project success but on a well-functioning marketplace
4. Less emphasis on contracts and more on evaluation of project economics, risk management, and project due diligence

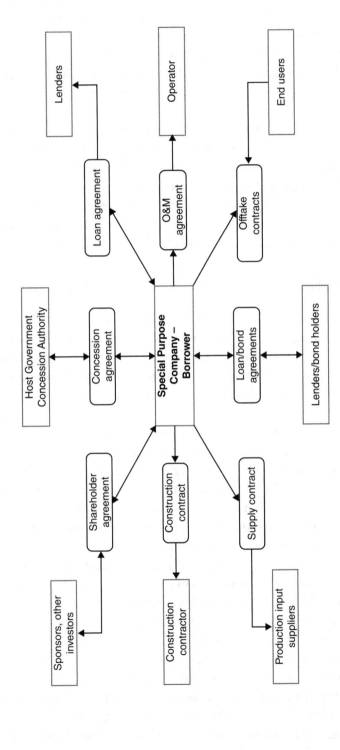

Figure 13.1 Simplified typical project finance structure
Source: Adapted from Merna, Chu, and Al-Thani (2010).

In the sections that follow we examine equity and debt investor requirements, structuring and financing options, the contractual basis, determinants of project financing, and how all the pieces are fused together in the project financing plan to direct choices in order to arrive at a successful financing close. Section 13.1 touches on the prerequisites and the various elements involved in the financing structure while the perspectives and expectations of equity investors, lenders, and other funding sources are examined in Section 13.2.

The project financing structuring framework, the decisions that must be made, and the process of advancing the project from the formation of the SPC to the financial structure phase are discussed in Section 13.3. The determining factors of project financing are presented one more time in Section 13.4. The integration of all the processes and evaluations are discussed in Section 13.5, which is a summary of how sustainable and efficient project financing comes together in the project financing plan.

13.1 ELEMENTS OF PROJECT FINANCING STRUCTURING

The purpose of project financing structuring is to identify the parties involved in funding, assess the financing options open to a project, and determine specific shares of funding and contracts and agreements needed. Hence, the components of financing structure are not only decisions that need to be made but, also, the selection of financing techniques and options to fund a project.

To begin with, for PPP deals, a common financing technique of host governments is land-financing variants, such as land contribution to build project facilities, sale of development rights, and betterment levies, which are a one-time tax on the increased value of property due to the project. Another PPP financing option is the one where a private sponsor is awarded a concession agreement and then uses it to raise funds to build and operate a project for the duration of the agreement.

The most common form of project financing is obtaining loans though the backing of contractual commitments of the offtaker to purchase the output produced. This, in essence, makes the offtaker a guarantor of revenue streams. For resource extraction projects, a production payments' scheme is created, whereby funds are advanced to build a project based on assigning a proportion of interest in oil and gas or mineral reserves to the sponsor. Another option is the advance payment technique, which involves the expansion of funds by a sponsor for project output to be developed and a sponsor agreement to purchase the output upon beginning of production. Lease financing is also used in some cases to have a project facility financed

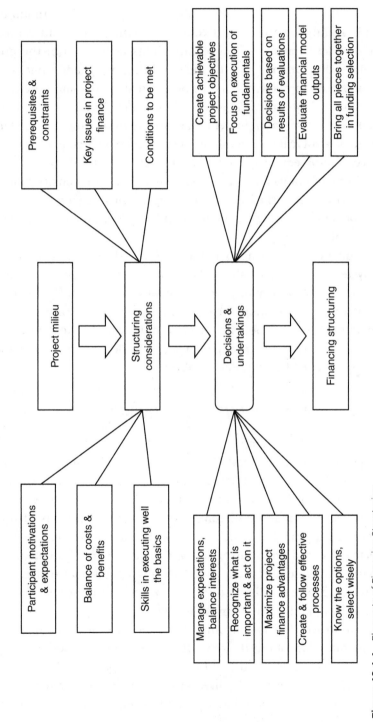

Figure 13.1.1 Elements of Financing Structuring

while it is owned by investors not related to the sponsor, who get tax benefits and then lease the facility back to the project company on a nonrecourse basis.

Decisions that have to do with equity structuring evolve around organizing and capitalizing the project company, management and control of its operations, and transfer of ownership rights at the end of the project company lifecycle. Other decisions include bringing in additional equity investors and how to resolve disputes between sponsors and other equity investors. On the debt-structuring side, a larger number of issues have to be considered to arrive at the right debt financing solution. Some of the lender considerations involve decisions about the country of sourcing of equipment and services, involvement of development agencies, local currency debt, use of government grants and loans, commercial loans for construction, and refinancing with long-term loans to cover operations. A summary view of project financing structuring components and considerations is displayed in Figure 13.1.1 above.

Project financing is to a good measure a risk-management method where a system is created to allocate risks to different project participants and minimize the volatility of project-company cash flows. The nature of the negotiated implementation or concession agreements narrows down the financing options and available financing techniques. It is those agreements that hold the project structure together and the development of a sound financing plan that make it implementable.

13.2 EQUITY AND DEBT INVESTOR REQUIREMENTS

The starting point of financing structuring is getting a good understanding of the objectives of equity participants and debt investors and what it takes to reconcile their diverse requirements. A key element of successful financing structuring is the financing strategy that lays out how the SPC will be financed optimally and consistent with the consensus of project stakeholder objectives. The financing strategy outlines the sponsor's process and steps to select funding sources and options to ensure adequate funding past construction completion and well into the operational phase. It also defines financing-related roles and responsibilities for project stakeholders in sufficient detail and clarity to make it effective.

Financial structuring is not only about the mix of different funding instruments but, also, about the drawdown schedule, the debt repayment profile and equity distributions, and the credit support and security packages required by debt and equity investors. For private sector sponsors, the financing strategy's success is judged by the adequacy of project internal rate of return (IRR), net present value (NPV), debt ratios, and short payback periods. For public sector stakeholders, financing strategy success is judged by getting the best value for money, which consists of least-cost funding, efficient project development, effective project outcomes for the money spent, and balanced distribution of project benefits.

What equity investors typically pay attention to in the analyses for financial structuring is a set of parameters coming out of the financial model that includes adequate return on investment measured by:

1. IRR, which is the discount rate that makes the project flows' NPV equal zero
2. Project NPV or risk-adjusted NPV, which is project NPV adjusted by the likelihood of occurrence in each period of operations
3. Payback period, which is the time required for an investment to be paid back from the project's cash flow
4. Profit investment ratio or profitability index, which is the present value of cash flows divided by the initial investment
5. Debt cover ratios that measure the project company's ability to generate cash flows to meet all its debt obligations
6. Debt service profiles, which is the repayment schedule of principal and interest amounts

In addition to sufficient upfront equity and commitment for future equity amounts to make a project bankable, project lenders closely examine the financial structuring parameters and look for and prefer the following:

1. Experienced sponsor company and project company management teams and a skilled and competent project team
2. Fixed completion date and contact price with appropriate guarantees and insurance and no technology risk and security from the engineering, procurement, and construction (EPC) contractor
3. Liquidated damages for delays, and performance and project company output guarantees
4. Interest rate and foreign exchange hedging contracts for significant operating cost items
5. Competitive project company output pricing, host government subsidies, and barriers to discourage new competitor entry
6. Strong and enforceable offtake and supply contracts and adverse regulatory noninterference
7. Adequacy of risk mitigation and a security package acceptable to all stakeholders

Because different stakeholders define success differently, a balance of private and public interests and objectives must be achieved. What sponsors look for in financial structuring needs to be consistent with lender requirements that, other things being equal, determine project bankability. Also, there are some preconditions to project financeability that apply to all projects and that are examined and monitored closely through all stages of project financing and include factors such as:

1. The host country's political and social stability and ability to deliver on contribution obligations
2. Identifiable project risks and the ability to mitigate them through contracts and agreements
3. Validation of project economic viability judged by the outputs of the project financial model
4. Accessible local and international debt financing and ECA and multilateral institution support

13.3 DECISIONS FROM SPC OWNERSHIP TO FINANCING STRUCTURE

The structure of project financing is the set of decisions needed to arrive at financial close. The key process elements of the financing structuring framework are shown in Figure 13.3.1. The project stakeholders are the sponsors, the host government authority, debt and equity investors other than the sponsors, and the ECAs and multilateral institutions involved in the project. The major decisions involve the SPC structure; the project structure, the risk structure, the contract structure, and the financing structure once relevant corresponding considerations are taken into account.

Having made those decisions, structuring project financing becomes the process of identifying the right funding channels, drafting and negotiating appropriate contracts and agreements, and selecting the best-suited financing instruments among several options. The result of these undertakings is the project financing plan, an illustration of whose development is presented in Figure 13.3.2, that directs the activities for both construction financing and long-term financing. The structuring process activities outlined in Figure 13.3.2 are a complement of the project financing-structuring framework, and the four major categories of activities involved are:

1. The financing structuring activities
2. The sourcing of finance undertakings
3. The evaluation of financing selected and negotiations
4. The financial closing steps

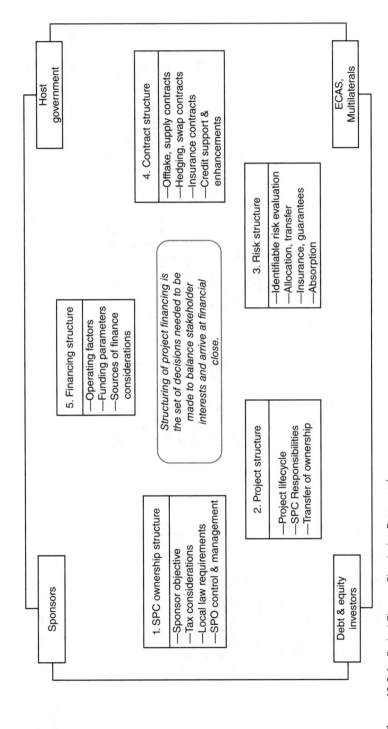

Figure 13.3.1 Project Finance Structuring Framework

271

Financing structuring activities

—Validation of project economic viability
—Risk evaluation & mitigation
—Sound due diligence
—Development of financial model
—Independent tests for project bankability
—Scoping out investor interest in the project
—Evaluation of financial model results
—Tweaking the financial structure to maximize returns to investors

Sourcing of finance activities

—Contact with potential sources of funding
—Preparation of project documentation
—Sketching out desired terms & conditions
—Obtaining proposals from debt & equity funding sources
—Private equity funds
—Large financial institutions
—Insurance companies
—Sovereign wealth & pension funds
—Other funding sources

Evaluation & negotiation activities

—Terms of financing, interest rates, fees
—Cover ratios & repayment schedule
—Timeliness & efficiency of proposal evaluation
—Negotiation to improve terms of funding
—Choice of lead bank/ arranger
—Negotiation of final term sheets

Financial closing steps

—Verification of working of financial systems
—Project stakeholder backing
—Conclude funding documentation

Figure 13.3.2 Financing Structuring Process Activities
Source: Adapted from Yescombe (2014).

A. Ownership Decisions

The project ownership-structure decision is made after evaluations and conclusions about the effects of the following:

1. Strategic, financial, competitive, and other objectives the sponsors expect to achieve from investing in the project
2. Upfront investment requirements and future investment contributions as well as the tax treatment of the SPC and benefits to be obtained in the host country
3. Constraints or conditions of the legal and regulatory requirements of the host country
4. Nature of the project, expected obligations, and control and management of the SPC

B. Project Structure Decisions

The project structure decision is also based on the life span of the project company operations, its responsibilities and obligations, and the terms and conditions of the ownership of its assets. However, the project structure to be negotiated has feedback effects on the ownership decision which, in turn, impacts the project structure. Once the SPC ownership structure and the project structure decisions are made and implemented, the project risk structure comes into focus after the feasibility study is completed and demonstrates the economic viability of the project which is, of course, conditioned by its risk structure.

The decisions on how to manage the project risk structure take place after the following process steps are completed:

1. Project risks and their root causes are identified and categorized as controllable and uncontrollable
2. Controllable risks are evaluated in terms of likelihood of occurrence and potential adverse impacts
3. Allocation of risks to the party best able to handle is made or sharing of risks in proportion to the benefits obtained by the project
4. Risk-avoidance efforts are made to minimize or eliminate the number of risks
5. Making provisions to absorb the risks that are uninsurable or have a low probability of occurrence
6. Obtaining guarantees from the parties where risks emanate from and insurance, credit support, and enhancements from the host government, ECAs, and multilateral institutions

7. Developing contingency plans to address unknown, uncontrollable, and black swan risks

---

Black swans are rare, random, unforeseen, and hard-to-predict events. They are considered outliers in the experience of environmental, political, business, technology and other fields but have large-scale impacts in these areas.

C. Contract Structure Decisions

The project contract structure requires the weaving of enforceable contracts and agreements to make the project bankable and provide adequate protection of shareholder interests. In cases where a host government authority participates in the project, the implementation or ceding agreements are a key part of the legal framework. These agreements involve decisions in every area they cover and when negotiated, they define the following:

1. The duration of the project life, licenses and permits required, and termination clauses
2. The roles and responsibilities of the parties involved
3. The project implementation arrangements that include bidding and procurement qualifications and project specifications
4. The host government's financial and in-kind contributions, grants, guarantees, and other kinds of support
5. The governing law and funding provisions and conditions precedent
6. The value of the project company assets at the end of the project agreement

Other elements of the project contract structure include several important parts, each of which entails decisions about acceptable levels of desired outcomes. Namely:

1. An EPC contract with an appropriate completion date, price, performance guarantees, and liquidated damages for delays and nonperformance
2. A sound offtake contract with quantity targets and price increases to offset inflation, equipment upgrades, and changes in tax treatment or tax-rate increases
3. Wide-ranging supply contracts for production inputs, supplies, and power and other utilities with price stability and quality clauses

4. Private and ECA and multilateral institution insurance contracts for risks not allocated or absorbed and third-party insurance policies

5. Credit support agreements, guarantees, counter-guarantees, hedging contracts, and other credit enhancements

6. A decent O&M agreement with performance, output, and quality clauses

D. Operational Decisions

The operational factors that play a role in financing structure decisions have to do with the term of the contract, the project cost and revenue forecasts, and the tax treatment of the project cash flows. Other operational factors impacting financing are the expected prices of the project company's output, inflation expectations, and the interest rate environment and financing costs. Factors influencing decisions about the sources of financing and funding instruments evolve around the following:

1. Project stakeholder equity contributions and their timing

2. Equity returns measured by the projects NPV or the investors' IRR

3. The debt service profile and debt ratios

4. Sponsor and other project stakeholder guarantees

5. Security on loans to the project company

Conclusions about the best choice of sources of funding and financing instruments are arrived at after operating and funding parameters are well considered and decisions are made on respective factors.

E. Financing Structure Decisions

The project financing structure is based on the results of analyses and assessments of the feasibility study results, the due diligence report, and judgments and decisions made concerning the structures mentioned earlier. Project financing structuring considers these factors and attempts to balance interests, costs, and benefits to arrive at an optimal structure; that is, the best possible outcome to be achieved that is acceptable to the stakeholders involved. The last factors considered are operational elements, funding parameters obtained from the project financial model output, and the sources and types of financing.

In project financing transactions, sponsor or developer equity is a prerequisite before other investors are brought into the project and commercial loans may be obtained. Equity and preferred equity decisions are influenced by evaluations on how the SPC is organized and planned to be capitalized, management and control of the SPC, how disputes between equity participants will be resolved, and the terms and conditions of the SPC's termination of operations. On the other hand, debt-financing decisions involve evaluations of sources of funding and availability, terms and conditions, compliance requirements, guarantees, insurance, and costs, advantages and disadvantages of different debt-funding options.

For projects in emerging countries, the first source of funding could be multilateral or regional development banks, followed by the host government's in-kind contributions. In most developing country projects, grants from the host government that provide initial funding are usually in local currency contributions. In both instances, government subsidies, tax relief, land and resource contributions, and government guarantees and counter-guarantees add to the basket of money flows to fund a project. Also, as a precondition to participate in a project, EPC contractors and technology and equipment providers are enticed to provide equity or debt to the project at costs comparable to those in financial markets.

Funding from host government subsidies is low on the list of sources of funding because, for the most part, it is indirect funding and usually involves dealing with bureaucratic processes. However, substantial benefits can be derived from funding via host government subsidies, which can take many different forms, such as:

1. Project company tax concessions, reduced tax rates, and tax holidays
2. Accelerated depreciation allowances and exemptions from import duties and export subsidies
3. In-kind subsidies such as land contributions, subsidized housing, utilities, etc.
4. Creation of free-trade zones and production subsidies
5. Cash grants, subsidized loans, loan guarantees, government insurance at reduced rates, credit subsidies and tax-free bonds

Senior commercial bank loans are used for different purposes, such as construction and operations, and different maturities; that is, short term and permanent (long term) financing. In many cases, commercial paper backed by the SPC's assets is used to fund ongoing operational expenses. Mezzanine loans are used in instances when equity investments and senior debt are not sufficient to cover all project costs. Junior bank loans are unsecured or subordinated loans, usually with no collateral behind the debt, and involve substantially higher interest rates. These loans are used for contingency funding purposes such as construction cost overruns. Project bonds are long-term financing instruments via public offerings or private placements and are used in large financings. Project bonds involve substantial costs to obtain a credit rating, preparing the bond placement information, and legal and marketing costs. Also, insurance to protect against the default of bonds is required for bond ratings BB or below as well as for loans.

Export credit finance and political insurance are integral parts of international project finance and play a major role in the project financing structure. Export trade finance is provided by the ECAs of the countries where equipment, technology, and services are sourced. They take the form of credit to suppliers or loans to buyers of equipment, technology, and services from the country the ECA provides credit insurance and financial guarantees. Also, political insurance from OPIC provides comprehensive coverage for losses to assets, investment value, or loss of earnings.

13.4 DETERMINANTS OF PROJECT FINANCING

An illustration of project financing's determining set of factors is shown in Figure 13.4. The first determinant is adequate equity investment by sponsors and the involvement of private and public stakeholders in the project, but with no or limited recourse to the owners of the SPC.

Once the primary determinants are satisfied, another set of factors defines an effective project financing structure and entails the following:

1. Economic and political state of the host country, the size of the project, and the funding needs

2. Updated sponsor and other investor analysis, and evaluation and equity contributions consistent with other project stakeholder expectations

3. Verification of continuity of stakeholder objectives and alignment consistent with updated sponsor objectives

4. Reasonableness of cost and revenue forecasts established by scrutinizing and testing the assumptions and underlying scenarios

5. Sound project-management processes and safeguards and the ability to integrate decisions effectively in the project financing plan

6. Project economic viability validated by a sound, independent, and critical assessment and supported by the findings in the due diligence report

7. Reassessment of project risk mitigation through allocation to parties best able to handle, insurance contracts, and counter-guarantees

8. Validation and verification of the due diligence findings by professionals engaged by the lenders' group

9. Verification of the adequacy of EPC, offtake, supply, hedging, and O&M contracts along with guarantees, financing support, and enhancements

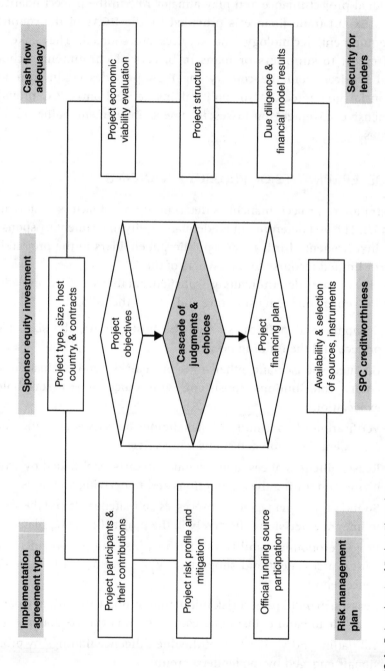

Figure 13.4 Determinants of Project Financing

10. Strong host government political support and enforceable offtaker and supplier contracts

11. Sponsor contacts, relationships, alliances, and understanding of processes and requirements of potential debt and equity sources

12. Availability of suitable cost of financing, support in local and hard currency, and interest rate and exchange rate hedging contracts

13. Participation of, support, and enhancements by ECAs and multilateral institutions

14. Satisfactory debt ratios tested though simulations of alternative plausible scenarios

15. Proper management of project company accounts according to lender covenants and restrictions

13.5 AMALGAMATION OF FINANCING

In previous sections we discussed elements of financing structuring, debt and equity investor requirements, the many decisions made in the project development stage, and the determinants of project financing. Following the process from creation of project objectives to financing decisions leads to creation of a project financing plan. A very important element missing from the discussion is the integration of different financing process components that are necessary to develop the project financing plan. The discussion of how all the different pieces and decisions come together to affect project financing is the topic of this section. It is aided by Figure 13.5.1, which is a summary illustration of how the integration of the project team's processes and work activities take place.

Once project evaluations and risk profiling and mitigation are completed, they form the basis of the project contracts and agreements and the due diligence report is where these pieces are integrated and summarized. Updating the financial model place takes place by integrating data, inputs, and parameters from the project characteristics, attributes of the project company, host government attributes, funding considerations, and validation from the due diligence report. Based on these updates, the financial model yields estimates of the debt-cover ratios, IRR, and NPV. Those estimates are further refined by inclusion in the model details about:

1. Equity investor motivations

2. Lenders' requirements

3. Tax and accounting treatment of debt

4. Loan particulars

5. Credit enhancements and support

6. Project specific considerations

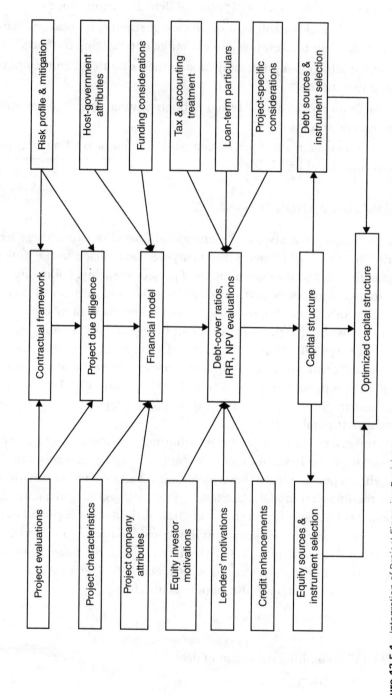

Figure 13.5.1 Integration of Project Financing Decisions

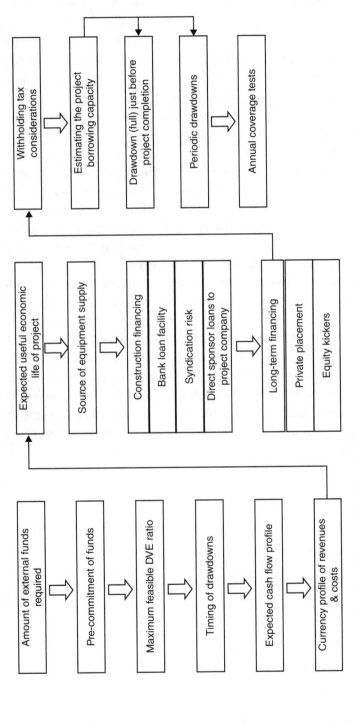

Figure 13.5.2 Illustration of Development of the Financing Plan

281

The refined financial model outputs determine the project's ability to generate sufficient cash flow to repay debt incurred, satisfy equity-investor requirements, and serve as a guide to the project's capital structure. At this junction, an interim project financing plan is created and an illustration of it is shown in Figure 13.5.2 above. But, this is not the end. In addition to upfront sponsor equity contributions and timing, additional funding and contingency financing needs are included and other equity sources and instruments are considered and evaluated.

Various equity and debt sources and facilities are assessed and the repayment schedule and loan fees are updated and input to the financial model. Only then can an optimized capital structure be determined and acted on to bring financing closure. The manner in which the integration of the parts needs to take place to create a competitive advantage demonstrates the significance of superior project management skills, capabilities, and experiences in structuring financing effectively. In large projects, however, the help and guidance of an experienced external financing advisor is valuable to facilitate the process and ensure smooth closing.

Figure 13.5.2 shows the series of elements needed to optimize the structuring of construction and long-term financing. Final decisions are made based on annual coverage ratios and tests and, if inadequate, the process is iterated until optimization is achieved. The project financing plan is a major milestone not only because it guides the financing structuring process but, also because it provides crucial support for creating a respectable information memorandum. The crucial importance of the project financial model lies with reaching a financing structure acceptable to both equity and debt investors and for that the reason the next chapter is focused entirely on that discussion.

CHAPTER 14

Project Financial Model

Assessing and Testing Financeability

project financial model is a representation of important qualitative and quantitative information. It contains assumptions, project schedules and operational and financial relationships in mathematical, deterministic models such as Excel spreadsheets. Stochastic project financial models are used in projects of prevalent uncertainties and because of their complexities they are only used in large project financings. A financial model calculates relationships and simulates the effects of forecast variables. Its output helps to plan and provides guide financial analysis and decision making in all phases of a project. As such, it is a key tool in the evaluation of the feasibility study results and in project development phase decisions. A summary of the main purposes served by a project financial model is displayed in Figure 14.1.

A project financial model is built right at the start of the project assessment stage and it is continuously expanded, updated, and improved as more information, data, analyses, and evaluations are completed. Because of its complexity and maintenance requirements, the project financial model is usually jointly developed by the sponsor-project team and the financial advisor with input from the lead-arranger bank. Its development is a process that begins with project definition and requirement information, data and qualitative assessments, expert opinions, assumptions about technical and financial relationships, the future operating environment, and changes in the drivers of the model. Then, it makes numerous calculations and shows scenario cash-flow projections for each project phase and provides financial information outputs.

The project financial model is important because its output is the basis for answering questions such as:

1. Does the project look promising enough at the start of its assessment to warrant substantial development expenditures?

2. When is the project financeable? What is an adequate return on investment (ROI); is it 5, 8, 10 percentage points above prime rate? What is a sufficient IRR? Is it 10, 13, 15% for the risk profile of a given project?

3. Are financial model results consistent with project stakeholder expectations and with due diligence findings?

4. Do financial model results confirm the logical consistency and reasonableness of underlying assumptions?

5. If for a certain situation or scenario the project financeability is in question, how can the project be made financeable? What changes and enhancements need to be made to improve its chances of financeability?

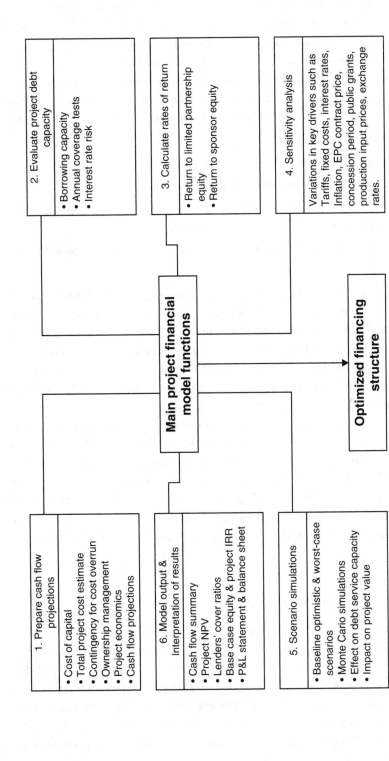

Figure 14.1 Purposes of the Project Financial Model
Source: Adapted from Finnerty (2013).

Sound project financial models are crucial in appropriate project financing structuring, but they cannot ensure appropriate project implementation and management of the project company. Therefore, they alone cannot guarantee project financial success. This is true even in cases where all financial ratios and indicators are in highly desired ranges. In the sections that follow, we discuss the uses of project financial models, inputs to and outputs of financial models, and the characteristics of sound financial models. It is important though, that the financial model discussion is linked back to:

1. Strategic and project objectives and development
2. Risk management and due diligence findings
3. Financing structuring processes and decisions that are made all along
4. Project financing plan elements and analysis
5. External financing advisor and consultant benchmarking and assessment

The sections that follow address the most important elements of the project financial model—a key component of project financing. The main functions and uses of the project financial model and how they determine project financing structuring are discussed in Section 14.1. Section 14.2 deals with the most impactful inputs to the project financial model and we acknowledge that lesser-impact inputs can make a significant difference in model outputs and give wrong indications.

The financial model calculations and outputs are presented in Section 14.3 but the scope of the discussion necessitates abstracting from a myriad of model structuring and calculation details. To complete the presentation of the project financial model, we examine the properties of good project financial models in Section 14.4. The project financial model discussion ends with the universal conclusion that the project financial model is the major pillar of financing structuring and that no project financing plan can be created without it.

14.1 USES OF THE FINANCIAL MODEL

The primary function of the project financial model is to guide financing structuring decisions. It serves as an instrument to account for and check all project costs and revenue projections, determine the amount of project debt required, and assess the project company's ability to repay that debt. Thus, it is the means to demonstrate the project's profitability, communicate its value creation from a common perspective and, when properly packaged, it is used in the information memorandum, presentations, and road shows to attract debt and equity investors. The list of functions the project financial model serves include the following:

1. Receive and process project specifications, data, assumptions and revisions; and function as a repository of all information collected, screened, and validated up to that point

2. Support high-leverage analytics, sensitivity analysis, and scenario testing and provide consistent and accurate financial parameter estimates

3. Conduct quick and reliable analyses and assess and respond to project-team requests and questions in support of contract negotiations

4. Provide project valuations for different stakeholder requirements or perspectives and report changes in project valuation due to changes in input factors

5. Assess and help decrease project risks and costs related to debt and equity investor-compliance requirements

6. Help with planning responses to unmitigated risks and black swans that could materialize at some point in the future

7. Provide insights into the project company's operations and the validate the adequacy of its business plan

8. Serve as a communications tool and convey a common set of project financials and evaluations across all project stakeholders

The project financial model is the foundation of the project financing plan because it combines all the important input feeds, processes them, and produces outputs that have varied uses in financial planning. Starting with a few project facts, it explicitly states sponsor expectations and objectives and lender requirements then, using assumptions based on expert opinions and cost and revenue forecasts, it builds a picture of what the project's economics look like. Thus, it is a crucial tool in sponsor analysis and evaluations as well as in a lenders' assessment of the project. It also serves the lenders' due diligence because it shows how well their requirements are met and assesses project viability. This is because the model captures details of project costs and revenues, the project company cash flow projections and, by extension, its credit worthiness and borrowing capacity which determine project bankability.

The analysis of the financial model results helps to identify and assess project risks, and determine or suggest additional risk mitigants that may be necessary to implement and subsequently to give indications of and influence the cost of borrowing. Financial model output guides project financing structuring decisions and by serving as input to the project financing plan, it determines feasible sets of financing structuring and guides many of the important financing processes. Additionally, one of the most important uses of the project financial model is its ability to test the reasonableness of assumptions used in building the models and to provide reasonableness checks for the model's structure and its results.

The cash-flow estimates coming out of the project model and the financial ratios are crucial in the analysis of project viability and financeability, which also enable the evaluation of the ROI for equity and debt investors. Another important function of the project financial model is to develop the project company's financial statements and periodic financial reports. Furthermore, practically all significant project negotiations are based on the project's financial-model results. In fact, financial-model results determine negotiation positions and decisions. In preparations for contract negotiations, the effects of initial, fallback, revised, and walk-away positions are determined by the financial-model results. During negotiations, the results of various proposals are evaluated and the impacts of counterproposals are assessed in order to guide negotiators' decisions.

Another useful application of project financial models is their ability to conduct sensitivity analysis of variation in the value of a single model driver on the cost and revenue output variables. When model drivers are varied randomly, the model outputs are simulations of impacts (Monte Carlo simulations) due to those changes that define the range of possible outcomes at different levels of probability. The use of model simulations is an essential tool to develop plausible scenarios and observe how they impact the output variables. Simulations are also a useful risk assessment and evaluation tool for various economic conditions and financial situations.

The financial model output is a requirement for the preparation of the project-information memorandum because it is the foundation for investor analysis and project evaluation. And because the project financial model can be used for black-swan simulations of extreme-event scenarios it is a valuable instrument for contingency planning. Additionally, it helps to plan actions for course corrections if certain events occur or changes need to be made in the project company's operations to achieve expected results.

14.2 FINANCIAL MODEL INPUTS

Project financial models need to be comprehensive and well-structured in order to be of value in decision making. This requires inclusion of all the key driving factors of costs, revenue, and the project company cash-flow arrangements. It also requires correct specification of relationships and feedback effects. In every case, the project lifespan and schedule of events are the first model inputs followed by estimates of the various costs involved, revenue projections, and host country factors. However, many of the final model inputs involve decisions based on earlier versions of the project financial model and other considerations. In other words, the project financial-model outputs induce changes that become inputs to the financial model. This takes place in a recursive manner until a steady state is arrived at and stakeholders reach a consensus view of project viability.

Capital costs are the major cost component that is determined by project requirements and performance specifications that, in turn, are determined by the sponsors' and host government's objectives and expectations. Besides capital costs, project-development costs are another major cost component, followed by the cost of project company production inputs, materials, and utilities. Project-company operating expenses are yet another important cost component along with the costs associated with the O&M agreement. Sometimes risk management costs, such as insurance premiums and hedging contract expenses, are separated from other costs in order to assess and allocate the cost of risk management to the right parties. In certain projects using rapidly changing technologies, the costs of equipment and technical updates are also kept separate. Other important factors are the depreciation and amortization schedules and resulting charges.

The project model inputs for the revenue side of the cash-flow equation vary substantially for different projects and are defined according to the expertise of the consultants developing the revenue forecasts. Revenue forecasts only require projections of the project company's output demand, i.e. the quantity sold over its lifespan, and the unit prices charged over that period. However, quantity-and-price forecasts require model inputs from assumptions concerning the impacts of:

1. The host country's macroeconomic variables, such as gross national product (GNP) growth, inflation rates, exchange rates, etc.
2. Industry structure, capacity, and competition changes
3. Megatrends, political, economic, social, technological, legal, educational, and demographic (PESTLED) trends, and industry-specific trends
4. Growth rate in the customer or user base and demand for the project company's output or expected market changes over the forecast period
5. Price changes needed to maintain a certain rate of return for regulated industries and price adjustments for unregulated markets

The drawdown debt schedule is determined by the construction timelines while the equity contributions schedule is determined by lender requirements and the project's debt capacity. On the other side, the debt repayment schedule is determined by the project company's debt load and its net cash flow. The loan covenants and restrictions are financial model inputs affecting uses of the project company's available cash flow and timing of distributions. Loan interest rates and fees along with equity funding costs are important project model inputs as is the applicable tax rate structure and refinancing costs and long-term debt requirements.

Project model inputs are continuously updated and fluid, and calculations are made in a recursive and iterative manner. Thus, in addition to factors that at some early point are fixed, there are some model inputs needed to initiate model calculations, such as the discount rate to be used in NPV calculations, the sponsor's target equity IRR, and factors whose nature is not known with certainty. Project-model calculations and output parameters stabilize when necessary analyses, assessments, verifications, and validations are performed. The model calculation results are used as inputs for the development of the financing plan, the project company's financial statements, and the project information memorandum. The project financial model calculations and outputs are the subject of the next section.

14.3 FINANCIAL MODEL CALCULATIONS AND OUTPUTS

The nature of interactions in the project financial model and its central role in project financing are displayed in Figure 14.3, which helps to visualize the tasks and activities performed in order to arrive at an optimized project financing structure. The annual amounts of cost and revenue projections are used to calculate the project company's annual cash flows and debt service requirements. Among the first order calculation from the project financial model outputs are the drawdown amounts of debt and equity in order to satisfy funding requirements.

After all calculations are performed, the project model outputs define the project debt service profile, which is used in repayment schedule negotiations. From these calculations various project parameters and ratios are calculated, such as:

1. Project sources and uses of funds, distributable cash, and directions for the project company's waterfall accounts
2. The project's NPV, which is the sum of the project's annual cash flows discounted at the sponsor company's weighted cost of capital. Sometimes, the profit-to-investment ratio is used instead of NPV, which is defined as NPV/initial investment. At other times, the project's risk-adjusted NPV is estimated to account for cash flow uncertainty each year

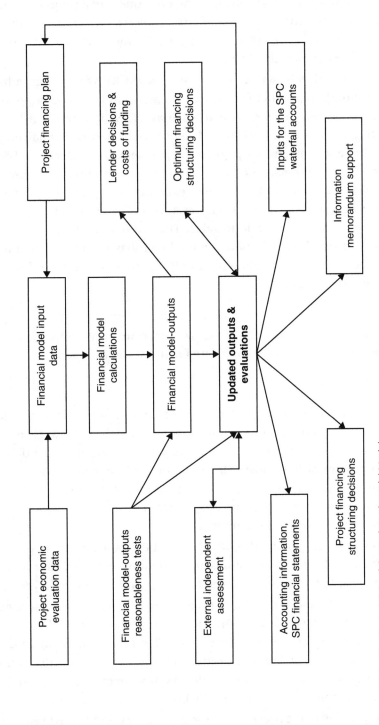

Figure 14.3 The Central Role of the Project Financial Model

3. The sponsors' or equity IRR, which is the rate that makes the project NPV equal to zero and the minimum sponsor IRR, is used as a cut-off point when assessing if the investment in a project is viable. The equity IRR for moderate risk projects in low-risk countries ranges from 12% to 15% a year up to 20% for projects in developing countries (Yescombe, 2014)

4. The annual debt service cover ratio (ADSCR), which is calculated from projections after the project company has been operating for at least one year. This ratio is defined as: ADSCR =annual net operating cash flow/annual project debt service, where annual project debt service is annual principal repayment plus interest. ADSCR is a basic summary of the project company's ability to raise the funds required to meet interest expenses and principal payments during a specific time period. But, it is one determinant of the level of debt the SPC is able to raise. The minimum ADSCR varies by project risk from 1.2 for accommodation-based contracts to 2.0 for merchant power plants without offtake contracts or price hedging (Yescombe, 2014)

Accommodation-type projects are social infrastructure projects such as schools, hospitals, prisons, elder care facilities, stadiums, etc.

5. Loan life cover ratio (LLCR) = NPV of net operating cash flow / (debt balance – service reserve amounts), where debt balance is usually senior debt at the time of calculation. This ratio gives lenders an indication of how many times the project' net cash flow over the project lifetime can repay the outstanding debt. The minimum initial requirement for average risk projects can be as 10% higher than the minimum ADSCR requirement

6. The average of annual ADSCR and LLCR ratios over the project's number of years of operations are better long-term indicators of coverage and, therefore, are given more weight in lending decisions

7. Project life cover ratio (PLCR) = Net operating cash flow before debt service for the project's entire life discounted at the rate of NPV/debt outstanding at time of calculation. This ratio is used in cases of cash-flow volatility that cause on-time repayment difficulties. Lenders usually want to see PLCRs anywhere from 15% to 20% higher than the minimum ADRCR

8. In projects that extract natural resources, two ratios are used in the evaluation of their financeability and reserve cover ratios. The first

ratio is the production-to-reserves ratio (PRR) to determine if reserves are depleted by production. The second ratio is the reserve life index (RLI) defined as: RLI = reserves/production, which shows the number of years of reserves assuming the project company has the ability to develop the source of the reserves

9. Debt-to-equity ratio (D/E). The debt-to-equity ratio determines the SPC's financial leverage and shows the share of assets being financed through debt. It is considered a long-term project company solvency indicator of the soundness its long-term financial policies. The debt-to-equity ratio varies by type of project and can range from 90:10 for accommodation based contracts to 50:50 for natural-resource extraction projects

10. Project-company financial statements are derived from the financial model calculations and—in addition to being used for tax calculation, financial analysis, and reporting purposes—they are used to check the validity of project model inputs and outputs

11. A valuable output of the project financial model is the model's sensitivity to results of different decision parameters due to changes in a single model driver or input. Through sensitivity analysis one can identify which single individual model input to change in order to help improve project economics and ensure its long-term viability

12. Sound development, simulation, and evaluation of different scenarios are only possible through the project financial model. Plausible scenario simulations for random changes in model assumptions and inputs are valuable because they define the outcome ranges of financial parameters and ratios under different probabilities of occurrence. Especially useful are black-swan event scenario simulations for rare but extreme shocks to the project company's operations

Since account agreements, waterfall account structures, and various precedents and conditions can be specified in the project financial model, the cascade of payments out of proceeds account is a model output requirement of lenders and sponsors and for that reason it must be tested and validated. Furthermore, the evaluation of the other project financial model outputs serves other useful functions and yields benefits which include the following:

1. Understanding the effects and impacts of changes in the amounts of project company debt capacity

2. Assessing the value of pursuing different short-term project funding facilities based on cost considerations

3. Incorporating the effects of different refinancing channels and facilities in long term financing decisions

4. Determining the appropriate project life span to ensure adequate loan repayment capacity and equity investor expected returns

5. Establishing the adequacy of credit enhancements to confirm profitable project company viability

6. Validating the reasonableness and ensuring consistency of both financial model inputs and outputs

14.4 PROPERTIES OF GOOD PROJECT FINANCIAL MODELS

The analysis of project financial model outputs is used to determine project financeability, the project company's borrowing capacity, and the type of funding to be raised. However, the quality of model outputs is affected by input factors that may be considered not very significant and yet turn out to have substantial impacts. Usually, the emphasis is on the analysis of outputs more than the scenario events and the description of the environment the project is taking place in, or on factors that determine the quality of good project financial models.

Experts in large project financial modeling development freely admit that such models become complex and prone to errors as soon as details are input into the model (Bodmer, 2015). Also, because the input variable interactions and feedback effects are not always well understood, models do not make correct calculations every time. Often, an inconsistency in financial model inputs results in large model-output errors and renders them inadequate to base decisions on them. Thus, in the remainder of this section, we present observations of project finance-model performance and lessons learned in this area.

The first element of reliable project financial models is correct translation of qualitative information to quantitative model inputs such as, for example, the assessment of a project-risk likelihood of occurrence and severity of impact based on the opinion of outside advisors. Sound judgment and a balance of perspectives and assumptions based on thorough analyses and evaluations is another aspect of respectable financial models. In such models, over-optimism is checked by independent reviews and the findings of the project due diligence. Comprehensiveness and inclusion of knowable and quantifiable model inputs and driving factors is essential because missing input factors cause erroneous model outputs. Therefore, complete checklists of input factors, data, and assumptions are created at the start of the undertaking and going over them to make sure no significant influencing factors are improperly considered or left out.

Validation of reasonableness of initial project requirements and specifications are a must in order for the feasibility study to recommend proceeding with the project from a sound basis of cost and revenue projections. Often, these essential determinants of costs become part of negotiations and result in changes of project viability and additional sponsor equity investments. Also, the completeness and reasonableness of scenario specifications are the foundation of the environmental structure the project financial model is built on. Here, elements such as the effects of industry structure developments, impacts of megatrends and subtrends, customer or user acceptance and ability to pay, and the effects of unmitigated risks are examples of both qualitative and quantitative factors that need to be incorporated in revenue forecasts, the key component in project cash-flow calculations.

A conservative approach to modeling with cost–benefit considerations in mind throughout should be prevalent in sound project financial models, and a balance of project-participant interests and concerns should dominate the development of model inputs. The latter is especially important in the allocation of risks and the stability of the structure the financial model is based on. Another important characteristic of good project financial models is that assumptions, their sources, and rationale are spelled out clearly and assumption updates, tests, and validations are well documented. Additionally, ongoing validation of information, data inputs, and relationships is necessary to ensure the reasonableness and reliability of project financial model-output parameters and ratios.

Independent verification of model input and output reasonableness, consistency, and validation at every financial model version and inputs update done by external advisors provides a higher level of confidence in the output parameters and ratios. But, how does one determine the reasonableness of model outputs? A test commonly used is evaluation of model-output ratios against previous sponsor and other project stakeholder experiences, and examining their behavior against comparable project statistics and industry averages. Is that enough to ensure model output reliability? No, it is not. Confirmation of realistic scenarios and sanity checks of outputs at each stage are necessary features of sound project financial models, as is sensitivity analysis that demonstrates how model-parameter changes could be made to achieve more efficient project financeability.

The properties of good project financial models discussed so far require a myriad of structure and input factor examinations. However, sound modeling practices and samples of project financial models for different types of projects are available on the internet, which confirm their complexity and show how to structure them. The absolute accuracy of project-model parameters and ratios cannot always be ensured because of the multitude of variables and inputs, events, and timing of events. What helps, however, is checking the validity of the project company financial statements with each project financial model run. That is because errors in financial statements are traceable back to model assumptions or inputs that can then be revised to more reasonable levels and produce corrected financial statements.

There is something to be said about model adequacy, simplicity, and parsimony with intense focus on a key cash-flow drivers being sufficient once the project feasibility study and due diligence have confirmed the quality and reliability of model inputs. Sound judgment is essential in discerning causes and effects of quantifiable and nonquantifiable project factors, but it is a challenging feat. For example, how does one compensate and balance sound model structure and inputs against less than effective communication, coordination, and cooperation among project stakeholders or contract noncompliance?

In addition to the attributes mentioned earlier that contribute to project financial model success, certain other practices strengthen the financial model's structure and enhance accuracy of its outputs. Examples of these practices include the following:

1. Using a modular approach to project financial model building is better as opposed to one large model performing all needed calculations in one module
2. Developing and maintaining a repository of input data, information, assumptions, outputs, and decisions made in different project stages
3. Ensuring that the project financial model addresses all sponsor strategic needs and standards and incorporates host government tax and regulatory requirements
4. Ascertaining the quality of assumptions and testing their validity in different project stages and their reasonableness on an ongoing basis using industry benchmarks and earlier project experiences
5. Building into the financial model checks and thoroughly testing it to eliminate gaps, circular logic, input errors, and wrong calculations

Additional useful lessons learned from financial model assessments that help developing sound models include the following:

1. Using best-modeling practices and software to build and test the financial model and provide ample documentation and easy to read charts
2. Demonstrating the financial model's logical structure, the flow of processing calculations, and application of specific tests

3. Maintaining data integrity, effective knowledge management throughout the project life cycle, and open communication and information sharing with all project participants

4. Subjecting the project financial model to independent, critical, and objective reviews and evaluations to ensure reliability and accuracy of its outputs

5. Ensuring that causality and feedback effects in scenarios tested are properly specified and their impacts checked for consistency and reasonableness

6. Documenting all decisions made by date, deciding party, project team acceptance, and other relevant factors

7. Including an evaluation of project-model performance in every project post-mortem analysis

CHAPTER 15

Trends Impacting Project Finance

Opportunities and Threats

n the new business development discipline, megatrends and subtrends are of crucial importance because of their potential effects on business strategy and the success of projects. Even though one has no control over them, how a business gets ahead of and adapts to them makes a difference. Hence, analysis of megatrends and their implications are a vital element of a sponsor company's strategic, financing, and business plans. What is more important than knowing which ones impact a business is what one does with that information to take advantage or avoid megatrends. Once their impacts are well understood by all stakeholders, they are used in decision making across all sponsor company organizations and in enhancing stakeholder cooperation.

Figure 15.1 shows trend components and illustrates that the assessment of trends first involves identification, then analysis of megatrends, subtrends, and PESTLED trend effects. To be of value, it also involves trend response planning. The term megatrend was popularized by John Naisbitt (1982), defined megatrends as global, broad impact, sustained forces of change that affect industries, economies, societies and cultures, and peoples' lives. The effects of megatrends are permanent and shape the business environment, competition, and the future of the world. Subtends on the other hand, are prevailing tendencies, movements, or progressions within or outside megatrends that persist over a period of time. Trends are different than fads in that trends are bottom–up determining actions, whereas fads are top–down phenomena of limited lifespan. Trends are also different than predictions, which are forecasts, opinions, projections, or extrapolations from trends and the two should not be confused.

Like project risks, the determination and evaluation of relevant global-trend impacts on a project are done properly in the early development stage of new projects and investment opportunities. An extension of this effort is the assessment of subtrends impacting the prospective investment country and the industry of the contemplated investment. For project financing purposes, however, it is as important to understand how trends and subtrends affect the project company and different project stakeholders as well. Namely, the sponsors and potential investors involved, the participating host government authority involved, the infrastructure construction industry, and the project finance industry participants. This understanding is important because trends:

1. Define to a significant degree the competitive environment and how doing business is changing
2. Provide insights on why and how project company output or consumer and user tastes are changing
3. Give indications of potential opportunities and threats currently and in the future

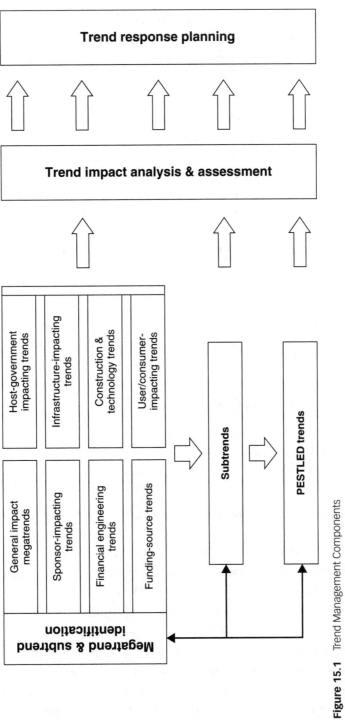

Figure 15.1 Trend Management Components

4. Help develop reasonable assumptions and scenarios and improve the project team's project evaluation ability and reliability of cost and revenue forecasts

5. Prepare the project company to realize the benefit or avoid the threat of their realization and prepare for appropriate responses

6. Trend analysis is a tool for critical thinking and strategic, scenario development, and effective new business development planning

Our discussion of megatrends and subtrends is of a cursory nature and it is partly based on discussions with clients, project consultants and advisors, and benchmarking study participants. Section 15.1 presents relevant trends to project finance, while Section 15.2 discusses the nature and origin of trends affecting project stakeholders and characteristics of trends impacting projects. Section 15.3 enumerates the demographic trends expected to continue into the future, while Section 15.4 highlights trends impacting technology and the infrastructure industry.

Trends that impact governments and their reaction to them are presented in Section 15.5, while trends that impact sponsors and debt and equity investors are discussed in Section 15.6. Trends impacting funding sources and financing of infrastructure projects and financial engineering are addressed in Section 15.7. Lastly, Section 15.8 addresses the process and resources used to identify and analyze relevant trends and assess potential impacts. It also sketches out how one may take advantage of trends.

15.1 MAJOR RELEVANT MEGATRENDS

The megatrends considered here are twenty years out, generally applicable to all types of infrastructure projects, well accepted and known, have global effects across infrastructure and project finance industries. They include the following:

1. The rise of the 7 Emerging (7E) countries, which are Brazil, Russia, India, China, Indonesia, Mexico, and Turkey (PWC, 2014)

2. Resource scarcity drives investment to projects focused on securing resources and economic development and less to projects to meet pressing health and social needs (KPMG, 2015)

3. Developers, sponsors, financiers, EPC contractors, and insures are going global (KPMG, 2015)

4. The development of smart cities to create substantial investment and business opportunities (KPMG, 2015)

5. Increased supply of infrastructure projects due to increased privatizations of government assets all over the world to meet budgetary or social needs (KPMG, 2015)

6. For the next 10 or so years, the emerging Asian countries (China, India, Indonesia, Malaysia, Philippines, Thailand, and Vietnam) will drive global infrastructure spending (KPMG, 2015)

7. Recognition of climate change around the globe and its causes will exacerbate resource scarcities, especially water, food, and energy. However, total food production has been estimated to grow significantly between 2010 and 2030 (Frost and Sullivan presentation)

The US National Intelligence Council (NIC) is an expert, reliable, and accurate source of global megatrend identification. In its 2010 assessment, which is still operating today, it considered the following megatrends as most impactful:

1. A trend towards a more closely knit and more complex international business system

2. Transfer of wealth and political influence from the West to the East continues into the foreseeable future

3. Scarcity of resources gives rise to geopolitical rivalries and the potential for increased conflict is present due to competition for food, water, and energy

4. New geopolitical strategic investors are emerging, such as national oil companies and Chinese resource extraction companies investing in infrastructure projects outside their countries

5. Terrorism and conflict will be major concerns as geostrategic risks rise and produce uncertainty

6. In response to wider access to lethal technologies and terrorism, a rise in homeland security and cybersecurity spending takes place and will continue in the future

7. Nongovernment organizations increase their international presence, but not with significant changes in their impact

8. The individual empowerment trend continues along with changing consumer tastes and the growth of consumers in emerging countries with ability to pay

9. The role of the US dollar in international transactions declines and the transition to a new international system has new risks

10. Dissimilar trends in aging populations between countries and within regions continue and geopolitical rivalries cause more disruptions than technological changes

11. Development of disruptive technologies, especially information technologies, affect all aspects of people's lives

12. Urbanization and the creation of megacities and megaregions that focus on urban mobility

15.2 MEGATREND SOURCES AND CHARACTERISTICS

Megatrends originate from good ideas, basic necessity factors, and innovation. In order to be sustainable, they also have reinforcement from the subtrends they generate and from the impact they have. Trends are developed from dynamic interactions with political, economic, societal, technological, legal, educational, and demographic factors. Changes in political and military power can trigger the development of trends that can be localized or broad and so can changes in economic systems. Legal and regulatory changes can set in motion trends affecting national economies, industries, and business models. Also, education and demographic changes can start the creation of trends that could impact the entire economy of a country for years to come.

Besides technological disruptions, the causes of megatrends and subtrends are associated with the following elements that underlie their development. In summary form, they are:

1. Unmet social needs, such as housing, health care facilities, schools, water treatment plants, etc.
2. Geopolitical, strategic, and military power shifts
3. Aging populations and increased urbanization around the world
4. Shortages of natural resources, the most important being water, food, and energy
5. New technology introductions and revolutionary product and service introductions
6. Governments reprioritizing economic development and growth plans
7. Changing consumer needs and tastes brought about by globalization

Megatrends are universal in nature; that is, they affect people's lives around the globe in varying degrees but have similar characteristics, the most important being:

1. They are closely interconnected and feedback effects back and forth between them reinforce each other
2. They produce conditions for the creation of new opportunities and innovation and also potentially adverse effects
3. Even though they are global, the impacts of megatrends are realized with different lags and impacts in different countries
4. Factors underlying megatrends are constantly changing and affect the direction, impact, and speed of trends

The effects of megatrends and subtrends on infrastructure projects can vary significantly across countries, industries, sectors and projects. However, their impact is evident in the following areas:

1. Engineering and design of plants and facilities and project specifications affecting costs
2. The models and structures used in project development
3. Bidding and procurement frameworks and systems
4. Project logistics and delivery to affect greater efficiencies
5. Project risks and opportunities that need to be well understood
6. Skills and experience to take advantage of them and create synergies or avoid them or minimize their impact
7. Increased need for additional knowledge, experience, and competencies in project development and financing
8. Development and funding of infrastructure projects, sources of funds, and instruments used

Given these trend characteristics, some basic questions that governments and sponsors need to answer in order to meet the challenges of and benefit by them include the following:

1. What knowledge, information, and skills and competencies are required to create efficient project bids and successful projects for all stakeholders?
2. How do sponsors cooperate with governments and other customers to ride trends and benefit both sides?
3. How can projects be built and financed smarter and more efficiently to obtain a competitive advantage under the effect of trends?
4. How can disruptive technologies be channeled to address urban transportation problems and water, energy, and food shortages?
5. What happens if sponsors, developers, technology and equipment providers, and governments do not meet the challenges of megatrends and subtrends?

15.3 DEMOGRAPHIC TRENDS

There is general agreement that demographic trends are a determining factor of the demand for infrastructure projects around the world. The National Intelligence Council (2012) studied the source of trends and their implications. These trends, which have been operative for a number of years, are expected to continue into the future:

1. An unprecedented and widespread aging in developed countries that puts pressures for increased social infrastructure projects
2. The growth of the global middle class around the world will maintain momentum
3. The growth of Muslim population will remain greater than other backgrounds
4. Population increase trends in China and India are lasting into the foreseeable future and these countries will achieve parity with the United States in human capital and science
5. Population decline trends present in sub-Saharan Africa, Russia, Eastern Europe, and Japan will persist
6. High immigration rates to the United States, Canada, and Australia continue due to demand for highly qualified professionals and increased population displacements
7. Asia, Africa, and Latin America will account for all the global population growth in the next 20 years
8. Ongoing urbanization by 2025 will increase the global urban population to around 57% and will drive water, transportation, and energy infrastructure projects
9. Social infrastructure spending will be determined by demographic shifts and by trends in education, health, and young and old population changes
10. Increased constraints on public finances are taking place due to aging populations and physical and cyberspace security concerns

The demographic trend impacts come primarily from three sources: The increased needs for basic needs of water and food; medical facilities and services; and public elder-care facilities and nursing homes. These trends, in turn, exert increased pressures on emerging and developing country government budgets to shift priorities away from other infrastructure projects. To support economic growth, however, governments are required to increase spending on educational facilities and urbanization project needs. The impacts of demographic trends are fairly easily forecasted and translated into needs governments consider in long-range planning. This will increase investment in social infrastructure projects and funding, primarily through the use of PPP models. However, the impact of trends on development infrastructure cannot be as easily assessed and investments in this area are primarily driven by economic growth needs.

15.4 TECHNOLOGY AND INDUSTRY TRENDS

Since the financial crisis of 2008, a tendency is observed towards increased importance and emphasis on rehabilitation of existing infrastructure as opposed to greenfield projects in countries with constrained government budgets and growth of the construction industry in emerging markets. The focus shifts to cities and urban area infrastructure needs and from the ability to fund projects to cost reduction of investment needs. At the same time, there is process innovation taking place in the preparation of project sites, logistics, and the use of new technologies, such as sophisticated logistics and project management software and applications of 3D printing that enhance the efficiency of the infrastructure-construction industry.

Organizational and contractual innovations are taking place and expected to continue, such as computerized inventory control, along with increased use of advanced equipment, tools, and materials, and development of super-supply chains. Further, there is increased attention paid to life-cycle infrastructure risk management that reduces project failures. Also, an important trend that is becoming apparent is one that links procurement, contracting, and project management models with asset operations.

Technology trends are probably the most impactful on the infrastructure industry and include new approaches to solving urbanization problems, and providing improved services and quality of life for people. In addition to the well-known trends in innovation and introduction of new information technology services, futurists like Thomas Fray (2015), talk about trends that will dramatically affect the development of infrastructure projects and construction, such as:

1. A transition of advanced countries to low-carbon economies around the world

2. New infrastructure models being used as the pace of new technologies speeds up

3. Driverless cars will become common in a few years and driverless highways require new road construction methods and integration with technology

4. "Space transportation on Earth," i.e. tube-transportation networks, will change the approach the transport industry by solving road congestion and construction problems

5. Atmospheric water harvesters installed in places where droughts are common will solve many of their water crises

6. Efficient, space-based power stations will be competing with existing terrestrial power plans to meet energy needs

7. Drone-delivery networks to speed up deliveries and make remote areas easier to deliver packages efficiently

8. High power, efficient mass-energy storage facilities and batteries are being developed to support powering new devices

9. Trillion-sensor infrastructure is emerging, which includes analytics, additive manufacturing, energy storage, ultra-low power wireless, network innovation, and operating systems

10. Disruptive new technologies including artificial intelligence, machine learning, augmented reality, the internet of things, etc.

11. New investment opportunities emerging in small biomass to energy projects in rural areas (KPMG, 2015)

Government budget constraints and higher sponsor project-development costs are forcing innovation and the introduction of new technologies to make projects and the infrastructure industry more efficient. Governments and the infrastructure industry are using new technologies and innovations in organizations, contracts and procurement, risk management, and project management. However, solutions to major urbanization-infrastructure needs involve additional new and futuristic technology introductions, costs, and challenges. Along with these solutions to infrastructure needs, come increased physical and cybersecurity challenges that create opportunities to address them effectively.

15.5 TRENDS IMPACTING THE GOVERNMENT SECTOR

Infrastructure project financing is impacted by trends observed in the public sector due to responses by governments and their attempt to get value for money invested. The following are trends observed in this area, but note that these trends may be more country specific and not of uniform impacts in every country:

1. Economic infrastructure gets higher priority than social infrastructure projects because spending on the former stimulates economic growth more that projects in the latter

2. There is an increasing use of PPP models and cofunding of infrastructure projects while governments are using better procurement approaches to ensure value for money

3. Governments are trying to reconcile the need for sound long-range planning with short-term political considerations and priorities

4. There is a trend towards decentralization and increased local public sector involvement in infrastructure projects

5. Governments use increased infrastructure spending to stimulate their economies because their balance sheets are becoming more constrained (Deloitte, 2013)

6. Government budgetary pressures result in projects being awarded on the basis of meeting requirements for local materials purchases, host country production and job creation, in addition to increased tax revenues

7. Governments are introducing policy reforms to attract investors in infrastructure projects and are making equity contributions towards the end of project construction to ensure that private investors stay in the project (Deloitte, 2014)

8. Development-oriented governments are taking steps to increase private investments in infrastructure through:

   a. Market reforms in several infrastructure industries

   b. Creating long-range plans for these sectors and separating infrastructure choices from political decisions

   c. Striving to achieve better infrastructure asset performance

   d. Paying attention to cities and focusing on urban population mobility (KPMG, 2015)

9. Governments are becoming more experienced with project financing techniques and requirements and are making the infrastructure sector more effective by reforming market structures and regulatory regimes of utilities (KPMG, 2015)

10. The shift of infrastructure project development from the public to the private sector is taking place along the transfer of infrastructure costs from taxpayers to consumers or users of infrastructure project services (KPMG, 2015)

The impact of demographic trends causes a shift to social infrastructure projects that is counterbalanced by the effect of government emphasizing projects supporting development and economic growth. Overall, the positive impacts of government impacting trends are balanced in favor of economic growth projects. Budgetary constraints are also causing governments to introduce reforms to attract infrastructure investments that promote needed economic growth and a shift from public to PPP projects that yield value for money spent. A positive impact of budgetary constraints is that governments are becoming more experienced in project finance techniques and shifting infrastructure costs from taxpayers to users.

15.6 TRENDS IMPACTING SPONSORS AND INVESTORS

All trends mentioned so far are affecting sponsors and investors directly or indirectly, but the following are trends generated by factors within these agents that have a direct impact on their mode of operations:

1. Sponsors, developers, and suppliers are looking for ways to further develop project financing skills and capabilities to obtain a competitive advantage in this area

2. Sponsors recognize the need to educate customers in project financing and evaluation of proposals and are developing programs to help public-sector customers

3. Project investors are careful to work within the host country's legal system and avoid corruption situations while they slowly obtain local knowledge, vet local partners, and learn the local culture and how to work with local institutions

4. Sponsors and investors increasingly look beyond contracts for risk management; that is, good contracts in form and flexible in the reality of enforcing them (Woodhouse, 2005)

5. The project due diligence is becoming more critical in effective risk management

6. As megaprojects become common, project participants become increasingly concerned about their complexity rendering them undeliverable or unprofitable

7. An investor preference and focus is emerging for investing in areas of low inflation, minimum systemic risk, and where financial risks are well managed

One of the helpful impacts of trends on sponsors and other investors in infrastructure projects is the transfer of project finance knowledge to governments and the restructuring of legal and regulatory regimes. The latter is also influenced by the intervention of official funding sources that require changes in order to reduce project risks and make them financeable. These effects make project development and financing easier to achieve effectively. Because governments look for effective and flexible contracts, the role of the due diligence is expanded to ensure more effective risk management. While investors look for low-risk projects, infrastructure projects are becoming more complex and costly to develop which, in turn, give incentives to sponsors to introduce innovations to make projects economically viable and they do.

15.7 TRENDS IMPACTING FUNDING SOURCES AND FINANCING

Official, government, and private sources of funding are affected directly by megatrends and trends in the areas discussed earlier. Gaps in funding for urgently needed economic development and social infrastructure projects are causing innovations in order to close those gaps. So, in addition to new players coming into the infrastructure financing market, new models of financing are introduced, such as regulated asset finance, project output-based aid, social impact bonds, and tax increment finance. The trends impacting funding sources and project financing include:

1. Overlooked markets, such as natural resource-rich Africa and other underdeveloped countries, are now considered for infrastructure investment opportunities

2. Private and public customers are becoming more experienced in project financing techniques (NIC, 2012)

3. China will outbid the World Bank with direct aid and foreign assistance to resource rich countries (NIC, 2012)

4. China is supporting building infrastructure around their trade corridors through funding by the Asian Infrastructure Bank, the China Development Bank, and China Exim Bank

5. The role of the US dollar in international transactions will diminish over time (NIC, 2012)

6. New models of project finance such as increased use of tax increment finance, social impact bonds, output based aid, and regulated asset finance with focus on inflation protection projects with minimal risks (Yescombe, 2014)

7. Increased importance of PPI and non-traditional funding sources (Brooking Institution, 2015) and increased crowdsource capital (World Bank, 2013)

8. Upward trend in global infrastructure fundraising for private equity investments

9. Need for transparency rises up the agenda (KPMG, 2013)

10. Political and regulatory risks rise up the agenda (KPMG, 2015)

11. Increased use of sovereign wealth funds and other state investment vehicles in China and the Gulf States (NIC, 2008)

12. New geopolitical investors such as China providing economic assistance to African countries and investing in petroleum and mineral resource extraction projects

13. Domestic lenders are becoming increasingly more sophisticated and provide a higher share of lending to infrastructure projects

14. Equity investment flow is matched by the development of the infrastructure bond market and the percentage of project bonds to loans is increasing

Creation of the New Development Bank and the Contingency Reserve Arrangement by the BRICS countries, the establishment of the Asian Infrastructure Investment Bank, the China Africa Development Fund, and the Silk Road Fund are ample evidence of trends to more infrastructure funding sources sponsored or led by Chinese institutions. These changes are creating trends that have global impacts, and other financing trends that affect sponsors and governments include:

1. Growth of project finance deals due to privatization of infrastructure assets and the need to increase productivity and stimulate economic growth

2. Globalization of the infrastructure fund market is increasing as more governments are privatizing infrastructure assets (Della Goce and Gatti, 2014/1)

3. ECAs and development finance institutions continue to be a driving force in the global project finance industry, but the role of multilaterals and development banks is shifting

4. Transactions are taking more time, have higher costs, and rely more on official funding (Deloitte, 2013)

5. Less long-term financing is coming from banks due to higher Basel IV reserve requirements and banks now cooperate with institutional investors to channel debt funds to infrastructure projects

6. Increased investment coming from investors such as equity funds and new private equity funds

7. Continued market growth for infrastructure projects through project pooling and the development of investment funds

8. Increased role of Islamic finance for large-scale projects in the Middle East and other Islamic countries

9. Rating companies conduct due diligence and project debt is priced according to the rating of the transaction

10. Increased focus on the balance of budgetary priorities and social project spending will be determined by a country's economic growth

11. Increased application of project finance in healthcare facilities, pharmaceuticals, real estate, and other industry projects

In summary, trends impacting funding sources and project financing show that the role of China will lead development of infrastructure projects not only in underdeveloped countries, but around the world. After China, Islamic financing will expand its influence in funding projects and this creates conditions for other sources of funding to increase their cooperation and pooling of funds. Because of the impacts of trends on project financing and other areas, projects are becoming more complex, take longer to complete, and involve higher costs. At the same time, project finance is increasingly being used to fund projects beyond infrastructure, such as in real estate, pharmaceuticals, and other industries. Also, Islamic financing and pension and sovereign wealth funds will play a significant role in the globalization of the infrastructure fund market.

15.8 ANALYSIS OF TRENDS AND THEIR IMPACT

The purpose of identifying and assessing trends is to evaluate their impacts on the business and to plan to take advantage of them or minimize adverse impacts. The different elements and the process of identifying trends and their impacts affecting the project company's operations are illustrated in Figure 15.8.1. The process begins with identifying megatrends, sub-trends, and PESTLED trends and determining which ones and to what extent they are relevant for a particular country and industry. At this junction, it is important to ensure that fads are separated from trends and determining how the relevant trends are likely to impact the industry the project company is in. This step is helpful in assessing trend effects on the industry structure and likely changes in the operating environment's competitive forces.

Once the effects of trends affecting the industry are well understood, the process examines how industry-relevant trends will affect the project company's future and determine the magnitude of impacts on its financial performance over its lifetime. The evaluation of trends impacting the project company specifically includes an assessment of trend effects on future technology; host country legal and regulatory changes; unmet customer/user needs and changes in preferences; and potential threats to the project company's success. While the process of identifying relevant trends is fairly straightforward, the quantification of their impacts requires a thorough analysis of analogs from competitors and other industries, and the evaluation and input of industry experts.

The identification of trends and their impacts on project finance deals is crucial because of project characteristics, sizable investment requirements, and required quality of financial projections to make projects financeable. The quantification of trend impacts requires building up strong competitive analysis competencies that support the sponsor organization's strategic

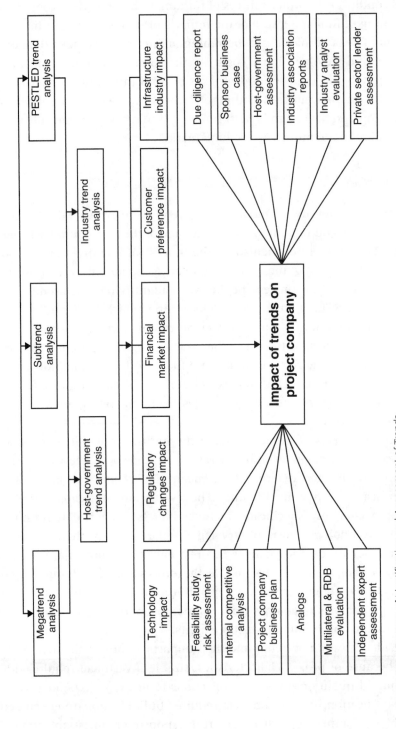

Figure 15.8.1 Process of Identification and Assessment of Trends

planning, business development, and PFO efforts. This involves activities such as:

1. Attending industry conferences and networking with others who are knowledgeable in identifying trends and have experience in quantifying their effects

2. Identifying industry leaders and watching actions of those industry leaders in response to trends impacting them

3. Doing host country market research and assessing competitor plans and initiatives there and in similar countries

4. Obtaining the views and opinions of industry experts and consultants and getting the insights of industry analysts

5. Reading industry reports and industry analyst commentaries and assessments about trends

6. Obtaining and evaluating opinions and predictions of futurists and analyzing their reports, academic articles, and papers on trends and impacts on different industries

7. Monitoring industry reports and checking trade magazines, such as the D&B First Research Industry Profiles and Frost and Sullivan's Market Analysis

8. Researching home and host country government reports on PESTLED trends and their effects on different industries

9. Getting the perspective of project bond rating agencies and insurance companies on the effects of trends on project finance transactions

10. Researching multilateral agency and ECA reports on future trends and developments in project finance

11. Leveraging the knowledge of relationships in various funding sources and obtaining their perspective on trends and future scenarios

12. Asking the right questions and listening closely to customers and users

A variant of Figure 15.8.1 is a sketch summary of the progression of identifying relevant trends and quantifying their impact on a project is shown in Figure 15.8.2, with assessment of trend impacts focused on:

1. Understanding the sources of trends and changes caused by them

2. Identifying areas of innovations affecting each project stakeholder

3. Evaluating impacts of technology changes on project pricing and project delivery

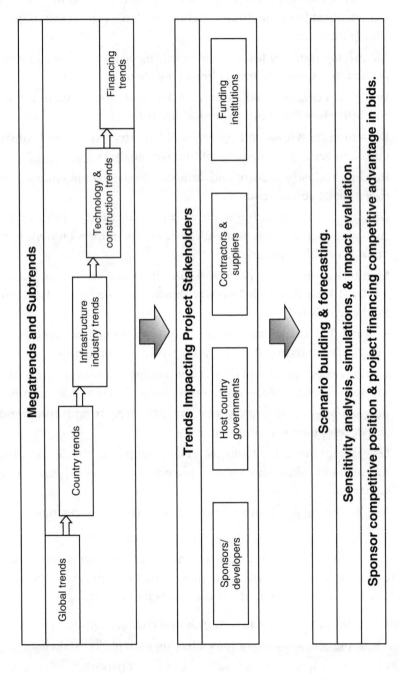

Figure 15.8.2 Progression of Quantifying Impacts of Trends

4. Quantifying and examining trend-impact scenario effects on the project financial model outputs

5. Assessing trend effects on sponsor competitive position and project financing

The first order in the assessment process starts with selecting the most relevant megatrends followed by a thorough host country environmental analysis and, having the benefit of the insights of futurists, determine how different trends are likely to affect the project company. Once the identification of country, industry, and company impacting trends is complete, trend impacts affecting the nature of a product or service and delivery are evaluated. How? By leveraging knowledge of industry experts, building plausible scenarios for forecasting models, and analyzing the effects of trends on pricing, demand, and the supply of the project company's output.

The evaluation of scenario outputs and sensitivity analysis facilitates a reasonably good assessment of the project company's SWOT analysis under the impact of trends. It also helps in the development of sponsor strategy and plans to deal with adverse trend impacts or prepare to take advantage of the opportunities presented by them. However, trend analysis and impact quantification are far more valuable when taking into account the impact of trends on all project stakeholders. This is needed because, for example, what impacts sponsors one way may affect equipment suppliers, host governments, contractors, and funding sources differently and/or with different lags. Note that ordinarily the evaluation of other trend impacts on stakeholders is of lesser rigor than that of on sponsors and the project company. However, differential impacts need to be considered and may require reconciling to satisfy adversely impacted parties.

What is also important in overall trend assessment is that trend impacts need to be evaluated for specific areas of a given project. Namely, impact evaluation on the following project areas:

1. Design, engineering, specifications, and requirements

2. Feasibility study, development, and sustainability

3. Competency and knowledge requirements

4. Procurement, logistics, and project delivery

5. Risk identification, mitigation, and enhancements required

6. Project economics, financeability, and funding

7. Costs and efficiencies and potential synergies

8. Sponsor company's competitive advantage in project development and financing

Once trends are identified, analyzed, and their impacts quantified, planning and preparation to take advantage of trends or avoid adverse effects take place. Here, the value added of experts in competitive analysis and strategic-decision forecasting are crucial in the development of response and expectation realization planning. Why? Because the various trend impacts need to be integrated into an overall project value impact. This requires extensive industry knowledge, skills, and experience, and seasoned judgment to make the integration by assigning appropriate weights to different trends.

CHAPTER 16

Project Finance

A Source of Competitive Advantage?

C ompetitive advantage is the superiority of a company that enables it to deliver a project, product or service at a lower cost, better quality, or in a manner that markets perceive as superior to that of competitors. It is the competencies and capabilities that a company can leverage to offer higher value by matching them to market opportunities when presented. Simply stated, it is what makes a company better than its competitors in the minds of customers and it is a key goal of business strategies and new business development to win bids and be more profitable than competitors. Sustainable competitive advantages are the unique, quantifiable, and substantial resources, assets, and capabilities that give a company an advantageous position over the long run and are difficult to duplicate. Sustainable competitive advantage is a short-term occurrence that may be replicated a number of times, but which is very difficult to maintain over long periods.

Competitive advantage is an important consideration in the business development and project finance disciplines because:

1. The selection of project proposals is based on least-total cost considerations, other things being the same

2. It creates a strong image of competence, financial strength, and trust to deliver on promises

3. It provides security and comfort to decision makers having selected a sponsor or developer that has a competitive advantage when things go wrong and problems arise

4. It is an ingredient of winning bids that is partly due to long-term relationships with construction contractors, equipment providers, funding sources, and insurers known for providing best value in their industries

5. Contract negotiations and agreements with sponsor companies possessing a competitive advantage gain approval from funding source decision makers quicker because of their positive reputation

6. Companies that have one type or another of competitive advantage deliver proposals that win contracts that deliver superior value to customers

Chapters 3 to 15 discussed the primary elements of what makes effective organizations, sound processes, and successful project implementation. Application of the understanding of what it takes to outdo competitors in project finance is a source of competitive advantage built on foundations such as:

1. Knowledge of the causes and sources of failures, learning from failures of project finance deals, and addressing reasons of project failures

2. Integrated project financing with strategic planning and new business-development processes and effective project management

3. Superior project finance organization competencies and capabilities applied to various project idiosyncrasies to provide effective financing solutions

4. Proper early project screening, planning, and development and management of stakeholder expectations

5. Clarity of roles and responsibilities of internal sponsor organizations and among other project participants

6. Thorough project economic evaluations based on sound strategic decision forecasting grounded on tested and reasonable assumptions and scenarios

7. Appropriately structured and negotiated agreements that are sustainable and enforceable in the project's host country

8. Thorough ongoing risk identification, assessment, and mitigation based on cost–benefit and best-able-to-bear considerations

9. Comprehensive due diligence that tests, verifies, and validates all aspects of project economics, risk management, and financeability

After a thorough due diligence is completed, other foundations of building a competitive advantage are based on the following:

1. Good understanding of megatrends and subtrends, their impacts on the industry and the project, and the ability to take advantage of them, create synergies, or avoid negative impacts

2. Well-structured, complete, and tested financial model and thorough testing and assessment of its outputs and their implications

3. Extensive knowledge of funding sources and facilities, experience with their products and processes, and global financing alliances

4. Breadth of experience in structuring successful project financings under different project and customer challenges and changing markets

In the sections that follow we look at successful project participant attributes from a competitive advantage perspective. Specifically, Section 16.1 deals with the common sources of competitive advantage necessary for the business development and project financing functions to be successful. The question of how a company would know that it has a competitive advantage is addressed in Section 16.2, which shows manifestations of competitive advantage, while Section 16.3 discusses strategies and options to strive for gaining competitive advantage. Section 16.4 is a reality check on whether creating and maintaining a competitive advantage in the long run is possible. It is based on interviews with project finance stakeholders and presents key findings of a benchmarking study on project finance best practices.

16.1 SOURCES OF COMPETITIVE ADVANTAGE

The well-known and commonly mentioned sources of competitive advantage that create an economic moat in any industry are the following factors:

1. Barriers of entry due to large capital investments required upfront or due to protection from industry regulatory regimes

2. Strategic assets, such as ownership of or access to resources, proprietary new technology, long-term contractual agreements, patents and trademarks, and other intellectual property

3. Exceptional skills and competencies developed and nourished and improved on an ongoing basis in areas affecting competitiveness

4. Low-cost, low-pricing ability due to economies of scale, flawless processes, and leveraging of buying power and long-term contracts with suppliers and contractors

5. Sponsor or developer experience and reputation that results in brand loyalty over time that makes customers prefer that brand over competitors'

6. Offering projects, products, or services that offer new designs, innovations, and quality improvements that enable a sponsor to increase prices without losing bids

7. Financial strength of a company with a strong balance sheet, high credit rating and access to capital, and the ability to invest in promising project opportunities as they come up

In the infrastructure industry, the sources of competitive advantage may differ from company to company, but are complementary to the universal sources of competitive advantage mentioned above and include:

1. Strategy drives project portfolio management, project screening, and selection, as well as project objectives and clarity of purpose

2. Project development objectives incorporate plans to meet customer needs and objectives and create a positive experience

3. Superior visionary senior management team accessible by the project manager and the project finance organization (PFO) well versed in project finance

4. Strong project finance skills and competencies yielding effective project development and financing implementation excellence

5. Project team support by highly experienced associates in bidding and procurement, competitive analysis, risk assessment and allocation, forecasting and scenario planning, and project financing

6. Unparalleled and unimpeded 360-degree communication, coordination, cooperation, and collaboration (4Cs) within the project team and between stakeholders

7. Best in class, collaborative, highly effective project management and stakeholder relationship management across all project phases

8. Appropriate project finance organizational structure, critical mass, culture, and prestige image with strong internal links, external alliances, and personal relationships

9. Presence and brand recognition in the region and preferably in the country undertaking the infrastructure projects or through joint ventures to deliver competitive bids

10. Close business contacts and personal relationships with current and prospective customers, funding sources, and ECA and multilateral agency decision makers

16.2 MANIFESTATIONS OF COMPETITIVE ADVANTAGE

Sponsor or developer organizations with some experiences in infrastructure project financing often ask the question: What are signs that indicate we could have or are on the way to achieving a competitive advantage? Some of the usual indications of presence of competitive advantage in project finance include:

1. Optimization of sponsor-project portfolios, giving customers more choices than competitors, and providing service differentiation, all of which create positive customer perceptions

2. Solid commitment to projects and significant equity participation that provide comfort to customers and which create bids considered better or of greater value for money spent

3. Lower total project costs and financing efficiency along with better project delivery experience that meets customer needs and expectations

4. All projects, except a few that are rejected as nonfinanceable, are effectively implemented and project companies are managed successfully to the end of project life

Responses given by infrastructure project participants to the question raised about how a company would know if it possesses a competitive advantage were fairly consistent and revealed the following indications:

1. Winning more project contracts than competitors that submitted lower bids

2. Focus on strategic objectives, intent, and creating and implementing successful project selection and development strategies

3. Continually adapting to changing external business environments and formulating project development and financing strategies to match strengths and capabilities to new market opportunities

4. Building core company strengths to enhance project success, paying close attention to relevance and appropriateness of project proposals, and focusing on financeable projects

5. Promoting continuous innovation and creativity in all aspects of project finance and further development of resources, skills, and capabilities

6. Sponsors that partner with and educate customers to create successful projects, obtain positive customer satisfaction feedback, and establish a preference for doing business with those sponsors

7. Projects that move along established processes with minimal disruptions, come to closing effectively, and implement project company business plans efficiently

8. The project sponsor company's financial reports reflect performance in or above the range of expectations

Many PFO skills and competencies are an essential part of competitive advantage. They are itemized below and when they are fully developed, they constitute an indicator of competitive advantage in project finance. Such PFOs must have capabilities and competencies demonstrated by the following properties exhibited in the course of project development and implementation:

1. PFO critical mass and proximity to decision makers along with immersion in corporate strategy, strategic intent, and the ability to translate them into achievable project objectives

2. Clearly articulated project strategy and objectives and consistency of corporate risk appetite with project risk

3. Extensive expertise and objectivity in competitive and strengths, weakness, opportunities, threats (SWOT) analyses and demonstrated competency in meeting all PFO roles and responsibilities

4. Accurate assessment of megatrends and trends in project finance and the host country's political, economic, social, technological, legal, educational, and demographic (PESTLED) conditions, and industry structure and competitiveness

5. Ability of the project team to anticipate, evaluate, and take advantage of trends by leveraging company's strengths to enhance readiness and maximize benefit

6. Complete, clear, and efficient core project development and financing processes and well-understood activities to be followed by the project team

7. Sound project screening and evaluation and conservative feasibility studies leading to thorough project assessments that ensure project economic viability and financeability

8. Unconstrained access to internal decision makers and unwavering support for effective project development, experienced bidding, and effective delivery of financing proposals

9. Highly effective project management and integration of processes, activities, and deliverables, extensive experience in all types of projects in the industry, and financing solutions to peculiar project and customer challenges

10. Demonstrated, unconstrained, all-around communication, coordination, cooperation, and collaboration within the project team and with other project participants

Other signs that indicate PFO progress to the point of attaining a competitive advantage include the following qualities and competencies. Notice, however, that these qualities translate to more effective and efficient project development and ultimately to more competitive project bids.

1. Sound competitive analysis; cost, demand, and revenue forecasting; project economic evaluation, and efficient and optimized project structuring

2. Thorough and objective due diligence, a clearly stated and presented report, and comprehensive life-cycle risk assessment, balanced risk allocation, and risk management

3. Ability to bring together diverse participant interests to reach consensus and effective negotiations and conflict management

4. Thorough knowledge and experience with optimal project structures and financial markets and instruments as well as skillful evaluation of lender and investor requirements, proposals, and their implications

5. Effective all-around internal and external relationship management and extensive contacts and personal relationships in funding sources

6. Thorough knowledge of the host government, ECA, and multilateral agency processes and requirements to get funding approvals efficiently

7. Skilled project financial modeling, evaluation, and interpretation of results and experienced in providing input to and evaluating project agreements and contracts

8. Competency in providing negotiation support, evaluation of proposals and counterproposals, and ensuring well thought out, cost/benefit analysis based, sustainable and enforceable contracts

9. Seasoned in creating sound project company business plans and operational targets and experienced in assessing critical success factors and performance indicators

10. Effective in the development of early warning systems and indicators and project company course correction planning

11. Ongoing monitoring of project company operations for objective evaluation of financial performance and variance analysis

12. Information and knowledge management and documentation and superior project post mortem analysis expertise

16.3 CREATING COMPETITIVE ADVANTAGE

Meeting customer project requirements and project financing are integral parts and expected of every proposal and sponsors and developers strive to obtain a competitive advantage in these areas. Gaining a competitive advantage in infrastructure project finance for a new business development is a concentrated effort. It requires sound organizational structures, proper political and relationship management internally and externally, suitable technical design and engineering, the right legal contracts and agreements, and appropriate financial engineering that fits particular project and customer needs.

A. **Organizational engineering.** Refers to creating the right organizational structures, developing competencies and capabilities, and ensuring all around communication, coordination, cooperation, and collaboration along with:

1. Appointing an outstanding overseeing management team that is accessible by the project manager and the project team for quick turnaround decisions and is supportive of project team roles and responsibilities

2. Establishing accountable and high-performance project teams responsible for creating and following problem free and efficient internal processes and systems

3. Independent, critical, and objective assessment of the company's strengths and weaknesses and ongoing search for competitive advantage factors from the set of its core competencies

4. Building, reviewing, and supporting core strengths against competitors and promoting innovation to maximize the set of

skills needed for successful project development and execution, and continuous productivity improvements

5. Matching core competencies to project opportunities as the external environment is constantly changing and positioning the company to compete with advantage in its core strengths, including project financing

6. Strong senior management support and adequately funded PFOs and project teams

B. **Political and relationship management.** This is probably one of the most protected aspects of winning project bids and an essential part of creating and developing competitive advantage. It involves several factors such as:

1. A high degree of understanding the customer's culture, needs and desires, constraints and limitations, and demonstration of commitment and personal support for decision makers

2. Getting down to the real customer needs and creating a receptive venue to present the superiority of financing proposals and get customer approvals efficiently

3. Obtaining and maintaining project political support by the ceding authority and the central and local government bureaucracies responsible for licensing and permitting

4. Business and professional links and personal relationships inside the company and external connections and relationships with counterparts in other stakeholder organizations

5. Understanding of the political environment, climate, and realities; the macroeconomic and social conditions of the country the project is in; the legal and regulatory regime; and the customer's ability to deliver on project requirements

6. Having the right people and processes assigned to manage relationships and project politics and issues as they arise on an ongoing basis for the course of project lifetime

7. Political and relationship management is built into every organization's processes and is the most important responsibility of the project executive and the project manager to ensure it is carried out effectively

Proper political and relationship management requires highly qualified, experienced, and managers who are sensitive to the local culture and are able to deal with all customer organization management levels. It also requires the ability to respond to customer needs with project proposal attributes that constitute customer value and end-user satisfaction. Relationship management needs the formation of alliances on a case-by-case basis with local influencers and funding sources to differentiate a project proposal and set it apart from those of competitors.

Often, political and relationship management is overseen by regional sales and support groups, which is appropriate. This, however, requires skilled and experienced relationship managers with good personal interaction skills, industry knowledge, and an ability to educate customers on project particulars and project financing. Relationship management is also important with debt and equity sources, ECAs, multilateral institutions, and regional agencies involved in project reviews and assessments, and final approvals.

C. **Suitable technical engineering and design.** This area deals with all aspects of project design, engineering and technology; equipment, construction, and project acceptance, and involves a number of factors. However, the way to get a competitive advantage through technical engineering begins with assessing correctly the technical capabilities of competitors and involves the following considerations:

1. The ability to assess customer and project needs accurately, validate them, and translate them into the competitively priced project design and engineering specifications

2. Develop and offer quality project design and engineering, appropriate equipment selection and quality, and technical specifications that meet customer needs and expectations

3. Superior depth, breadth, and versatility of project designs and engineering to create value that meets customer specifications based on brand strength, warrantees, and guarantees

4. Leading the technical aspect of the project feasibility study and development to control project costs to levels likely to win proposals, assessing technical project risks, and helping in risk mitigation

5. Testing the technology and equipment to be used and ensuring they meet project requirements and specifications in line with managing cost components and providing professional opinion to lender engineers in the due diligence and its report preparation

6. Closely monitoring construction progress to make sure the project is delivered on time and within budget and performance according to project specifications

7. Providing better technology updates, excellent support, and reliable service during the lifetime of a project asset and at transfer of ownership to the customer

8. Leveraging the history of company reputation, technological and project success, market position, and a record of customer feedback and adapting proposals to customer needs

D. **Financial and legal engineering.** This is concerned with developing a project finance competitive advantage based on the creation of an economic moat in conjunction with a web of tightly knit legal contracts and agreements. In addition to having the proper PFO and legal team organizations working closely together, the following considerations are instrumental:

1. Monitoring of megatrends, country PESTLED trends, industry trends, and customer or user needs and tastes and willingness and ability to pay

2. Effective project screening, development, economic evaluation, due diligence, risk management, comprehensive and well-structured financial model, and financing plan and financing structuring

3. Superior knowledge and experience in project finance sources, instruments, review and approval processes, and bringing projects to effective and efficient closing by leveraging relationships and alliances

4. Investment in skills and competencies, project team development, and technology in the areas of competitive analysis, strategic decision forecasting, and project financing

5. Development of a sound, complete, and well-tested project financial model inputs, outputs, and evaluation of ratios confirming project financeability, meeting investor expectations, and optimizing the project financing solution

6. Introducing financial product innovations, and process improvements that are known to result in delivering superior project financing and overall project competitiveness

Much like financial engineering, the legal engineering part is a necessary but not a sufficient requirement to create a sustainable advantage, although the two combined and executed effectively may yield a competitive advantage on a project-by-project basis. Legal engineering considerations are the factors mentioned in the discussion of successful contract attributes and include the following:

1. Clearly stated and reasonable project objectives and customer expectations managed to reasonable levels

2. Well-defined project scope and clarity of what needs to be done and clarity of participant obligations and roles and responsibilities

3. Early participation of the PFO and the project team and all around, unimpeded 4Cs characterizing the contract development process and sound vision and contract objectives

4. Attention paid to prerequisites to drafting effective project contracts having been satisfied

5. Early involvement of the PFO in contract preparation and structuring and ensuring 360-degree open communication, cooperation, coordination, and collaboration

6. Comprehensive contract planning, negotiation process, and assessment of negotiation results by the financial model

7. Balance of participant interests using unambiguous language and fair, balanced, and cost–benefit based risk allocation

8. Real commitment of the contract parties to project success throughout its lifecycle

9. Skilled and highly qualified legal staff and project team managers assigned to support drafting of legal documents

10. Independent and critical review and evaluation of contracts by external legal experts

11. Creation of a project contract-management system for contract administration, auditing, and control

16.4 COMPETITIVE ADVANTAGE REALITY CHECK

There are differences of opinion on whether sustainable competitive advantage can be obtained by sponsors through project financing, but there are exceptions. Interestingly, opinions on whether competitive advantage can be obtained through project finance vary along the lines of interest of project participants. In order to assess the issue objectively and get a reality check, results of a benchmarking study which focused on the following three questions are presented:

1. What needs do customers seek to satisfy through project finance?

2. Can a sponsor company create a competitive advantage in project financing?

3. What are the required practices and support structures to establish a competitive advantage using project finance?

Study participants included customers, industrial companies, financial advisors, commercial and investment banks, law firms, and the IBRD and IFC parts of the World Bank in order to obtain a comprehensive, balanced, and diverse view on project financing competitive advantage. Hence, the results of the study are presented from the perspectives of sponsors and developers, customers, project financing advisors and sources of funding, law firms, and other project finance participants.

A. **Sponsor–Developer Perspectives**

There is agreement among well-established sponsors and developers that project financing is necessary to get competitive advantage and win bids. However, there is a divergence of opinion about smaller firms that lack project volume and resources to strive for competitive advantage. Some of the views offered by sponsor and developer group participants are the following:

1. Project finance is a critical capability for sponsors and developers to have internally or through external relationships

2. There is disagreement and perceptions coincide with vested interests on whether a developer can create a competitive advantage through project finance, but there is agreement that project finance is required to compete in infrastructure industries

3. Sponsors and developers believe that superior understanding and management of the project finance process can lead to competitive advantage. This requires the PFO to understand well the marketplace, facilitate relationships that help the transaction, focus on the process, validate financing structures with banks, and help with loan underwriting

4. Total cost minimization, helped by lower financing costs, is the principal reason for developing project financing capabilities

5. Project sponsors and developers need to lay out how project finance can support their business strategy. That is, they should have a clear vision and the ability to sustain the course initially laid out

6. Sponsors cultivate relationships, but alliances are on one-by-one case basis because financing institutions are common carriers of capital and relationships are productive, but exclusive alliances are not

7. It is good to have a series of informal alliances, but prefer developing relationships with a few global institutions that can provide advice early on what is possible and eliminate not financeable projects early

B. **Customer Perspectives**

Customers generally confirm that financing is required, but lowest-cost financing is not sufficient to win bids and they use total project solution costs instead to judge different proposals. The views stated are consistent across the set of customers interviewed and include the following points:

1. Customer interest in project finance is driven by lack of cash and a desire to share risks, obtain better credit terms, and maximize value for money

2. Customers evaluate bids on a bottom line basis but lack experience with innovative financing methods. They feel that the longer the financing term, the better the deal

3. Sponsors and developers demonstrate commitment to a deal by bringing significant equity and accepting a larger share of project risk

4. Risk sharing with sponsors/developers is important and so is off balance sheet financing and value for money for the host government

5. At times, government entities may constrain financing alternatives that could be used in a project due to established rules and regulations

6. Customers need to be educated on the processes of project financing and financial instruments

7. Customers look at the total project solution and do not select a proposal because of the financing and its lower costs alone

8. For credit-impaired customers, project financing is very important and the lowest price generally wins bids

C. **Financiers Perspectives**

The necessity of project financing to win bids is confirmed by PFOs and financiers, but their views diverge on whether long-term competitive advantage can be obtained except only on a project-by-project basis. Some of the other views expressed are summarized below and include the following:

1. Leading sponsors have centralized PFOs that are independent and possess critical mass to strive for competitive advantage that may or may not be sustainable over the long run

2. Customer needs for project financing are not always clearly or correctly stated in their RFPs and successful PFOs recognize the need to educate customers on project financing and evaluation of proposals

3. There is no magical bullet. Innovative or effective financing proposals are those that meet customer needs, which vary by project and help win bids

4. There is no off-the-shelf financing arrangement in project finance; every project is different, and proposals are carefully tailored. This is an area of potential to create a competitive advantage through project financing solutions

5. Differences in costs are minimal across competing proposals, but the risks of poorly thought-out financing arrangements is enormous and impacts both sponsors and customers

6. Leading PFOs are versatile in applying a wide variety of specific techniques to specific situations, but in build, operate, and transfer of ownership (BOT) projects and its derivatives, the transfer part is difficult to negotiate and is disliked by sponsors and developers

7. ECA financing is the first choice and bulwark of project finance when supplier content is high, especially when its effectiveness is supplemented with ancillary support from other government sources

8. Lease financing, where the transaction is tax driven and the customer rents the project company assets, may be well suited for technology and credit impaired customers

9. Skills, competencies, and experience are required to get a competitive advantage and include: speed, leadership and triage

In project finance deals, speed is affected by experienced people preventing and avoiding unnecessary delays. Leadership means using senior people, capable of leading project development and financing effectively. Triage is a critical experience in cutting to the chase and identifying the projects that are not financeable early.

D. Other Participants Perspectives

Contractors, equipment providers, and law firms maintain that competitive advantage cannot come from project financing alone. The totality of the project proposal makes the difference and wins bids and for that to happen, the interests and concerns of these participants must also be considered. Key points made by these contributors are summarized in the following responses:

1. Customer needs and competition are often driving contractors and equipment suppliers to become project sponsors and developers

2. Advisors, contractors, and law firms confirm the importance of lowest total-project costs, but downplay the significance of lowest financing costs alone

3. Equipment suppliers and contractors believe that project finance enables them to ensure lower total project costs and give them a competitive advantage

4. The objectives of all project stakeholders must be considered and different criteria must be met because lenders focus on debt-cover ratios, customers on lowest cost, and sponsors and developers look to maximize their after-tax return on equity

5. Contractors, equipment providers, and legal advisors agree that sponsors and developers need project financing to compete, but they do not view it as a source of competitive advantage by itself

6. Every proposal submitted by successful suppliers includes financing, but since financing techniques cannot be patented, project financing alone cannot create competitive advantage

7. Project financing is offered to be competitive and a contractor or supplier gets eliminated from future projects if they do not offer it

E. **Competitive Advantage Requirements**
   Participants with expertise in different areas of project finance disagree on its role in creating a sustainable competitive advantage and division of opinion falls along lines of self-interest. The various perspectives are compressed in the following statements:

1. Lawyers and some financial advisors feel that sustainable competitive advantage is not possible because deal structures are public knowledge and because of the commonality of available financing instruments and funding sources

2. Outsourcing aspects of project finance is worthy of consideration when there is uncertainty regarding a company's ability to develop sustainable competitive advantage using project finance

3. Constraints to competitive advantage through project finance come mostly from conservative financing approaches and limited experience and tools

4. Sponsors and developers report five sources of competitive advantage: A clear vision of project finance goals, bringing equity to the deal, having experienced project teams, developing strong relationships, and meeting customer needs

5. Competitive advantage requires a clear vision and enterprise capabilities that support project finance. That is, vision concerning project financing processes, identification and screening, risk assessment and mitigation, economic assessment, commercial structuring, and closing

6. Enterprise capabilities needed for competitive advantage through project finance require appropriate corporate and PFO organizational structure and culture, the right image, sound core processes, strong skills and competencies, efficient systems, selective alliances, and understanding of customer financing needs and requirements

7. Success in project finance requires a team orientation, access to quick decisions, and tenacity because of massive negotiating and finalizing contracts and agreements

8. Experienced professionals with knowledge of global markets and key participants are needed where experience is defined as: Having worked on deals through closing, possessing knowledge of financing sources, instruments terms, and knowing key participants; namely, advisors and experts, and principals in local government and finance

It is interesting to note that benchmarking-study participants considered competitive advantage in project financing from the contract finance and financial engineering perspective alone and not as part of new business development. Hence, the resulting general view that competitive advantage cannot be obtained through project financing. When a different participant group with a broader, new business development perspective was interviewed, three major points came through very clearly:

1. Assessment of competitive advantage in the infrastructure industry does not necessarily apply to other types of projects or industries

2. Competitive advantage can be achieved when the success factors of project development and financing go beyond contract finance and financial engineering are incorporated throughout

3. Sustainable competitive advantage in the era of coopetition may be possible through partnerships and joint ventures

The potential for acquiring or developing a competitive advantage in infrastructure projects through project finance can be realized only if both customer needs and requirements are fully met and the sponsor company delivers proven advantages to customers that competitors cannot. Figure 16.4 is a clearly illustrated summary of key points on competitive advantage. One point, however, has been left out from participant responses: Using lessons learned in previous projects through post mortem analysis. Successful sponsors are using post mortems to improved processes, productivity, and reduce project development costs and total bid costs.

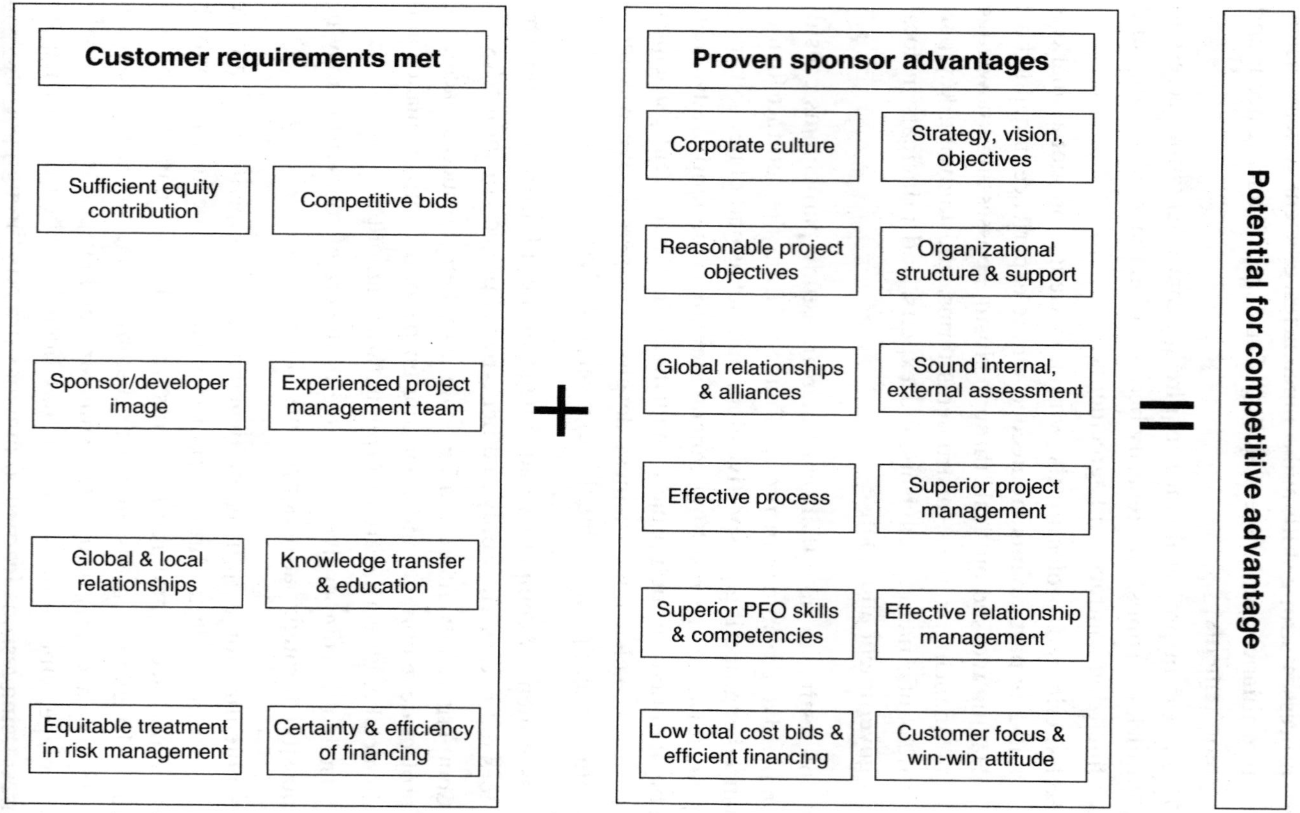

Figure 16.4 Project finance competitive advantage.
Source: Long Range Planning Associates.

Successful global infrastructure sponsors and developers possess project finance and overall company competitive advantage because they:

1. Assess accurately the likelihood of winning bids early in the screening phase by understanding well customer needs and ensuring all customer and project requirements are met

2. Determine whether and how they can meet customer and project requirements and offer competitively priced bids that include efficient project financing

3. Structure projects more effectively by putting themselves in the customers' and competitors' heads and developing projects more effectively by putting themselves in their competitors' position

4. Evaluate in a parallel effort to what extent they possess the needed advantages and if they are worth acquiring them to compete or to outsource them

5. Evaluate in the final step the two sides of the equation to determine whether there is potential for obtaining a competitive advantage knowing that financing alone may not always enable them to do so

Common Project Finance Abbreviations

ADB	Asian Development Bank
AfDB	African Development Bank
ALOP	Advance loss of profits (insurance)
BAB	Build America Bonds
BDFI	Bilateral Development Finance Institution
BII	Business Interruption Insurance
BIS	Bank for International Settlements
BLT	Build, lease, transfer
BOC	Breach of contract
BOO	Build, own, operate
BOT	Build, operate, transfer
BTO	Build, transfer, operate
CAR	Construction all risk (insurance)
CC	Construction contractor
CEAR	Construction and erection all risks (insurance)
CF	Compare one thing with another
CFD	Contract for Differences
CGF	Credit Guarantee Finance
CIRR	Commercial Interest Reference Rate
CLO	Collateralized Loan Obligation
COD	Commercial Operation Date
CP	Condition precedent
CTA	Common Terms Agreement
CUP	Cooperative Underwriting Program (offered by MIGA)
DBFO	Design, build, finance, operate
DFI	Development Finance Institution
DPC	Design Procurement and Construction
DSU	Delay in start up
EBRD	European Bank for Reconstruction and Development
ECA	Expert Credit Agency
EFSI	European Fund for Strategic Investments
EIA	Environmental impact assessment
EIB	European Investment Bank
EPC	Engineering Procurement and Construction
ERDA	Energy Research and Development Administration
ETF	Exchange Traded Fund
FIM	Final Information Memorandum
FMC	Facilities Management Contract
GIC	Guaranteed Investment Contract
GOCO	Government owned, contractor operated (private sector)
GPA	Government Procurement Agreement (WTO framework for public procurement)

GPL   General Public License
GST   Goods and services tax, eg. VAT
IA   Implementation Agreement
IDA   International Development Association
IDB   Inter-American Development Bank
IFC   International Finance Corporation
IFI   International Financial Institution
IIT   Infrastructure Investment Trusts
IMF   International Monetary Fund
IPP   Independent Power Producer
IPPF   Infrastructure Project Preparation Facility
IRB   Industrial Revenue Bonds
IsBD   Islamic Development Bank
ITN   Intention to negotiate
LGPL   Lesser General Public License
LGTT   Loan Guarantee Instrument for Trans-European Transport Network Services (EIB)
MARAD   Maritime Administration
MDB   Multilateral Development Bank
MDFI   Multilateral Development Finance Institution
MIGA   Multilateral Investment Guarantee Agency
MIRR   Modified IRR (IRR calculation w/reduced reinvestment rate for cash taken out)
MLP   Master Limited Partnership
MPP   Merchant power plant
MRG   Minimum Revenue Guarantee
NEPAD   New Partnership for African Development
NRE   Non-Recurring Engineering
NTP   Notice to proceed
OBA   Output Based Aid
ODA   Official Development Aid
OPIC   Overseas Private Investment Corporation
PAB   Private Activity Bonds
PBCE   Project Bond Credit Enhancement (the result of using EIB project bond initiatives)
PCG   Parent Company Guarantee or Partial Credit Guarantee
PEFCO   Private Export Funding Corporation
PFI   Private Finance Initiative
PIDA   Program for Infrastructure Development in Africa
PIM   Preliminary Information Memorandum
PMS   Performance Management System

PPA	Power Purchase Agreement
PPF	Public Private Funds
PPI	Private Participation in Infrastructure
PPIAF	Private Public Infrastructure Advisory Facility
PPP	Public-Private Partnership
PPPI	PPPs forInfrastructure
PQQ	Pre-Qualification Questionnaire (in public procurement)
PRG	Partial risk guarantee
PRI	Political risk insurance
PSC	Public sector comparator
PURPA	Public Utilities Regulatory Policy Act
QIB	Qualified Institutional Buyer
REIT	Real Estate Investment Trust
RPI	Repayment Protection Insurance
RWA	Risk-weighted asset
SAD	Service availability date
SCD	Service commencement date (SAD = SCD)
SFI	State financial institutions
SIB	State Infrastructure Bond
SIBs	State Infrastructure Banks (U.S.A.)
SPC	Special purpose company
SPV	Special purpose vehicle
TAF	Technical assistance facility
TFS	Technical feasibility study
TIF	Tax Increment Finance
TIFIA	Transportation Infrastructure Finance & Innovation Act
USAID	U.S. Agency for International Development
VFM	Value for money
VGF	Viability gap funding

Commonly Used Project Finance Definitions

63-20 Issuance. State and local governments can issue tax-exempt debt through the creation of nonprofit corporations pursuant to IRS Revenue Ruling 63-20. Bond proceeds can then be used by private developers to finance and build transportation facilities.

Accommodation project. An availability-based or private finance initiative (PFI) model contract relating social infrastructure projects such as schools, hospitals, prisons, government offices, etc.

Angola model. Construction of infrastructure projects in return for the right to extract natural resources.

Assumptions book. A register of source data and assumptions for the financial model.

Availability contract. A project agreement with a contracting authority under which it pays the project company for the right to use the project.

B loan. Participation by a private sector lender in a loan made by a multilateral development finance institution (MDFI).

Banking case or Base case. The projection of cash flow shortly before financial close, agreed between the project company and an offtaker or the contracting authority.

Bilateral DFI. A development finance institution (DFI) in a particular country providing loans and equity to projects in developing countries.

Buyer credit. An export credit agency-supported loan to an importer of equipment for a project.

Capital grant. Payment by a contracting authority of part of the capital cost of an availability based or other PFI-model project.

Capitalized interest. Interest during construction that is added to the debt principal amount.

Collateralized loan obligations. A way to syndicate bank loans to insurance companies or pension fund and the process is known as securitization.

Concession agreement. A government contract giving a company the right to operate a business subject to negotiated terms and conditions.

Concession. It is a PPP in which the general public pays user charges in the form of tolls, fares, or other charges for using the facility and it is used in the PFI model as well.

Contingency. Unallocated reserve in the project construction budget, covered by contingency finance.

Contract mismatch. Incompatible provisions between a project agreement and one or several project contracts.

Convertible securities. They are bonds or convertible preferred shares that allow the holder to exchange them for a stated number of shares of the project company's common stock.

Corporate finance. Usually refers to a loan against a company's balance sheet and existing business and it is an alternative to project finance.

Cost benefit ratio. The ratio of net present value (NPV) of the benefits of a project to the NPV of its costs over a project's lifecycle.

Counter party risks. Technical and financial capacity risks related to all parties with which the project company has project contracts.

Credit default swap. It is a credit derivative that is a privately negotiated contract. Its value is derived from the credit risk of a bond, a bank loan, or some other instrument and the credit risk is taken by a party other than the lender.

Credit enhancement. Provision of a guarantee, standby loan, or other additional financial security for a project financing.

Cross-collateralization. The sharing of security between different groups of lenders in a project.

Debt acceleration. It is a drawdown procedure where debt can be drawn during a much longer availability period and its common use is in concessions.

Debt accretion. Increasing the debt amount during the operation phase of a concession, based on traffic growth above initial projections.

Debt sculpting. It is a way for principal repayment obligations of the project company to be calculated to ensure that principal and interest obligations are matched to the strength and pattern of the cash flows in each project period.

Defects liability period. The period after project completion during which the construction contractor is obliged to remedy any defects on the project's construction.

Direct agreements. Agreements between lenders and partners signing contracts with the project company, which protect the lenders' interests under these contracts signed by the offtaker or contracting authority.

Dividend trap. Inability of the project company to pay dividends, despite having cash available to do so, because of accounting losses.

Dry closing. Signing of a loan agreement and project contracts subject to subsequent conditions.

Economic infrastructure. The infrastructure essential for the functioning of an economy, such as transportation, communications, energy, water and sewage and social infrastructure.

Enclave project. A project whose products are exported for which payment is received outside the host country.

Equity bridge loan. Finance provided by lenders during the construction period for the amount of equity investment.

Export credits. Guarantees or insurance provided by ECAs to lenders and direct loans to the project company which are linked to export sales from the ECA's country.

Final information memorandum. The information memorandum on the project company used for syndication.

Financial assessment. A systematic approach to determine the commercial viability of a project to all project participants. It is performed by the project sponsor and it is considered viable if it is validated by lenders.

Financial close. The date all project contracts and financing documents are signed and conditions precedent to initial drawing of the debt have been fulfilled.

Forward contracts. They obligate the holder to buy a specified amount of a particular asset at a stated price on a particular date. Most forward contracts are for commodities or currencies and the specified future price is called the exercise price.

Franchise. The right to operate existing public infrastructure project and receive user payments. It is different from a PPP because no substantial new investment is required by the private sector operator.

Fronting bank. A bank acting as a channel for an interest rate swap.

Futures contracts. They obligate the holder to buy a specified quantity of a particular asset at a specified exercise price at a specified date in the future. There are futures contracts for precious metals, industrial commodities, currencies, and other financial instruments.

Government support agreement. A project contract that creates the legal basis for the project and under which the host government agrees to provide various kinds of support and guarantees.

GPA. An agreement on government procurement, the framework for public procurement under the WTO.

Gross up. An increase of a payment to compensate for tax deductions.

Implementation agreement. A contract between a project company and a developing country host government that allocates political and financial uncertaintyrisksin a project financing. Implementation agreements are not normally needed in industrialized countries.

Incomplete contract. A contract in which the parties cannot provide for all possible outcomes.

Information memorandum. A marketing document presented by the project company to prospective investors after a confidentiality agreement is signed and a brief investment summary has been reviewed.

Institutional PPP. An operating project company in which the contracting authority sells part of the equity to an investor who is actively involved in management of the company.

Intercreditor.   Refers to the relationship between different groups of lenders.

Interest buy down.   Reduction in the interest rate in exchange for providing more equity in the project.

Interest rate equalization.   The interest subsidy provided by ECAs to banks to cover the difference between the banks' cost of finance and commercial interest reference rate (CIRR).

Investment insurance.   Political risk insurance provided to investors by ECAs, DFIs, or private insurers.

Islamic finance.   It refers to financial activity in which Muslims engage in and it involves traditional financial and investment techniques and structures that are tailored to comply with Sharia principles.

Leverage.   The debt-to-equity ratio.

Life cycle.   The renewal or replacement of major project company equipment at the end of its operating life.

Limited recourse debt.   This is debt that carries a repayment guarantee for a defined period of time for part of the total principal or until a milestone is achieved; e.g. until construction is complete or the project reaches a minimum level of output is a subset of non-recourse debt. The difference is that at least some portion of the debt becomes non-recourse at some point.

Linear project.   A project involving construction of a facility over a long stretch of land, such as a road.

Liquidated damages.   The pre-agreed level of loss when a contracting party does not perform under a contract.

Loan agreement.   The agreement between a project company and its lenders such as a credit agreement or a facilities agreement.

Mandate.   The appointment of a bank as lead arranger.

Mandatory costs.   The additional costs of funding a loan which commercial banks charge to a borrowing project company.

Mark to market.   Calculating the current value of a swap or its breakage cost.

Mechanical completion.   Under an EPC contract, confirmation that the project can meet the required performance and operating criteria.

Mini perm.   A loan for the construction period and first few years of project operation to be refinanced in due course by long-term debt, which is known as a Hard Mini Perm.

Modified IRR.   An IRR calculation with a reduced reinvestment rate for cash taken out of the project.

Notice to proceed.   It is given from the project company to the construction contractor to begin the project works.

OECD Consensus provisions. Starting as a Gentlemen's Agreement among OECD countries, it has evolved and has specific provisions to bring order to official export financing.

Options. An option gives its holder the right to do something, without the obligation to do it. A call option is the right to buy an asset and a put option is the right to sell an option.

PFI Model contract. A project agreement with a contracting authority under which it pays a project company for the right to use the project. It is also referred to as an availability contract.

Pooled equity vehicles. These are companies formed by an existing operating company to own and manage certain specified types of projects. They give investors geographic diversity and opportunities to invest in projects alongside an experienced operator.

Private activity bonds. A method of raising finance for PPP projects in the US municipal bond market.

Private finance initiative. A way to transfer responsibility of financing government projects and the risk of failure away from the government and into private sector hands.

Private participation in infrastructure. Refers to participation in privatized and private sector infrastructure and PPPs.

Process plant project. A project where there is an input at the end of the project that goes through a process within the project and emerges as an output, such as power generation and water treatment.

Project agreement. The contract between the project company and an off-taker or contracting authority to design, construction, finance, and operation of a project and which is the main security for a project financing.

Project development. Refers to the prebid stage process of preparing for and structuring a new project that has three distinct phases: origination of a project, negotiating and formalizing the project contracts, and mobilizing financing.

Project finance. It involves creation of a legally independent project company financed with nonrecourse debt and equity from sponsors to build single purpose capital assets usually with a limited life cycle.

Project preparation facility. Funding for a contracting authority to engage advisors to develop a PPP project.

Public sector comparator. A calculation of the life time cost of a project if build and operated by the public sector to compare with the expected cost of a PPP project.

Public–private infrastructure advisory facility. It is a multi-donor trust fund that provides technical assistance to governments in developing countries for PPI projects.

Public–private partnerships. These are arrangements that vary from full private ownership subject to government approval and oversight, to public projects in which the private partner serves as a financial contributor to the government-sponsored project. They are governed by negotiated contracts that specify public and private responsibilities, impose public regulation of safety, require quality of service, and often restrict user fees.

Qualified institutional buyer. An institutional investor to which Rule 144A bonds can be sold.

RAB Finance. Regulated asset based finance is a method to raise funding for a project using a regulated ROI.

Regulatory capture. It refers to the tendency of a host country independent industry regulator to be overly influenced by activities it is regulating.

Retainage. The portion of each payment under the construction contract retained by the construction company as security until commercial operation date.

Rule 144A. A U.S. Securities & Exchange Commission rule modifying a two-year holding period requirement on privately placed securities to permit qualified institutional buyers to trade these positions among themselves.

Secondary investors. These are investors purchasing some or all of the sponsors' shareholding in a project after the construction is complete.

Secondary loss. A loan guarantee by a public sector entity on which a payment or loss only occurs if the loss on the project is greater than the senior loan outstanding.

Section 129 loans. Section 129 of Title 23 allows federal participation in a state loan to support projects with dedicated revenue stream including tolls, excise taxes, sales taxes, real property taxes, motor vehicle taxes, incremental property taxes, or other beneficiary fees.

Securitization. The process where interests in loans or a group of assets are packaged, underwritten, and sold as asset-backed securities. Structuring enables lenders to transfer some of risk of project company loan ownership to parties willing to manage them for a profit.

Senior lenders. These are lenders whose debt service takes priority over the debt service of mezzanine or subordinated debt and distribution to investors.

Shadow tolls. They are tolls based on usage of the project but are payable by the contracting authority rather than the general public.

Site legacy risk. The risk of pre-existing contamination on the project site.

Social impact bond. It is a bond in which repayment depends on achieving specific social outcomes.

Standby finance. Funding made available if the project company's cash flow comes below projections.

State infrastructure banks (SIBs).   US banks that provide mezzanine support for transportation projects using federal funding.

Structural risk.   A contract mismatch in project finance projects.

Subrogation.   It is the right of an insurer or guarantor to take over an asset on which an insurance claim or guarantee has been paid.

Sukuk bond.   A bond based on Islamic principles.

Sunset date.   The last possible date for completion of construction of a project before failure becomes an event of default.

Swap credit premium.   The credit risk margin charged on an interest rate swap.

Swaps.   These are contracts obligating two parties to exchange specified cash flows at specified intervals. In an interest rate swap, cash flows are determined by two different interest rates in the same currency. In a currency swap, cash flows are based on the interest rates in two different currencies.

Syndication.   The process by which the lead arranger reduces its underwriting by placing part of the loan with other lenders.

Take and pay contract.   A contract under which the purchaser pays an agreed price for the project company's output produced, but is not obligated to purchase.

Take or pay contract.   A contract under which the purchaser must buy the product or make payment in lieu.

Target repayments.   A flexible repayment structure to allow for temporary project company cash flow deficiencies.

Tax increment finance.   A method of raising finance for urban development by imposing higher taxes on properties whose values appreciated by a project.

Term loan B.   A long-term loan with low amortization in its earlier years, and/or a balloon repayment, provided by an institutional lender.

Termination sum.   The compensation payable by the offtaker of the contracting authority for the early termination of a project agreement.

Third-party liability insurance.   Insurance against damage or injury caused by the project to third parties.

Third-party risks.   Risks that parties not involved with the project contracts may affect the completion of the project.

TIFIA finance.   Finance for transport infrastructure projects provided under the US Transportation Infrastructure Finance and Innovation Act of 1998 and subsequent legislation.

Tolling contract.   An input supply contract in which the fuel or raw material is supplied free and the project company is paid for processing it.

Tranche. Separate portions of a loan or investment that may be provided by different parties on different terms, or for a specific purpose rather than financing the project as a whole.

Tripartite deeds. Direct agreements between lenders and the parties signing project contracts with the project company protecting the lenders' interests under these contracts.

Undertakings. These are representations and warrantees. Confirmation by the project company of the facts on which financing is based and acceptance of liability for any error.

Unitary charge. A service fee or payments by the contracting authority under the PFI model contract; e.g. contact payment, tariff, user charge, payment mechanism.

Unwind cost. It is also known as breakage cost, it is the cost for early termination of an interest rate swap, fixed rate loan or bond, an inflation indexed loan, or an inflation swap.

Value for money (VFM) The basis on which an offtaker or contracting authority decides whether to transfer project risks to a project company.

Variation bonds. These are bonds with the right to increase the amount of a bond issue after it has been placed in order to cover additional capital expenditures.

Viability gap funding (VGF). A construction subsidy for a concession project.

Warrantees. These are guarantees against poor construction or failure of equipment after project completion, provided by the construction contractor.

Warrants. A warrant is a long-term call option issued by a company and it entitles the holder to buy shares of the firm's stock at a stated price for cash.

Waterfall or cascade. This is the order of funds' disbursement priorities under the financing documentation for the application of the project company's cash flow.

Windfall gains. Politically sensitive profits made by investors in PPPs resulting from debt refinancing or sale of their investment.

Working capital. The amount of funding required for inventories and other costs incurred before receipt of sales revenues.

Wrapped bonds. Bonds guaranteed by a monoline insurance company; that is, an insurer who repays the principal and interest on a bond should the issuer default.

Bibliography

Bala, B. K., F. M. Arshad, and K. M. Noh. *System Dynamics Modeling and Simulation*. Springer, 2016.

Baker & McKenzie. "Power Shift: The Rise of Export Credit and Development Finance in Major Projects." *Infrastructure Journal*. www.baker&mckenzie.com.

BBVA. Financing PPPs: Project Finance. 2006. www.oecd.org.mena/governance/37147349.pdf.

Blanc-Brude, F. *Rethinking Infrastructure: Voices from the Global Infrastructure Initiative*. McKinsey and Company, 2014. www.mckinsey.com/industries/capital-projects-and-infrastructure/our-insights/voices-on-infrastructure/voices-on-infrastructure-voices-from-the-global-infrastructure-initiative.

Bodmer, E. *Corporate and Project Finance Modeling: Theory and Practice*. Wiley, 2015.

Brealy, R. A., C. A. Ian, and M. A. Habib. "Using Project Finance to Fund Infrastructure Investments." *Journal of Applied Corporate Finance 9*, no. 3(Fall 1996):25–39.

Collan, M. *Ciga-Investments: Modeling the Valuation of Very Large Industrial Real Investments*. Doctoral Dissertation, Institute of Academic Research, November 2004.

Cuthbert, N. *A Guide to Project Finance*. Denton Wilde Sapte, 2004.

Damian, A., J. Hendrickson, and B. Wicke. *Mexico's Utility Reform: Investment Opportunities in an Emerging Market*. Deloitte, 2004. www2.deloitte.com/us/en/pages/consulting/articles/mexicos-utility-reform-investment-opportunities-in-an-emerging-market.html.

Davison, A. "Default Rates for Project Finance Bank Loans Improve." *Moody's Investor Services Global Research*, March 2015. www.moodys.com/research/Moodys-Default-rates-for-project-finance-bank-loans-improve--PR_319921.

Davis, H. A. *Project Finance: Practical Case Studies*. Euromoney Publications, 1996.

Della Croce, R. "Trends in Large Pension Fund Investment in Infrastructure." *OECD Working Papers on Finance, Insurance and Private Pensions 29*, OECD Publishing, 2012.

Della Croce, R., and S. Gatti. "Financing infrastructure—International Trends." *OECD Journal: Financial Market Trends* (2014/1).

Deloitte. *Funding Options—Alternative Financing for Infrastructure Development*, April 2013.

Dewar, J. *International Project Finance*. Oxford University Press, 2011.

Dewar, J. *International Project Finance: Law and Practice*. Oxford University Press, 2015.

Du Plessis, W. *Why Development Finance Is Vital for Africa's Projects*, Baker & McKenzie, 2013.

EFCA, *Project Financing Sustainable Solutions – Reassessing Priorities, Adding Value Through Innovation*, May 2001. www.efcanet.org/portals/EFCA/ELOKET/1429/pr_fin_final.pdf.

Ernst & Young, *The Upside of Disruption: Megatrends Shaping 2016 and Beyond*, November 2013.

Ehlers, T. Understanding the Challenges for Infrastructure Finance. *Bank for International Settlements Working Papers 454*, August 2014.

Esty, B. "Why Study Large Projects? An Introduction to Research in Project Finance." *European Financial Management* 10 (2004): 213–224.

Esty, B. C. "Improved Techniques for Valuing Large-scale Projects." *Journal of Project Finance 9* (Spring 1999).

Esty, B. C. *Modern Project Finance.* Wiley, 2004.

Esty, B. C. *The Economic Motivations of Using Project Finance*, Harvard Business School, 2003.

European Investment Bank. *EPEC PPP Guide*, 2015. www.eib.org/epec/g2g/.

Fabozzi, F. J., and P. Nevitt. *Project Financing*, 6th ed. Euromoney Publications, 1995.

Fazoul, M., K. Khan, and J. Parra. Financing Large Projects: Using Project Finance Techniques and Practices. Prentice Hall, 2003.

Finnerty, J. D. *Asset-Based Financial Engineering.* Wiley, 2013.

Flyvbjerg, B., M. Garbuio, and D. Lovallo. "Delusion and Deception in Large Infrastructure Projects: Two Models for Explaining and Preventing Executive Disaster." *California Management Review* 51, no. 2 (Winter 2009): 170–193. 2014. https://arvix.org/pdf/1303.7403.pdf.

Frey, T. *2050 and the Future of Infrastructure.* August 4, 2014. www.futuristspeaker.com/business-trends/2050-and-the-future-of-infrastructure/.

Frost & Sullivan, *Looking through the Crystal Ball: Megatrends that Will Shape the Future of the World*, www.slideshare.net/meghhamka/mega-trends-presentation.

G20 Development Working Group. *Assessment of the Effectiveness of Project Preparation Facilities in Asia Final Report*, Adam Smith International, 2014.

Gatti, S. *Project Finance in Theory and Practice: Designing, Structuring, and Financing Private and Public Projects*, 2nd ed. Academic Press, 2012.

Gatti, S. "Government and Market-Based Instruments and Incentives to Stimulate Long-Term Investment Finance in Infrastructure." *OECD Working Papers on Finance, Insurance and Private Pensions No. 37* (2013).

Gatti, S. *Project Finance in Theory and Practice: Designing, Structuring, and Financing*, 2nd ed. Academic Press, 2013.

Gelb, A., S. Tordo, H. Halland, N. Arfaa, and G. Smith. *Sovereign Wealth Funds and Long-Term Development Finance: Risks and Opportunities.* Policy Research working paper no. WPS 6776. World Bank Group, 2014.

Gevero, A. S., and M. C. Baker. *Annual Global Project Finance Default and Recovery Study, 1980–2014*, S&P Global Market Intelligence, June 2016.

Ghadar, F. *Financing Third World Development.* University Press of America, 1987.

Global Infrastructure Basel. GIB Grading for Sustainable Infrastructure. 2014. www.gib-foundation.org/gib-grading.

Gutman, J., A. Sy, S. Chattopadhyay. *Financing African Infrastructure – Can the World Deliver?* Economy and Development at Brookings, March, 2015. www.brookings.edu/wp-content/uploads/2016/07/AGIFinancingAfricanInfrastructure_FinalWebv2.pdf.

Hall, J. *7 Ways to Identify and Evolve with Industry Trends*. 2016. www.inc.com/john-hall/7-ways-to-identify-and-evolve-with-industry-trends.html.

Hingham, A., C. Bridge, and P. Farrell. *Project Finance for Construction*. Rutledge, 2017.

Hoffman, S. L. *The Law and Business of International Project Finance*, 3rd ed. Cambridge University Press, 2008.

International Project Leadership Academy. *Examples of Failed Projects*. www.calleam.com/WTPF/?tag=examples-of-failed-projects&paged2.

Gomez Ibanez, J. *Regulating Infrastructure*. Harvard University Press, 2006.

Gomez Ibanez, J., and J. F. Meyer. *Going Private: The International Experience with Transport Privatization*. Brookings Institution Press, 1994.

Jain, N., F. Katsuki, A. Lal, E. Pitsilis, and J. Sengupta. *Deepening Capital Markets in Emerging Economies*. McKinsey & Company, April 2017.

Jawad, I. *World's Top Trends to 2025 and Implications to Business, Society, and Cultures*. Frost & Sullivan, 2014. www.investinbsr.com/ipaforum/wp-content/uploads/Iain-Jawad-IPA-Forum-2014-Presentation.pdf.

Kabirkham, M. F., and R. J. Parra. *Financing Large Projects: Using Project Finance Techniques and Practices*. Pearson–Prentice Hall, 2003.

Kensinger, J. W., and J. D. Martin. "Project Finance: Raising Money the Old Fashioned Way." *Journal of Applied Corporate Finance1*, no. 3 (Fall 1988): 6–100.

Khan, M. F. K., and R. J. Parra. *Financing Large Projects – Using Project Finance Techniques and Practices*. Pearson–Prentice Hall, 2003.

Klein, M., J. So, and B. Shin. *Transaction Costs in Private Infrastructure—Are They too High? Note # 95*, World Bank, October 1996.

KPMG. *Emerging Trends for 2013: Trends that Will Change the World Over the Next Five Years*, 9th ed. Foresight, February 2013.

KPMG. *Advisory*. Project Management Survey Report. KPMG, 2013. www.kpmg.com/NZ/en/IssuesAndInsights/ArticlesPublications/Documents/KPMG-Project-Management-SurveyReport-2013.pdf.

KPMG. *10 Emerging Trends for 2015—Trends That Will Change the Work of Infrastructure Over the Next Five Years*. KPMG Foresight, 2015. https://home.kpmg.com/content/dam/kpmg/pdf/2015/11/emerging-trends-EN-2015.pdf.

KPMG. *Infrastructure—Emerging Trends*. KPMG, February 15, 2015. www.kpmg.com/ro/en/home/media/press-releases/2015/02/infrastructure-emerging-trends-2015.html.

Lang, L. H. P. *Project Financing in Asia*. Elsevier, 1998.

Lieberman, I. W., and C. D. Kirkness. *Privatization and the Emerging Equity Markets*. World Bank, 1998.

Lo, A. W., and S. K. Narahariseth. "New Financing Methods in the Biopharma Industry: A Case Study of Royalty Pharma Inc." *Journal of Investment Management* 12, no. 1 (2013): 4–19.

Lynch, P. *Financial Modeling for Project Finance*. Euromoney Publications, 1996.

Macdonald, B., and M. Wilkins. "Lessons Learned from 20 Years of Rating Global Project Finance Debt." *Standard & Poor's Rating Services Credit Week*, January 2015.

MacKenzie, W., and N. Cusworth. "The Use and Abuse of Feasibility Studies." *Proceedings of the Project Evaluation Conference."* Melbourne, Australia, June 2007, pp. 65–76.

McGraw Hill Construction. *Mitigation of Risk in Construction: Strategies for Reducing Risk and Maximizing Profitability.* Smart Market Report, 2011.

McKinsey & Company. *Urban Mobility at a Tipping Point,* McKinsey Center for Business and Environment, 2015.

McKinsey Global Institute. *The Future of Long-Term Finance: Backup Material, Report for Group of Thirty,* November 2012.

McNichol, D. *Construction Goes Global: Infrastructure and Project Delivery Across Borders.* AIG, 2015.

Merna, A., Y. Chu., and F. F. Al-Thani. *Project Finance in Construction: A Structured Guide to Assessment.* Wiley–Blackwell, 2010.

Merna, T., and G. Owen. *Understanding the Public Finance Initiative: The New Dynamics of Project Finance.* Asia Law & Practice Publishing Limited, 1998.

Millet, P. *Lending and Borrowing in Ancient Greece.* Cambridge University Press, 1991.

Moody's Investor Service, *Infrastructure Default and Recovery Rates, 1983-2012H1, Special Comment,* December 2012. www.moodys.com/research/moodys-project-finance-bank-loans-continue-to-demonstate-resilience--PR-363018.

Morrison, R. ed. *The Principles of Project Finance.* Taylor & Francis, 2016.

Naisbitt, J. *Megatrends: New Directions Transforming Our Lives.* Warner Books, 1982.

National Intelligence Council. *Global Trends 2025: A Transformed World,* November 2008.

National Intelligence Council. *Global Trends 2030: Alternative Worlds,* December 2012.

Nevitt, P. K., and F. J. Fabozzi. *Project Financing,* 2nd ed. Euromoney Books, 2005.

Niehuss, J. M. *International Project Finance in a Nutshell.* Thomson Reuters, 2010.

OECD. *Infrastructure to 2030 Vol. 2—Mapping Policy for Electricity, Water, and Transport.* Organisation for Economic Co-operation and Development, 2007. www.oecd.org/futures/infrastructureto2030/40953164.pdf.

OECD. *Survey of Investment Regulations of Pension Funds.* Organisation for Economic Co-operation and Development, July 2008. www.oecd.org/finance/private-pensions/40804056.pdf.

OECD. "Financial Market Trends." *OECD Journal 106* (2014/1).

OECD. *Pooling of Institutional Investors Capital—Selected case Studies in Unlisted Equity Infrastructure.* Organisation for Economic Co-operation and Development, April 2014.

OECD. *Arrangement on Officially Supported Export Credits.* Organisation for Economic Co-operation and Development, November 27, 2015. http://www.oecd.org/officialdocuments/publicdisplaydocumentpdf/?doclanguage=en&cote=tad/pg(2015)7.

OECD. *Due Diligence Guidance for Responsible Business Conduct: Meaningful Stakeholder Engagement in the Extractive Sector.* Organisation for Economic Co-operation and Development, 2016. http://mneguidelines.oecd.org/OECD-Guidance-Extractives-Sector-Stakeholder-Engagement.pdf.

OECD Capstone Project. *Quantifying the Costs,* Benefits and Risks of Due Diligence for Responsible Business Conduct. Organisation for Economic Co-operation and Development, June 2016.

OECD. Working Papers on Finance Insurance and Private Pensions. No. 29, December 2016.

Oxford Economics & PWC. *Capital and Infrastructure Spending—Outlook to 2025*. PwC, 2017. www.pwc.com/cpi-outlook2025.

O'Neil, J. D., Hunton & Williams LLP. *Worldwide Annual Review*, Infrastructure Project Financing. Financier Worldwide, 2012. www.hunton.com/files/publication.

Orr, R. J., and J. R. Kennedy. "Highlights of Recent Trends in Global Infrastructure: New Players and Revised Game Rules." *Transnational Corporations 17*, no. 1(April 2008).

Pritchard, D. M. "Public Finance and War in Ancient Greece." *Greece and Rome 62*, no. 1 (March 2015): 48–59.

PwC. *Capital Project Infrastructure Spending—Outlook to 2025*. www.pwc.com/cpi-outlook2025.

PwC. *Trends, Challenges, and Future Outlook*, 2014. www.pwc.co.za/infrastructure.

Ranong, P. N., and W. Phuennam. "Critical Success Factors for Effective Risk Management Procedures in Financial Industries." Master's thesis. Umeå School of Business, Spring 2009.

Singh, S. *Top 20 Megatrends and Their Impacts on Business, Cultures, and Society*. Frost & Sullivan. www.gilcommunity.com/files/8613/6139/4213/the_new_mega_trends_-_Sarwant_Singh_-_FrostSullivan.pdf.

Slivker, A. What is project finance and how does it work? (available to faculty & staff), 2011. http://ebook.law.uiowa.edu/ebook/sites/default/files/Anastasia%20FAQ.pdf.

Slivker, A. *What Is Project Finance and How Does It Work?* April 2011, p. 15. www.Scribd.com/document/106661961/Project-Finance-Manual.

Standard & Poors. *Annual Global Project Finance Default and Recovery Study 1980–2014*. S&P Global Market Intelligence, June 2016.

Seljas, J. C. *Global Trends in PPP & Project Finance Markets, Ernst & Young*, October 2013.

Smith, R. C., and W. Ingo. *Global Financial Services: Strategies for Building Competitive Strengths in International Commercial and Investment Banking*. Harper Business, 1990.

Sy, A., and J. Gutman. "Top Five Trends in the Changing Landscape of African Infrastructure Financing." *Brookings Institution—Africa in Focus*, 2015.

Tan, W. *Principles of Project and Infrastructure Finance*. Taylor & Francis, 2007.

The Infrastructure Consortium for Africa, Effective Project Preparation for Africa's Infrastructure Development, 2014 ICA Annual Meeting, Cape Town, South Africa, November 2014. www.icafrica.org/fileadmin/documents/Publications/Effective_project_preparation_in_Africa_ICA_Report_31_October_2014.pdf.

Triantis, J. *Navigating Strategic Decisions: The Power of Sound Analysis and Forecasting*, CRC Press, 2013.

United Nations. World Population Prospects: 2015 Revision. http://www.un.org/en/development/desa/publications/world-population-prospects-2015-revision.html.

VanWee, B. "Large Infrastructure Projects: A Review of the Quality of Demand Forecasts and Costs Estimates." *Environmental Planning B: Urban Analytics and City Science34*, no. 4(August 2007): 611–625.

Vintner, G. D. *Project Finance*, 2nd ed. Sweet and Maxwell, 1998.

Walker, C. *The Rise of Export Credit and Development Finance in Major Projects*. Baker & McKenzie, 1998.

Weber, B., M. Staub-Bisang, and H. W. Alfen. *Infrastructure as an Asset Class: Investment Strategy, Sustainability*, Project Finance and PPP. Wiley, 2016.

Wiener, D., and N. Didillon. *Financing Sustainable and Resilient Infrastructure by Creating a New Asset Class for Institutional Investors*. Global Infrastructure Basel, 2016.

Woetzel, J., N. Garemo, J. Mischke, M. Hjerpe, and R. Palter. *Bridging Global Infrastructure Gaps*. McKinsey Global Institute, June 2016. www.mckinsey.com/industries/capital-projects-and-infrastructure/our-insights/bridging-global-infrastructure-gaps.

Woodhouse, E. J. *A Political Economy of International Infrastructure Contracting: Lessons From IPP Experience*. Working Paper #52, Stanford University, September 30, 2005. http://pesd.fsi.stanford.edu/sites/default/files/PESD_IPP_Study,_Global_Report.pdf.

World Bank. *Financial Inclusion Strategies—Reference Framework*, June 2012. https://siteresources.worldbank.org/EXTFINANCIALSECTOR/Resources/282884-1339624653091/8703882-1339624678024/8703850-1339624695396/FI-Strategies-ReferenceFramework-FINAL-Aug2012.pdf.

World Bank. *Crowd Funding's Potential for the Developing World*. Information for Development Program/The World Bank, 2013. https://www.infodev.org/infodev-files/wb_crowdfundingreport-v12.pdf.

World Bank and G20 Investment and Infrastructure Working Group. *Success Stories and Lessons Learned: Country, Sector and Project Examples of Overcoming Constraints to the Financing of Infrastructure*. World Bank, 2014. www.g20.utoronto.ca/2014/WBG_IIWG_Success_Stories_Overcoming_Constraints_to_the_Financing_of_Infrastructure.pdf.

World Economic Forum and Boston Consulting Group. *Strategic Infrastructure Mitigation of Political and Regulatory Risk in Infrastructure Projects*. World Economic Forum, February 25, 2015. https://www.weforum.org/press/2015/02/report-mitigating-political-regulatory-risk-for-successful-infrastructure-projects/.

Yescombe, E. R. *Principles of Project Finance*, 2nd ed. Elsevier, 2014.

Index

Page references followed by *f* indicate an illustrated figure or photograph; and page references followed by *t* indicate a table